A list of books in the series appears at the back of this book.

BETWEEN RACE AND ETHNICITY

BETWEEN RACE AND ETHNICITY

Cape Verdean
American
Immigrants,
1860–1965

Marilyn Halter

UNIVERSITY OF ILLINOIS PRESS
Urbana and Chicago

Publication of this work was made possible in part by a grant
from the Ellis Island–Statue of Liberty Foundation.

This book is printed on acid-free paper.

Library of Congress Cataloging-in-Publication Data

Halter, Marilyn.
    Between race and ethnicity : Cape Verdean American immigrants,
1860–1965 / Marilyn Halter.
        p.   cm. — (Statue of Liberty-Ellis Island Centennial series)
    Includes bibliographical references and index.
    ISBN 0-252-01997-0 (acid-free paper). — ISBN 0-252-06326-0 (pbk. :
    alk. paper)
    1. Cape Verdean Americans—History. I. Title. II. Series.
E184.C24H34   1993
973'.0496658—dc20   92-33344
                                                                   CIP

To the memory of

Flora Britto Monteiro
Antonio Jesus
Mary Da Rosa Barros
Antonio "Tote" Cabral
Joseph Ramos
Manuel E. Costa
and to
Faith "Corday" Rivera, 1939–87

Contents

Illustrations follow page 98

Preface: Of Marginal Natives and Multiple Identities

Almost a decade ago when I began this project I thought that by dealing solely with the *history*—not the sociology, anthropology, social psychology, or politics—of Cape Verdean American immigration, I could avoid grappling with issues of identity that, as an outsider or non-Cape Verdean, I rationalized were not appropriate terrain on which I should tread. I would document with proper detachment and distance, but with a clear sense of who I was and was not vis-à-vis the Cape Verdeans, the history of this unique racial-ethnic group. And I actually managed to write a decent doctoral thesis on the topic without directly engaging the sticky questions of identity, race, and ethnicity except in the most tentative way. I am not meaning here to denigrate my past work for not having approached the topic differently. At the time it represented where I stood and seemed the safest route to travel. Through further study and personal interactions, my own consciousness of these issues, and my exposure to the larger theoretical questions, particularly the debates around identity politics, have expanded and changed my perspective. And I realize now that intellectual work of this kind is always in process. Even as I write this new positioning into the manuscript, I am aware that my orientation will continually transform itself so long as I continue to live and think among various racial and ethnic populations, including the Cape Verdeans.

Currently, in fact, I am directing a comparative study of recent immigrant entrepreneurs that includes six different racial-ethnic populations. While I am overseeing the research on British West Indians, Greeks, Puerto Ricans, Dominicans, and Haitians, I am doing the empirical work on the Soviet Jews myself. I embarked on this aspect of my new research with much enthusiasm, realizing it would be the first time I have studied *my own people*. Three of my grandparents emigrated to the United States at the turn of the century from the Pale of Settlement in Russia. And so, as I interview the proprietor of a skin care salon who hails from the Ukrainian city of Odessa, I realize that I am gazing into the face of a woman who could pass for my Grandma

Clara—that her recipes for skin creams are derived from vegetation that grew from my own ancestral roots. Yet, at other times, for example, as I am trying to grasp the meaning of the longings expressed by a member of the Moscovite emigré intelligentsia, I myself am wishing for the familiarity I experience in the company of my Cape Verdean friends. For despite the tie of Jewishness, this recent emigrant from Moscow is much more Russian than Jewish identified and the kinship I feel with Cape Verdean American culture, in this case, prevails. Thus, I realize that as a granddaughter of Russian Jews, I will certainly at times feel at home with the subjects of my current research but that I can also register equally strong identifications with my Cape Verdean associates that are not so readily explained. Now, rather than consciously trying to evade the questions of identity formation that constantly bubble to the surface in any reading of the Cape Verdean experience, I try to explore its dimensions. What also concerns me at this time is just what it is that my long involvement in the Cape Verdean community and history can tell me about my own ethnicity and color in addition to what I may be able to say about Cape Verdean identity as an outside interpreter.

These methodological as well as theoretical concerns arise when seriously undertaking an interdisciplinary approach that applies a social scientific orientation to a historical problem. For historians, unlike anthropologists, are not required by convention to reveal their own relationship to the object of inquiry. However, I must say, that I have yet to meet any historian who does not enjoy learning about how their colleagues may have arrived at their various choices of research topics. Indeed, often the first thing we do is to devour the acknowledgments of a newly published book (not simply to see if we are credited!) for some glimpse of this more personal trajectory when it appears that no other clues will be offered in the text. Nonetheless, it is certainly neither expected nor required that we historians put ourselves into the narrative. In contrast, anthropologists, by this point in the evolution of the discipline, are almost mandated to spell out their own subjectivities in relation to their chosen field of study.

How, then, should the historian conducting ethnographic research with living subjects proceed? My first approach was to treat this particular endeavor at writing history no differently from other works in the field of new immigration studies. But then, in part, through discussions with colleagues in related disciplines, I began to think that entering into the history I tell can only enhance its value to the various audiences that will read the contents. Just as the findings of classic anthropological studies of "exotic" cultures conducted by members of colonizing societies are now recognized as limited because of the inevitably skewed perspectives resulting from that very colonial relationship (though that does not mean these are useless scholarly efforts but rather alerts us to how we would best read such works), historians, too, can sharpen their analytical tools by being cognizant of their own positioning in relation to their historical subject. Yet, I am not simply arguing here for a self-centered confessional style. There are many possibilities, for the most part yet to be written, of ways to present this kind of interpretation.

How, then, to begin to explain how a Jewish girl from Northern Minnesota (whose real claim to fame is having attended Bob Dylan's Bar Mitzvah) ended up researching and writing about Cape Verdeans — an Afro-Portuguese population residing primarily in the coastal cities of southern New England? Certainly growing up on the richly multiethnic Mesabi Iron Range could be said to have foreshadowed my later interest in immigration, race, and ethnicity, but it is still a long stretch to the focus of my current preoccupations.

My own migration east to the "foreign" land of Massachusetts in 1969 to attend Brandeis University, a sudden plunge into the midst of energetic human rights, social protest, and counter-cultural activity, clearly was also formative. Yet it is somehow fitting, if ironic in retrospect, that my initial adaptation to the dominant New England culture in this period was mediated by a Jewish-based educational institution. For even as I attempted to negotiate regional Yankee society — as I was groping toward the center — I found myself at the same time, expanding my multiethnic universe reaching toward those individuals even more marginalized than I was.

By the mid–1970s, largely through chance and circumstance, I found myself living and working in southeastern Massachusetts, the heart of the Cape Verdean American community. Through my community involvements, friendships, and interest in local history, I was drawn into close association with Cape Verdeans. In 1983, in part because of encouragement from my Cape Verdean friends, I went back to graduate school to write a dissertation on the history of the Cape Verdean immigration to this country. I feel greatly privileged to have had the unparalleled opportunity of witnessing the Cape Verdean experience from up close — through visits to the island homeland, participation in Cape Verdean cultural events, and having been welcomed into the homes of Cape Verdean residents and been treated to that very special *Crioulo* hospitality.

What I now understand to be perhaps the best explanation for the draw of the Cape Verdean American community for me, as well as the ease I often feel amidst it, has to do with a compatibility that stems from a shared sense of liminality, that in-between, neither here nor there station, of which anthropologist Victor Turner has so eloquently written.[1] As the following pages will elaborate, Cape Verdeans, like the Jews, are diaspora peoples who have played the historical role of middlemen or brokers between colonizing and colonized societies. Furthermore, the overarching theme in the history of the Cape Verdean American experience has to do with never having belonged to a clearly defined racial or ethnic group. The discomfort of not belonging, the invisibility of residing between race and ethnicity, reverberates in my own experience of Jewishness. The first time I heard Cape Verdeans playing "Jewish" geography—the United States community being small enough that you can often trace new Cape Verdean acquaintances to known family and neighborhood names—and saw the delight and comfort expressed when the mapping is a success, I knew I was on some kind of familiar ground. Furthermore, the knowledge as a Jewish American that at different times in history, Jewishness was considered to be an "inferior" racial category as well as the universal ambiguity of the label of Jew as being simultaneously a religious, ethnic, and/or cultural configuration, made both the borderland positioning and variegated inflections of Cape Verdean representations of identity known territory to me. The struggles that I have witnessed among Cape Verdeans to be *seen* as well as their ability to traverse the worlds of white and black both allowed me in and tapped into my own history as "marginal native"—that is, never fully belonging but within the periphery of understanding.[2] Whether, as a school girl in Minnesota, when I was always the only Jewish pupil in the classroom, or at Brandeis, having been one of the few midwesterners and from a rural background among the predominantly urban east coast student body, or as is the case today, being Jewish and white amidst the Catholic, Cape Verdean community of color—to name some of the more obvious ways that I have found myself not *of* a particular sociocultural grouping but rather marginally native to it—this liminal social placement, while often lonely, can also offer unique perspectives and insights.

While I can never know precisely how Cape Verdean Americans experience the complexity of issues of identity, I can begin to comprehend these intricacies as a white female Jewish scholar informed by the liberation and civil rights movements of the last three decades. Thus, the way that I have experienced the multidimensional aspects of Cape Verdean identity formation opened up all the other ambiguities and permutations of identity. Most importantly, the realization that color may be more complex than black and white led me further to question the fixity of other deeply held ideas and forms of binary oppositional categorization, such as male/female or gay/straight.

Still rooted in the daily life of a multiracial working-class community, still interacting at many different levels with Cape Verdeans and other peoples of diverse cultures, still engaged in scholarly projects of living history, still discovering my own multiple identities, the more academic questions of renegotiating the boundaries of traditional disciplines and remapping the terrain of those ever-present configurations of race, ethnicity, gender, social class, and sexual preference cease to be merely abstractions. For above all else that I have learned from my long association with the Cape Verdeans is an understanding of the malleability of social categories, a knowledge that continually challenges, expands, and ultimately enriches my world.

After presenting a paper based on my research at a conference at Brown University several years ago, a long-standing leader in the Cape Verdean American community presented me with a button that read "I'm Proud to Be Cape Verdean." Although I was deeply touched and honored to receive it, I actually prefer the wording of the pin given to me one summer at a Cape Verdean Independence Day celebration. Cape Verdeans characteristically greet one another with a warm and affectionate embrace. This button asserts, "I'm Not Cape Verdean, but Kiss Me Anyway."

NOTES

1. See especially selections from Victor Turner, *The Ritual Process: Structure and Antistructure* (New York: Aldine de Gruyter, 1969), pp. 94–113, 128–30; Victor Turner, *From Ritual to Theatre: The Human Seriousness of Play* (New York: Performing Arts Journal Publications, 1982), pp. 20–61.

2. This term comes from the title of Morris Freilich, *Marginal Natives: Anthropologists at Work* (New York: Harper and Row, 1970)

Acknowledgments

The completion of this project resulted from two very distinct stages of research and writing and, consequently, the wonderful support I have received over the years has primarily come to me from two differing groups of people. I conducted the research and wrote the first draft of the manuscript in a nonacademic setting during an extended leave from graduate school. Working in isolation from academia in this period, I thank the many individuals in the Cape Verdean American community who helped me to see, as an outsider, from within. I am particularly grateful for my close association in this phase, with Ron Barboza, a brilliant freelance photographer, whose ardent quest to visually capture the Cape Verdean experience has inspired my own efforts to document this story in words. Thanks also to Joaquim A. Custodio, who was an invaluable consultant and whose oral history is central to the concluding chapter of the book. Both also provided contacts and accompanied me to interviews, as well as read early drafts. The map of the Cape Verde Islands in this volume was drawn by Ron. Almost fifteen years ago, I met Carol Pimentel, my first Cape Verdean acquaintance who quickly became a dear friend and who has, over the years, enthusiastically introduced me to many members of the Cape Verdean community. I warmly thank all those who have opened their doors to me for interviews and who have so generously shared their memories. My lively traveling companions on my first trip to Cape Verde, especially Richard Gonsalves and Joanie Andrews, enriched my experience there and contributed to a greater understanding of the relationship between Cape Verdean Americans and their island homeland.

Paul Cyr, curator of special collections at the New Bedford Free Public Library, first revealed the ship manifest records to me and contributed his compilation of arriving vessel data. He also located accounts in the North Carolina press of the Bark *Vera Cruz VII* and found the 1924 reference to Albert Jenks's article on Cape Verdean immigrants. Paul's continued commitment to making Cape Verdean source materials available to the public have greatly enhanced this study as well as benefited the local population. The late Manuel E. Costa, Sr. made my initial investigation into the existing secondary sources on Cape Verdean Americans easier by having contributed his collection of materials on this subject to the Genealogy Room of the New Bedford Free Public Library. Assistance with compiling the quantitative data came from Dan Georgianna, Rita Moniz, John Bennett, and the staff of the Southeastern Massachusetts University Academic Computer Services, especially Joy Martin.

During this first period, I can remember reading the acknowledgments of my favorite authors of social history texts and wishing that I, too, had people in my field to thank for reading drafts or study groups that have provided stimulating intellectual exchanges, but upon returning to academia in 1987, I developed a circle of colleagues who have given me just that kind of essential professional support and whose debts, I have now incurred as well. Before naming these individuals, however, I first want to express my deepest gratitude to Sam Bass Warner, who sustained me throughout both phases of this process, maintaining the lifeline between the university and my fieldwork base. He was the key to enabling me to get this study off the ground by welcoming me back to graduate school and offering a thorough reading of the manuscript, enthusiastic support of my research efforts, and spirited confidence in my career goals.

Several colleagues generously read drafts of working papers or chapters and provided helpful commentary or pertinent references. They are Silvia Pedraza, Lawrence Fuchs, Judith E. Smith, Andrew T. Miller, Joyce Antler, Ronald Edsforth, Antonio Carreira, Clara E. Rodriquez, Jeffrey Bolster, Donaldo Macedo, Heriberto Dixon, David Goldberg, Nancy Hewitt, Yukiko Hanawa, Joseph Boskin, Donna Gabaccia, and especially Richard Lobban, who invited me to coauthor the second edition of the *Historical Dictionary of the Republic of Cape Verde* and who has steadily supported my scholarship in this field. I also want to thank Roger Daniels, series editor; Rita D. Disroe, manuscript editor; Jim O'Brien, who indexed my book; and the two anonymous reviewers, particularly the thoughtful and detailed response of the lengthier critique. Joseph D. Thomas provided copies of photographs, several oral history tapes and many useful references. Portions of chapter 3 were printed in his 1990 edited collection, *Cranberry Harvest: A History of Cranberry Growing in Massachusetts*. I have also benefited from the institutional support of Boston University's Institute for the Study of Economic Culture and from a Wellesley College faculty award.

The women of my "work" group—Bettina Borders, Kathlyn Condon, Elizabeth Bennett, Mary Farmer, Janet Freedman, Donna Huse, and Sandee Krupp—have offered crucial personal and professional support throughout this effort as well. Several colleagues and friends in related disciplines provided invaluable sustenance by giving their unwavering encouragement and sound advice. No one could ask for a more terrific cheering squad. Thanks to Susan Reverby, Jeffrey Rubin-Dorsky, Sheila Katz, Jeffrey T. Sammons, Lynn Weiner, Blanche Linden-Ward, Lois Rudnick, Evelynn Hammonds, VèVè Clark, Kathryn Preyer, and especially Robert French, Kate Gyllensvard, and Charles Everett Pace, who, among other things, taught me to respect the incubation phase of a project such as this one.

Finally, I want to thank my family—both the new Cape Verdean members, Jonathan and Portia DePina and Marcy Stoddard—and my eleven-year-old son, Conor, who was a toddler when I first embarked on this project. From time to time during the course of the research, Conor would ask me, "Mommy, are we Cape Verdean?" His question always gave me the delightful opportunity to explain to him just who the Cape Verdeans are and to realize anew how fortunate we have been to be so closely connected to this remarkable group of people.

BETWEEN RACE AND ETHNICITY

Introduction: The Cape Verdeans—All Shades, All Hues

A profound analysis of cultural reality removes the supposition that there can be continental or racial cultures. . . . The fact of recognizing the existence of common and special traits in the culture of African peoples, independently of the colour of their skin, does not necessarily imply that one and only one culture exists on the continent. In the same way that from the economic and political point of view one can note the existence of various Africas, so there are also various African cultures.

> —Amilcar Cabral, leader of the successful struggle for the independence of Cape Verde and Guinea Bissau, 20 February 1970

The story of American immigration, when written in other form than that of lifeless statistics, has many strange chapters. Perhaps there is no more curious chapter than that of the people of the Cape Verde Archipelago.

> —Albert Jenks, anthropologist, 1924

Many inhabitants of the Cape Verde archipelago, twenty-one islands and islets in a crescent shape stretching from 283 to 448 miles off the west coast of Africa, have immigrated to the United States, constituting a little-known racial-ethnic group in this country, the Cape Verdean Americans.[1] Though relatively small in numbers, these Afro-Portuguese settlers represent the only major community of Americans of African descent (albeit of mixed ancestry) to have voluntarily made the transatlantic voyage to the United States.[2]

Most historians agree that the Cape Verde Islands were uninhabited until the mid-fifteenth century when Portuguese explorers landed there,

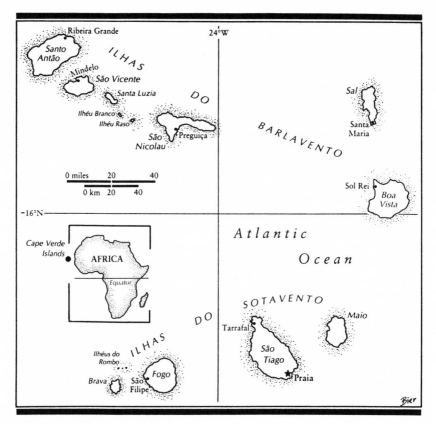

Figure 1. Map of the Cape Verde Islands.

although some historians maintain that the Cape Verdes may have been known to Arabs and Africans before the Portuguese discovery.[3] Actually an Italian navigator, Antonio da Noli, sailing with a Portuguese expedition, is credited with first coming upon the archipelago in 1455.[4] For over five hundred years, until 1975, when the islands became an independent nation, known as the Republic of Cape Verde, the inhabitants lived under Portuguese colonial rule. In the early years of colonization, the Portuguese tried to establish large-scale sugar and cotton plantations on the islands using a system similar to that which had already been implemented in southern Portugal, the Algarve, the Azores, and Madeira. Almost from the very beginning of settlement, West African slaves were being brought to the Cape Verdes to labor on the plantations, but the arid climate of these Sahelian islands prevented truly successful commercial cultivation of the land. What soon became more important to the Portuguese than agricultural production was the strategic location of the archipelago as a crossroads in the expanding slave trade. Situated near the Guinea coast and on the Trade Winds route to Brazil, the Cape Verdes served as an entrepôt for the distribution of goods both legal and clandestine, for supplying foreign vessels with needed supplies and salt, and for transporting slaves to the New World.

As these exchanges were taking place, the sparse Portuguese population intermingled with the greater numbers of slaves to produce a rich and distinctive Cape Verdean society and culture. From the start, the island population was ethnically diverse. Among the Europeans, in addition to the Portuguese were Genoese, Castilians, and Spaniards while it has been estimated that a minimum of twenty-seven different West African ethnic groups were represented among the early settlers.[5] Because of the inhospitable climate and isolation of the archipelago it was always difficult to attract white migrants. Adventurers and refugees, including Jews fleeing persecution[6] as well as criminal and political exiles or *degredados,* made up much of the Portuguese influx. The *degredados,* who comprised a significant proportion of the white settlement, began arriving as early as 1500. Oftentimes their banishment to the Cape Verdes was temporary, but, in some cases, they did remain permanently. Exiled without their families, the *degredados* formed liaisons with slave women, increasing the mulatto sector which was as likely to have free status as not. Some of these settlers also crossed over to mainland Africa to trade along the rivers of Upper Guinea, forming a broker class. Known as *lancados,* they organized trading relations between African chiefs and visiting European ships, often marrying African women during their stay. The role of middleman would reassert itself at various points in the history of Portuguese colonization, particularly under the Salazar régime when Cape Verdeans were utilized as government administrators in the other colonies.

Another factor that contributed to a easing of distinctions between master and slave and that also expanded the free black population resulted from the frequent pirate attacks on the islands. During these assaults, landowners would flee to the mountains and in the ensuing confusion, their slaves too would run away to the interior, forming autonomous communities, particularly in the mountaintops of the island of São Tiago. In addition to these self-liberated slaves, unlike the system in the United States, Cape Verdean slavery was marked by frequent manumissions. Freedom was granted routinely for good behavior as well as for those considered to be descended from the master, including nieces and nephews as well as sons and daughters. During periods of extended drought conditions, slaves were let go because of severe shortages of food and the absence of a demand for their labors. In those periods, however, while freed from political bondage, these individuals then had to face dire economic circumstances with large numbers succumbing to starvation. Finally, at no point in the history of the governing of the archipelago were there legal sanctions prohibiting interracial marriages or liaisons.[7] Consequently, by the twentieth century, almost the entire population of the Cape Verdes was made up of people of mixed descent.

Hence, in this mesh of African ancestry, Catholicism, and Western presence, it has not always been possible to discern whether the European or the African influence predominates. Rather, the interweaving has been so complete that it is most appropriate to speak of the evolution of a separate culture with its own distinctive customs, folklore, cuisine, music, literature, and, finally, language. Though based in Portuguese and several West African languages, the mother tongue of the Cape Verdean people is a full-fledged, creolized language of its own, called *Crioulo*.[8] The official language is still Portuguese, but *Crioulo* is the vehicle of everyday communication in Cape Verde for everyone at all levels of society. Although varying from one island to another, it became a defining feature of the Cape Verdean cultural identity that has been transmitted to the United States and other parts of the world.[9]

Always plagued by scanty and erratic rainfall, the effects of the dry climate in the Cape Verdes were exacerbated by colonial mismanagement of the land,[10] so that by the end of the eighteenth century, the people of the Islands were experiencing severe and recurrent drought with its resulting famine and high mortality. Unable to escape overland to more favorable conditions, the young Cape Verdeans seized the chance to leave home in search of a better life as crew aboard the United States whaling ships that were beginning to arrive at the archipelago's protective harbors. American merchant vessels were already a familiar sight, as by this time the Islands had become a regular stopover in the trade with the west coast of Africa, the Canaries, Brazil, and other parts of the world.[11] Beginning in 1816, the United States established consuls on two of the islands, São Tiago and São Vicente. Furthermore, in the 1840s and 1850s in an effort to curtail the imports of slaves, the United States formed its African Squadron, a fleet of sailing cruisers used to further the antislavery mission by boarding suspected ships and seizing their human cargoes. Some of these vessels were based in Cape Verdean ports.

Especially as Yankee seamen began to lose interest in whaling due to decreasing profits in the industry, the ship captains looked to the

Cape Verde Islands in order to recruit hands who could be paid less money than their American counterparts. At the same time, because of the impoverished conditions, the men of the archipelago were eager to obtain a berth on a whaler, no matter what the pay, as a means to escape the constant suffering.

The Cape Verdean recruits quickly earned a reputation as valued seamen who made up a disciplined and able crew. Despite their skill and desirability as whalers, however, they were routinely allotted the lowest rates in the division of profits and were frequently subject to harsh treatment in the mariners' hierarchy because of discrimination based on race and ethnicity.[12] The exploitation of their labors at sea foreshadowed a similar prejudice that they would face in their land-based occupations once the immigrants began to settle in southeastern New England.[13]

By the late nineteenth century, with the advent of steamship travel and the decline of the whaling and sealing industries, the old sailing vessels became obsolete and were therefore available at a very low cost. Some of the early Cape Verdean immigrants took advantage of this opportunity to buy up these old Essex-built "Gloucester Fishermen." They pooled their resources and converted them into cargo and passenger ships, known as packet boats, for regular sailings between fixed destinations. With the purchase of a sixty-four-ton fishing schooner, the *Nellie May,* Antonio Coelho became the first Cape Verdean American packet owner. He hired a former whaleman as captain and the ship set sail for Brava in 1892.[14]

Before long Cape Verdean American settlers owned a fleet of these former whalers and schooners that regularly plied between the ports of New Bedford and Providence and the islands of Cape Verde, particularly Brava. Thus, in a situation unlike that of most immigrant groups, black or white, the Cape Verdeans came to have control over their own means of passage to this country.

During the same period, cheap sources of labor were being sought for the expanding textile mills and the cranberry bogs of southeastern Massachusetts. Larger numbers of immigrants were arriving to fulfill the demand, fleeing their land of continual hunger. In the first decade of the twentieth century, drought conditions became even more intolerable, accelerating the economic disintegration of the Islands. The people booked passage on the packet ships, with the hope of surviving through emigration to America. This movement continued steadily until the enforcement of the restrictive immigration laws of 1921 and 1924.

It is this history of Cape Verdean immigration to and settlement in southeastern Massachusetts that I will examine in the following pages.

To date, a comprehensive study of the Cape Verdean American experience has not been written.[15] The relatively small size of the population accounts for some of the inattention, but the invisible nature of Cape Verdean ethnicity stems from other factors as well. Deirdre Meintel, the only American anthropologist to have done extensive field work in the Cape Verdes, concluded that the continued obscurity of Cape Verdeans in this country parallels their historical lack of recognition within the colonial empire, a phenomenon she called "double invisibility":[16]

> The social invisibility Cape Verdean Americans experience as a small, Afro-American ethnic group, is nothing new to them. Time and again the insignificance of the archipelago in Portugal's empire was made clear; for example, by the lack of maritime contact with the metropole for years on end, the indifference of the Portuguese government to the plight of the islands during droughts, and even by the new social science texts, introduced during the colonial wars, that were oriented to the larger, more economically valuable, mainland colonies.[17]

Moreover, in part because of the ambiguity of their regional placement, not only have Cape Verdeans been eclipsed from Portuguese history, they have also been marginalized in the field of African Studies despite their long-standing socioeconomic and political ties to continental Africa. Thus, to acknowledge the social identity of Cape Verdean Americans is to have some cognizance of the Cape Verde Islands themselves, a part of our world history and geography lessons that has traditionally been overlooked.

Another explanation for why this group has been neglected derives from the manner in which white racism has functioned in North American society. Historically, racial classification in the United States has been an oversimplified matter of black or white, a dichotomy that has virtually obliterated cultural differences among people of color. The Cape Verdean Americans are an example of such cultural invalidation with their history having been systematically ignored. Even more recent studies that have been done in the wake of ethnic revivalism, such as Stanley Lieberson's *A Piece of the Pie: Blacks and White Immigrants Since 1880,* have failed to note the place of this group in our past. In this book, the author has amassed an abundance of data to explain why white immigrant groups have fared better than blacks in America. While he touches on the histories of other nonwhite groups besides native blacks, such as the Japanese American settlement, he makes no mention of Cape Verdeans. This omission is not surprising and is typical of the literature on the subject. What is glaring is that in his discussion of newcomers to this country from 1890 to 1924, he inaccurately asserts that, "As for blacks, there was virtually no voluntary migration from either Africa or some of the areas of black settlement in the New World."[18] This gap in our collective knowledge of the history of Cape Verdean Americans has detracted from even some of the better attempts at multicultural research.

Finally, those who have previously embarked on studies of Cape Verdean Americans have been continually frustrated in their efforts by the absence of reliable sources necessary to produce a profile of this population.[19] Again, as a result of the hegemony of a dualistic racial system, the U.S. Census and other official records have subsumed the Cape Verdeans under other broad categories, most often as "Portuguese" but also as "African Portuguese," "Black Portuguese" and "Atlantic Islanders." This confusion has discouraged many a researcher on the subject. My own work has only been possible through the discovery of a previously unexamined source: ship manifests that specifically name the Cape Verdeans and that have enabled me to cull a wealth of demographic information about this group.

That the history of this distinctive ethnic and racial group in America has not yet been systematically recorded is reason enough to suggest such an undertaking. But the story of Cape Verdean American immigration is of particular significance when considered in the framework of recent historical scholarship that compares the adaptation and social mobility patterns of native blacks with European immigrants during the process of large-scale urbanization and mass migration that occurred in the late nineteenth and early twentieth centuries in this country.[20]

Here is a people who immigrated to the United States freely as Portuguese colonials and who identified themselves in terms of ethnicity but who, because of their mixed African and European ancestry, were looked upon by the rest of society as a racial category. Although the Cape Verdeans sought recognition as Portuguese Americans, the "white" Portuguese, chiefly from the Azores and Madeira, disassociated themselves from them. From very early on in their settlement here, Cape Verdeans were excluded from Portuguese national parishes, social clubs, and neighborhoods. At the same time, the Cape Verdeans chose not to identify with American blacks. Their Catholicism tended to keep them apart from the primarily Protestant African American population but, more powerfully, the Cape Verdean Americans quickly perceived the adverse effects of racism on the upward mobility of anyone considered nonwhite in this country. Though no match for the pervasive racial discrimination, Cape Verdeans also had to confront the virulent anti-Catholic sentiment rife at the time of their immigration to the United States.

Furthermore, the Anglo or dominant culture regarded Cape Verdeans as black not only because of a biologically defined and rigid racial structure but also because of social class. The jobs they were able to obtain were the same type of menial jobs held by black Americans and as a result, their place in the economy of southeastern New England was not very different than that of African Americans. Thus, the definition of race that was imposed upon them was based not only on the color of their skin but also on the role they played in the local economy and social structure.

Because of their unique geographical location as well as their ethnic and racial identification, the Cape Verdean experience does not readily fall into either the literature on black migration from the rural south to the urban north or that of southern, central, and eastern European immigration to the shores of America. However, certain ideas resulting from this theoretical material can still be of use as applied to the particular example of the Cape Verdean Americans. Conversely, the Cape Verdean case itself can serve to further illuminate the historical experience of both white and black immigrants and migrants in the United States.

Very broadly speaking, the work on black migration and European immigration falls under one of two conflicting interpretations. The classic assimilationist theory, when applied to southern rural blacks, depicts them arriving in northern cities much as the European peasant did. Unfamiliar with the urban environment or industrialization, they were accorded the lowest paying jobs, lived under poverty conditions and suffered from family disorganization. In time, however, over at least one generation, they began to overcome these odds and, like the other immigrant groups before them, were able to get themselves onto an upwardly mobile track and finally make the adjustment to city life. This model of urban adaptation has been called "ethnic succession" and can be applied to European immigrant groups as well.[21]

In the case of both the descendants of slaves from the South and the European newcomers, urbanization would effectively wipe out the vestiges of premigration culture as the migrant accommodated to the new society. Each successive wave of immigrants would make it into the middle class but at the expense of cultural disintegration and individual anomie.

At the other extreme is more recent research on urban adaptation. These efforts argue that new arrivals to the city retained their premigration culture and emphasize that race and ethnicity are independent factors that can account for varying patterns of adjustment and social mobility among different ethnic groups.[22] From this point of view, the migrant is seen as being more in charge, less a pawn in the urbanization process. Family continuity and preservation of the old ways persisted despite the tremendous turmoil of uprooting. Whether ex-slaves or peasant immigrants, the settlers used their various cultural backgrounds to facilitate accommodation and survival in the new environment. In some cases, moving to the city strengthened traditional customs rather than accelerating assimilation.

In fact, the adaptation process, especially in the case of the Cape Verdeans, was much more complex than either of these interpretations suggests. At best, the ethnic succession model incorporates the phenomenon of race in terms of African American exceptionalism. Within ethnicity theory the experience of slavery and its legacy of institutionalized inequality is recognized as being a special obstacle to the black population in the adaptation process. Without minimizing the extent of rabid anti-immigrant bias in this country, it is now clear that racial minorities have encountered a different kind rather than a different degree of prejudice than white ethnic groups have faced, an institutionalized form of discrimination that is deeply embedded and tenaciously endures.[23] Only African Americans were enslaved, Native Americans nearly exterminated and removed to reservations, and Japanese Americans—not German or Italian Americans—relocated to concentration camps during World War II, to cite some of the most striking examples of the differing consequences of racism versus ethnocentrism. Moreover, prevailing racist attitudes have been the major deterrent to the kind of successful adjustment that the ethnic succession approach postulates.[24]

A further limitation of the ethnicity paradigm when applied to foreign-born blacks in particular is the absence of recognition of the diversity of cultures *among* racial minorities in the United States. African Americans are seen within this construct as simply another ethnic group, an undifferentiated population. Like the larger society itself, the discourse of ethnicity theory reveals a biracial rather than multicultural mode of analysis. Ethnic differences within the black population are too often overlooked in the scholarship on race relations as well. The peculiar but widely held belief that whites—whether Anglo-Saxon, Polish, or Greek—are defined by ethnicity, while blacks are defined by the color of their skin alone, persists. As the sociologists Michael Omni and Howard Winant succinctly state: *"Blacks in ethnic terms are as diverse as whites."*[25] This concept has been missing within the entire body of literature on the history of North American immigration,

race, and ethnicity, resulting in a seriously flawed interpretative framework with which to work.

Related to the idea of cultural homogeneity among migrants of color
is another myth that permeates the scholarship on immigration; that
is, the belief that all our forbears came from Europe. For example, the
usual assertion in our history books or, for that matter, in immigration
texts, is that the first restrictive immigration laws were passed in the
early 1920s, when the doors slammed shut. To make such a statement
is to completely ignore the Chinese Exclusion Act, passed over 40 years
earlier in 1882 and subsequently renewed several times, the first such
prohibitive immigration legislation.[26] Yet, this error is commonplace in
the literature, the result of seeing United States immigration solely in
terms of European arrivals. As Ronald Takaki states and reiterates in
the very title of his fine history of Asian Americans, *Strangers from a
Different Shore*, "Eurocentric history serves no one. It only shrouds
the pluralism that is America and that makes our nation so unique,
and thus the possibility of appreciating our rich racial and cultural
diversity remains a dream deferred. Actually, as Americans, we come
originally from many different shores—Europe, the Americas, Africa,
and also Asia."[27]

Certainly, the policy makers were acutely aware, though clearly not
appreciative, of the varying shores from which the second wave arrivals
came as is evidenced by this rationale given by an authority on immigration policy in support of the 1921 quota act:

> We believe that our best interests will be served by keeping the
> United States as far as possible a white man's country. Our own
> history, as well as the history of other countries, affords many examples
> of the serious difficulties that arise when members of very diverse
> races come into intimate contact. We cannot assimilate the yellow,
> brown, and black races. . . . There is need at the present time of
> excluding other dark skinned races, a need which will undoubtedly
> increase unless some action is taken. From 1899 to 1922 there were
> admitted to this country over 115,000 African blacks, and during the
> same period more than 25,000 West Indians other than Cubans. One
> would think that our Negro problem was already large enough without
> adding to it that way. . . . But it would seem, since we have applied
> the principle of exclusion to such people as the Chinese and Japanese,
> that we should go the whole way and totally exclude the black
> immigrant-aliens. The barred zone should be extended to Africa and

also to the West Indies, especially to Jamaica and the Bahamas, to stop the coming of blacks from those quarters.[28]

While immigration scholars would do well to differentiate ethnicity within racial categories and to recognize the varying continental origins of immigrants, it is of equal importance to grasp the links that have been made between racial minorities by those representing the dominant culture. For example, what is the relationship of the history of anti-Asian bias to discrimination against blacks in the promulgation of white racism in this country?

Including immigrants of color and including those who have migrated here from places other than Europe presents a formidable challenge to each of the major theories of assimilation where racial minorities have been incorporated by analogy only. This problem exists whether utilizing the traditional paradigm of the melting pot or the concept of Anglo-conformity, which posits a dominant Anglo-Saxon majority culture under which all others should be subsumed. Even subscribing to the more currently popular model of cultural pluralism that allows for the possibility that ethnic groups can coexist, each retaining their varying cultural forms without fusing into one another nor having to submit to Anglo-Saxon supremacy, is not fully adequate to explain the experience and adaptation patterns of certain immigrant populations. The failure of all American assimilationist theory to date is that race, if discussed at all, is treated as a derivative of ethnicity. Or similarly, the tendency in the scholarship is to meld together ethnicity and race, using both terms interchangeably as if they were the same. Furthermore, all three models emphasize the European immigrant to the exclusion of Asian, African, Hispanic, and Caribbean groups, all of which have had a significant presence in this country even before the recent wave of immigration.[29]

While the Cape Verdean people do represent a blend of racial and ethnic elements in their cultural identity, it is necessary to distinguish the racial and ethnic aspects of their history to best understand the meaning of their experience in the United States. It has not been useful for scholars to conflate the two social categories, in part because what often occurs is that the European or white ethnics become the norm. The particular issues of being a racial minority in this society get lost, as with the example, given above, of the recurring obliteration of the history of discrimination against Chinese Americans. Studies of those populations that are simultaneously racial and ethnic groups are of particular value in their potential to reveal the most to us about the social nature of each of the categories.

My analysis of issues of race and ethnicity among the Cape Verdean immigrants turns on a theoretical premise that views race as a social construction. Race, in this context, is no longer solely a by-product of ethnicity or social class but, indeed, has an epistemology of its own. Omi and Winant in *Racial Formation in the United States* emphasize the malleability of racial meanings, arguing convincingly that race cannot be seen as an ahistorical phenomenon or physical fact. Rather, it is an ever-changing set of notions subject to the influence of shifting ideological and power structures within society. This reformulation of race can be understood both in terms of external social perceptions and from the point of view of a people's own self-identification. In her pivotal 1982 essay, "Ideology and Race in American History," Barbara Fields writes, "Ideas about color, like ideas about anything else, derive their importance, indeed their definition, from their context."[30]

Over twenty years ago, in *White Over Black: American Attitudes toward the Negro,* Winthrop Jordan brilliantly deconstructed the language and rationale for enslavement in this country. He traced the origins of the earliest white ideas of blackness and the evolution of this racial imagery down to the antebellum period in the United States, arguing that English beliefs about black inferiority were already in place before the development of the slave system. By so doing and although he is writing in the tradition of the intellectual historian, in this case utilizing a theory of psychosexual analysis, his interpretation demonstrates the fluidity of racial notions, implicitly refuting the concept of race as a biological and fixed category. Interestingly, given the subject of this book, the first example Jordan gives us of initial contacts between Africans and the English occurred in 1564 at the Cape Verde Islands: "The most arresting characteristic of the newly discovered African was his color. Travelers rarely failed to comment upon it; indeed when describing Negroes they frequently began with complexion and then moved on to dress (or rather lack of it) and manners. At Cape Verde, 'These people are all blacke, and are called negros, without any apparell, saving before their privities.' "[31]

The theory of racial formation needs to be further elaborated to strengthen the view of race as a factor, like gender, which is historically constructed and which changes social meaning in time and place. Such an approach to ideas about race owes a debt to the body of knowledge that has been developed among feminist scholars. Writings such as Joan Scott's prize-winning book, *Gender and the Politics of History,* help us to understand that women's and men's roles are not rooted in nature but that, in fact, they are always subject to historical construction.[32] Gender as a tool of historical inquiry offers a conceptual framework that looks at the changing ideas of womanhood and manhood and ways in which actual behavior has met these prescriptions. Likewise, in the United States racial classification has historically been viewed in rigid categories of black and white. Yet, the Cape Verdeans are an excellent example of a nonwhite immigrant group whose ethnicity has been obscured and whose racial self-concept and labels have shifted over time, falling into categories of identification that are historically nuanced, complex, and ever-changing.

Theoretical models of ethnicity, of social class, and of nationality have taken precedence in the literature, but have been woefully inadequate when applied, as they have been, to racial minorities. In fact, a person can be white one day and black the next, or an individual's race may change simply by moving from one country to another.[33] In societies with more fluid racial structures and at times when historical conditions allow greater possibilities for flux, education, wealth, and other cultural or economic factors can have as much importance or more than phenotype or skin shade in determining one's social position. Hence, in her study of Jamaicans, Nancy Foner speaks of individuals who "change" color in Jamaican society as their life circumstances shift while Karen Blu found that the American Lumbee population who were initially regarded as a race but who perceived themselves as "a people" (in ethnic terms) have now reconfigured their own identity so that they are currently considered an ethnic group by all.[34] If race really is a biological fact, then why is it that states have had to engage in such lengthy judicial deliberations to legally and socially designate racial identities? And how is it that governments differ in the official labeling of certain populations as racial groups? Jews were a race in Nazi Germany; South Africans define the Japanese as "honorary" whites. Several of the oral history accounts in this volume illustrate the evolution of varying racial identifications in time and place within a single lifetime.

Sometimes, however, self-definitions do not match the assigned social designations, leading to psychologically painful consequences. This kind of personal turmoil stemming from a sense of being unseen is a recurrent theme in the Cape Verdean life histories as well. Omni and Winant discuss the psychosocial origins of such a crisis of identity: "One of the first things we notice about people when we meet them (along with their sex) is their race. We utilize race to provide clues about *who* a person is. This fact is made painfully obvious when we encounter someone whom we cannot conveniently racially categorize—someone who is, for example, racially mixed or of an ethnic/racial group with which we are not familiar. Such an encounter becomes a source of discomfort and momentarily a crisis of racial meaning. Without a racial identity, one is in danger of having no identity."[35]

The absence of an identity is precisely how one journalist titled his commentary on the Cape Verdean immigrant—"A People without a Race."[36] Also unable to readily classify the Cape Verdeans by race, another referred to them as "the green people," taking literally the translation of Cape Verde.[37] Confusion about identification crops up often in the literature about and by Cape Verdeans. "Black, White or Portuguese? A Cape Verdean Dilemma," an oral history by a Cape Verdean American woman, speaks directly to these contradictions.[38] Neither black nor white, but sometimes white, at other times black, African, Portuguese, brown, even *green*, Cape Verdean immigrants are continually having to redefine their identity. And it is not simply a matter of changing self-definitions. In terms of successful adaptation, how they are defined by others often has had greater social and economic significance than how they see themselves.

Yet the experience of invisibility is certainly not peculiar to Cape Verdean Americans alone. On the contrary, it is an issue they have in common with other black ethnic groups in this country, familiar and troubling to all. Carlos Guillermo Wilson refers to Afro-Hispanics as "los excluidos" (the excluded ones). On Black Cubans, Heriberto Dixon writes, " 'To be or not to be' that is the question facing black Cubans although they may not be aware of it. Are they a black minority within the larger Cuban minority? Or, are they a Cuban minority within a larger black minority?" and in another of his articles on this subject, he simply begins with the title, "Who Ever Heard of a Black Cuban?" In *Puerto Ricans: Born in the USA,* Clara Rodriguez calls her chapter on race "The Rainbow People" and speaks of dialectical distance, the phenomenon of Puerto Ricans caught between two polarities. Haitian immigrants, too, express the contradictions and ambiguities of being a "minority within a minority."[39]

According to Roy Simon Bryce-LaPorte, "Black immigrants operate—as blacks and immigrants—in the United States under more levels of cross-pressures, multiple affiliations and inequalities than either native blacks or European immigrants. . . . On the national level, they suffer double invisibility, in fact—as *blacks* and as *black foreigners*."[40] Once again the term *double invisibility* emerges as a way to understand the Cape Verdean experience. While Meintel used the phrase to refer to the confluence of Cape Verdean obscurity, both within the system of Portuguese colonialism and in terms of social identity, Bryce-LaPorte suggests a meaning that is reminiscent of the underside of W. E. B.

Du Bois's paradoxical notion of African American "two-ness." According to Du Bois, "two-ness" reflects both the spiritually empowering and deeply conflictual nature of the double consciousness that blacks inevitably experience in American society.[41] Yet because of the potentially crushing force of white cultural dominance, the possibilities for obliteration are twofold as well. Certainly, Ralph Ellison understood this phenomenon in relation to blackness when in his introduction to the novel *Invisible Man* he declared, "despite the bland assertions of sociologists, 'high visibility' actually rendered one *un*-visible—whether at high noon in Macy's window or illuminated by flaming torches and flashbulbs while undergoing the ritual sacrifice that was dedicated to the ideal of white supremacy."[42]

For the Cape Verdean immigrants or perhaps, for all people of color in the United States, the struggle to be seen, the extent to which identities have been eclipsed is so exponential, that "double" may not suffice to name it. Rather, the invisibility is a multiply configured legacy, the result of centuries of global colonizing efforts based on notions of racial inferiority. At the very least, then, this study is an attempt to provide a coherent history and explanation of the Cape Verdean experience that will assist in making this people of mixed racial and ethnic background a less invisible, more recognizable entity.

Perhaps because the United States has had a history of institutionalizing racism within such fixed genetic categories as compared to other societies, even those with a history of slavery such as Brazil or even the Cape Verde Islands themselves, it has been more difficult for American historians to view race as anything but a physical attribute. Yet it must be understood that the intellectual past that we inherit, the privileging of certain kinds of knowledges, in this case the powerful theory and methods of biological determinism were also historically constructed.[43] That the social or cultural dimensions of race in the United States have been less generally evident does not mean that race in this country is more inherent than elsewhere. Exploring the history of a foreign-born population of color, such as the Cape Verdean migrant to this apparently immutable bipolar racial system, gives us an opportunity to jar essentialist notions of race that have permeated our understandings of the United States racial order. It also points to the need to collapse the traditional and arbitrary division between black history and immigration studies, a schism that reflects, in part, the tendency of historians to think of race relations primarily in terms of the African American experience alone.

While the Cape Verdean example raises questions initially concerning the changing racial meanings of black and brown, those who deal with the social construction of race need not make the mistake of only focusing on people "of color" when analyzing shifting definitions. Some of the best work, like Jordan's *White Over Black* or Marlon Riggs's 1987 film, *Ethnic Notions,*[44] are not actually about blacks but rather are interested in how whites conceptualize the "other," whether African or African American, both in terms of racial and sexual constructs. They are as concerned with what racial imagery can tell us about *Anglo*-American culture as about black society.

However, we ought to take this approach one step further and ask the same questions about whiteness as we do about being black when discussing race. That is, how has the idea of being "white" changed over time and just what color is "white" anyway? Did not the "white" Portuguese immigrants—those from mainland Portugal, the Azores and Madeira—already bring with them their own autonomous racial baggage—that of colonizers toward the colonized, that of migrants who back at home were also socially white, not black, but whose ethnicity still held connotations of Moorish, hence, dark-skinned ancestry in this country? The entire second wave of southern and eastern European migrants were arriving in a period of rabid nativistic sentiment that rested in part on the fear that white Anglo-Saxon purity would be undermined by the infusion of darker-skinned peoples. Perhaps, part of the process of adaptation and legitimization for the "white" Portuguese in the United States was to learn to become "*whiter*" than ever in the new society and to do so by purposefully defining themselves in sharp contrast to the "black" or Cape Verdean Portuguese. At the conclusion of his pilgrimage to Mecca in 1964, Malcolm X came to understand "whiteness" as a social construction in a profoundly transformative moment for him:

> It was when I first began to perceive that "white man," as commonly used, means complexion only secondarily; primarily it described attitudes and actions. In America, "white man" meant specific attitudes and actions toward the black man, and toward all other non-white men. . . .
>
> You may be shocked by these words coming from me. But on this pilgrimage, what I have seen and experienced has forced me to *rearrange* much of my thought-patterns previously held and to *toss aside* some of my previous conclusions. . . . During the past eleven days here in the Muslim world, I have eaten from the same plate, drunk from the same glass, and slept in the same bed (or on the same rug)— while praying to the *same God*—with fellow Muslims, whose eyes were the bluest of blue, whose hair was the blondest of blond, and

whose skin was the whitest of white. And in the *words* and in the *actions* and in the *deeds* of the "white" Muslims, I felt the same sincerity that I had felt among the black Africa Muslims of Nigeria, Sudan, and Ghana.

We were *truly* all the same (brothers) — because their belief in one God had removed the "white" from their minds, the "white" from their behavior and the "white" from their attitude.[45]

Largely through analysis of legal documentation, Virginia Dominguez begins to grapple with these issues, including the examination of the meaning of white in her study of Creoles in Louisiana, *White by Definition*. She explains:

> To begin with, the existence of alternative definitions of *Creole* and of alternative criteria by which persons come to be identified as Creoles undermines a number of common assumptions about ethnic identity. . . .
>
> For one, most individuals have a large number of potential identities by ancestry alone. A person who moves back far enough in the family genealogy is likely to find ancestors of different national origin, social class and in many cases even racial origin. . . .
>
> But there is more. The dispute between the two sectors of Louisiana's population that identify themselves as Creole, in addition, hinges on the status connotations of the labels *Creole, white,* and *black*. . . . Thus, to identify someone as Creole is to invoke in the course of a particular conversation historically linked connotations of social and economic status.[46]

Furthermore, not only can a creole, mulatto, or biracial identity stir up uneasy historical questions of social and economic standing, it can also visibly connote a problematic sexual history as well, a factor that, perhaps more than any other aspect of crossing the fixed boundaries of racial definition, makes people extremely uncomfortable even in the contemporary social milieu. It is instructive here to remember that the Cape Verdean immigrants were beginning to arrive in large numbers during the latter half of the nineteenth century and into the twentieth, a period that coincides with the zenith of what could be termed, in the language of social psychology, a national phobia concerning interracial intimacy. The specter of the reproductive legacy resulting from widespread miscegenation under slavery (white male/black female) precipitated much of the fear of racial intermingling in these years. The near maniacal preoccupation with prohibiting contact between the races reached its height at this time with widespread southern vigilante action in the form of lynch mobs acting under the pretext of protecting white women from free black male sexuality. While Omi and Winant above, certainly make an important point in their description of what typically occurs in an encounter with a person of mixed racial heritage when they state that "Without a racial identity, one is in danger of having no identity," at other times it is not merely the *absence* of recognition that triggers a crisis of racial meaning. Rather, peering into the face of a multiracial person can unveil the existence of a cross-racial sexual liaison—living proof that this strict legal and social taboo has been violated, a realization that disturbs the state of denial about such activity that operates in most peoples' consciousness about race and sexuality. Under the gaze of the person whose security and worldview depend upon a clear, state-sanctioned separation of black and white, the mestizo becomes a sexual transgressor. More than simply facing an individual of indeterminate racial background, what transpires in this case is an even more complex and unsettling clash of racial meanings. When significant numbers of people cannot be readily categorized, it threatens to undermine the entire system of social classification.

Finally, in addition to questioning received notions of racial and ethnic categorization, this study endeavors to overcome another limitation of much of the work in the field of immigration history. For the most part the story of American immigration has been written from the perspective of an assumed male actor, although it is the case that in the last several years the trend has begun to reverse itself.[47] In part to combat the traditional approach, some recent publications have focused solely on the female experience. Although there are noteworthy exceptions within the latest scholarship that do successfully intersect analysis of gender, race, ethnicity, or social class, in monographs such as this study, where a particular ethnic group is the subject, women, if present at all, are usually lumped in with the children and known only as the "family" of the [male] migrant.[48] To insure that the female voices would be heard above the clatter of immigrant family activity, approximately half of my oral histories were conducted with women.

As has been shown to be the case with women of other ethnic groups migrating during this period, Cape Verdean women rarely were involved in formalized institutional activities such as labor unions or mutual benefit societies. Rather, their lives were lived through informal kinship, neighborhood, church, and workplace connections within the ethnic enclave. Like African American and other racial-ethnic women, the vast majority of Cape Verdean female migrants, whether single or married with children, worked outside the home. They labored primarily as pickers in the cranberry bogs along Buzzards Bay and Cape

Cod, Massachusetts, or as domestics in urban neighborhoods adjacent to the Cape Verdean community. A smaller number worked in the textile mills of southeastern New England but held the lowest paid and least desirable positions, under hiring practices based on race and ethnicity as well as gender. The Cape Verdean immigrant woman's accommodation to the labor market and the ways that her family and work responsibilities converged as she found strategies to support family survival will be addressed in this volume.

More challenging has been the attempt to explore the interplay of issues of gender with the variables of race and ethnicity within this framework. While I had consciously attempted to give equal attention to women's voices from the onset of the project, gender analysis was not an initial priority of this work. Since the research phase was completed, I have come to recognize the extent to which a fully integrated interpretation based on gender serves to strengthen our understandings of all other aspects of the immigrant experience. Yet, this book remains centrally concerned with issues of race and ethnicity. My hope as of this writing has been to simply raise the question of how the social construction of Cape Verdean racial/ethnic identity may itself be gendered.[49]

In the chapters that follow I will demonstrate ways that Cape Verdeans do resemble the other "white" ethnic groups arriving during the period of mass migration. Moreover, in many respects, the newcomers from the Cape Verde Islands were a classic sojourner immigrant population. Yet, unlike their European counterparts, the Cape Verdean arrivals faced a country of racial as well as ethnic hostility. Their decision to relocate in this country began a long and challenging search for a distinctive social identity within North American society.

The daily life of the cranberry pickers who settled on Cape Cod will be contrasted to that of the city dwellers who worked on the docks and in the mills and households of the wealthier residents in New Bedford. Many Cape Verdeans had a seasonal rural/urban migratory patterning, working the bogs in the late summer and fall, back to the city and the factories in the winter. In this sense the rural and urban communities were not such separate entities. Like some communities of southern African Americans, Cape Verdeans spanned a rural/industrial continuum.[50] This comparison will be approached from the perspective of how rural and urban experiences differed when put through the crucible of racial definitions. The question of what it meant in relation to cultural adaptation and economic advancement for a people with African ancestry to have emigrated to a country of racial hostility out of a self-willed search for opportunity and flight from hardship versus forcible capture and enslavement will also be explored. Although the Cape Verdean American immigrants have never been free of the difficulties that have stemmed from having to reconcile their mixed European and African ancestry with a society that exhibits such sharp racial differences, it will be seen that the ethnic communities that they did establish in southeastern Massachusetts facilitated adaptation in the primary period of settlement.

These questions will be addressed using a variety of sources. Reconstructing the history of Cape Verdean Americans has been hampered by a scarcity of written materials as well as the absence, noted earlier, of accurate population records. Official governmental sources on Cape Verde itself are also extremely limited, like the record of the entire modern history of Portugal during the period between 1920 and 1974, the era of the Salazar dictatorship and the formation of *Estado Novo,* the "New State." As political freedoms disappeared so were any vestiges of critical inquiry squashed. Records were haphazardly kept with no attempt to systematically preserve or catalogue them. Wide gaps in official documentation exist from these long years of authoritarian rule and neglect.[51]

Official Census figures have not been of use in defining the Cape Verdean immigrant population; therefore, I sought to locate an alternative source of reliable data and found it in the record on microfilm of the actual passenger and crew lists of arriving vessels from the Cape Verde Islands to the port of New Bedford, Massachusetts. These ship manifests, required first by the United States Secretary of the Treasury and then by the Secretary of Commerce and Labor, contain an abundance of information on each arriving alien. Passenger lists of vessels coming in from the Cape Verde Islands cover the period 1860–1934.[52] In all, a total of 23,168 entries arriving on 450 different voyages were recorded, providing a solid demographic base from which to proceed.

Like many other recent works of the new social history, this study has benefited from anthropologist Clifford Geertz's model of ethnographic research both in terms of its validation of the significance of lived experience and in the interest in a dynamic and multitextured cultural analysis.[53] However, by using both statistical data and "thick description," my hope is to avoid the pitfalls of solely relying upon either approach. The potential limitations of applying Geertzian semiotics to historical inquiry have been compared by Ron Walters to "those of quantification, its methodological rival in social history. Both tend to freeze theory at a middle level short of anything all-encompassing. Both can turn in on themselves to an obsession with method over content. Each ironically, has the potential to divorce itself from the gritty experiences of the common folk it intends to study, the one by reducing people to numbers, the other by elevating them to literature."[54] In fact, the two methods can be complementary. Rich ethnographic data in the form of oral accounts that individuate human experience serve to enliven the numbers while the statistics are a constant reminder that this is not the unraveling of a make-believe world, an intriguing plot in a work of historical fiction. Rather, real life histories are being explicated. These are episodes filled with possibilities for symbolic analysis, but nonetheless played out within the social realities of the power structures, racial climate and economic conditions existent in the United States during the late nineteenth and early twentieth centuries.

The other sources essential to this study are the personal recollections of the Cape Verdean immigrants themselves.[55] There are still living today Cape Verdean Americans who can give firsthand accounts of the process of settlement in the early part of this century, bringing to life and complementing the quantitative data furnished by the logs of the packet ship trade. Alone, the individual narratives would not have been adequate to support broader historical conclusions, yet they became invaluable when presented in conjunction with the demographic findings and the available secondary sources. While the statistical analysis sets the stage for the drama of the immigrant experience, the life histories are the dialogue, a script filled with a range of emotion and private testimony that transcends the more static evidence of the public record.

The oral history approach has by now become an accepted method of historical research, offering important insights into the lives and struggles of ordinary people. Perhaps the greatest contribution that this methodology has facilitated, however, is in gaining access to the folk history of groups whose heritage might otherwise be lost. This is particularly true of cultures that have a predominantly oral rather than written tradition. Cape Verdeans are such a people. The *Crioulo* language is a primarily spoken one, as are all creole languages. Only in very recent years has there been a systematic attempt to preserve it in written form.[56] Furthermore the oral histories themselves can become documentation for future researchers, despite the emphatic statement that "unlike historians, anthropologists create their own documents," made by Roger Sanjek in the preface to his recently published and delightful collection, *Fieldnotes*.[57] When it comes to the work of the oral historian, this disciplinary distinction dissolves. Just like the anthropologists, we, too, generate primary source material to add to the documentary pool.

The period of time covered in this work lent a special urgency to the interviewing process. The first generation of immigrants who are still with us are now in the twilight of their lives. Several of the respondents have passed away since this research was undertaken, and others were either hospitalized or too ill at home to be able to participate in repeat sessions. Their memories are a precious gift to us. As one former whaler so wisely pronounced, "The whales can still be saved. But the whaler can only be remembered by his stories."[58]

In conducting my interviews, I was always accompanied by a trusted member of the Cape Verdean community, a procedure which resulted in a much more quickly established rapport with the respondents.[59] It also meant that cultural and linguistic nuances that might be difficult for an outsider to discern were usually recognized as such and an attempt at explanation would be made during the course of the taping.[60] In many instances, I already knew, in some other capacity, the individual being interviewed, which also enhanced the quality of the oral accounts. At the time of my first trip to the Cape Verde Islands in 1984, I was one of a handful of non–Cape Verdeans in this country to have journeyed to the archipelago. Once this investigative expedition was completed, news of the visit impressed the local Cape Verdean community with the seriousness of my effort. Before long, word spread that I was hard at work on this project and subsequently, it would not be an unusual occurrence for me to be stopped on the street by a Cape Verdean American acquaintance with a request for me to interview a family member. Such was the eagerness of some to ensure that the history would be written and that their own legacy would not be lost in it. Hence, the usually challenging tasks of locating and making contact with willing subjects for oral interviews as well as gaining their confidence fell into place with relative ease. The oral histories that I myself was able to generate for this study were supplemented by a sprinkling of additional excerpts from the narratives of Cape Verdean immigrants that have appeared in published form in recent years.[61]

The rich and varied Cape Verdean oral tradition has produced an original and noteworthy literature that is undeniably Cape Verdean and should not go without mention here. In spite of the dominant prestige of the Portuguese language, some Cape Verdean writers such as Pedro Monteiro Cardoso, Eugenio Tavares and Sergio Frusoni have boldly and proudly used *Crioulo* as the medium in their mission to describe Cape Verdean life. Love of their homeland and the inconsolable pangs of separation are themes that recur again and again in the literature. The *Crioulo* epigraph that introduces the pivotal novel of Cape Verde, *Chiquinho,* reads: "Corpo, qu'ê nêgo, sa ta bai; Coraçom, qu'ê fôrro, sa ta fica. (The body, which is a slave, departs; the heart, which is free, remains.)[62]

Through the *morna*—a distinctive Cape Verdean literary form consisting of poetry put to music and conveyed through gestures and dance—the hardships and hopes of the people are lyrically phrased. It is an expression of nostalgia and longing, of *saudade,* with elements resembling the African American blues. But, unlike the blues, the words to the *morna,* have, as often as not, dealt with the anguish of departure. For it was only in emigration, through leaving what they loved the most, that the Cape Verdeans could take control of their lives, support those dear to them and catch a ray of hope for survival. It is one of the great ironies in the history of the Cape Verdean people that the emigrants to America have been so economically dependent upon occupational ties to the water, whether in maritime jobs or working the moist swampy land of the bogs. Meanwhile their homeland has been parched with drought, the scarcity of water being a fundamental historical constant. The fate of these "eternal emigrants" is poignantly expressed in the well-known *morna, Nha Destino (My Destiny),* that follows. The story of how their destiny was reached and what happened to those who completed the journey unfolds in the chapters ahead.

A

NHA DISTINO

I

Olim na meio di mar.
Tâ sigui nha distino
Pâ caminho d'América. . . .

II

E cê triste n'dixa nha terra
Sima e triste n'dixa nha mae.
Sodadi mora na nha pêto . . . .
Dixam bai pâ câ morrê.

III

Bai terra longe . . . .
Edistino di home . . . .
Edistino sem nome . . . .
Qui no tem qui cumpri . . . .

B

MY DESTINY

I

I'm already in the middle of the sea.
O follow my destiny
Sailing towards America

II

It's sad to forsake my country,
But it is sadder to leave my mother.
Let us go fast, otherwise the longing
kills me, crushing my breast.

III

It is a Cape Verdean destiny
To go far away from his land
It is a cruel destiny
We must all accomplish.[63]

NOTES

1. The names of the ten major islands grouped with any nearby islets are given below. Many thanks to Ron Barboza for compiling a complete

listing of Cape Verdean islet names and locations and for contributing this information to my study. Cape Verdean American immigrants have originated from all of the nine islands that are permanently inhabited. (Santa Luzia is uninhabited.)

Santo Antão
Ilheu do Boi

Boa Vista
Ilheu de Sal Rei

Brava
Ilheu Grande or Baixo
Ilheu Luz Carneiro
Ilheu Sapado
Ilheu de Cima

Fogo

Santa Luzia
Ilheu Branco
Ilheu Raso

Maio

São Nicolau

Sal
Ilheu de Rabo de Junco

São Tiago
Ilheu de Santa Maria

São Vicente
Ilheu dos Passaros

Because this population does not fit neatly into a category based on race or ethnicity alone, I have used the hyphenated term "racial-ethnic." The theoretical implications that this method of categorization raises will be discussed in later sections of this chapter.

2. While many individual Cape Verdean Americans today would group themselves under the broader category of African American, this identification is by no means universal. On the contrary, for the first generation of settlers, about whom this study is primarily concerned, most simply saw themselves as Portuguese, in some cases, going to great lengths to distinguish themselves from the African Americans. Nonetheless, the geographic placement of the archipelago—its proximity to the African continent, as well as the substantial African influences, both demographic and cultural, support the validity of pointing out the voluntary nature of their passage to the United States and of including them in the African diaspora. The complicated parameters of these questions of identity will be addressed at length in the text.

Note also that throughout his discussion of emigration in his recent dissertation, "The Roots of Cape Verdean Dependency, 1460–1990" (Ph.D. diss., University of Minnesota, 1990), pp. 121–31. Paul Barrows puts the word voluntary in parentheses arguing that the economic, climatic, and political conditions on the islands were so abysmal as to virtually force people to leave. Still, the migrants came of their own volition, unchained.

3. See A. H. de Oliveira Marques, *The History of Portugal from Lusitania to Empire,* vol. 1 (New York: Columbia University Press, 1972), p. 136; António Carreira, *Cabo Verde: formação de uma sociedade escravocrata (1460–1878)* (Porto: Imprensa Portuguesa, 1972), pp. 294–95.

4. T. Bentley Duncan, *Atlantic Islands: Madeira, the Azores and the Cape Verdes in Seventeenth-Century Commerce and Navigation* (Chicago: University of Chicago Press, 1972), pp. 18–19. Several conflicting dates for the initial sighting of the islands have been put forth by various authorities. Duncan's research, however, appears to be the most accurate on this point.

5. Carreira, *Cabo Verde: formação* pp. 316–34.

6. Jews first came to the island of São Tiago as refugees from religious persecution during the Inquisition. They were shunned by the wider society and confined to a separate ghettolike community in the city of Praia. During the early nineteenth century, Jewish Miguelistas fleeing once more, came to settle in the mountains of São Antão, where there are still traces of their presence in the three Jewish cemeteries on that island and in the name of the village of Sinagoga, where it is said that they gathered in prayer. (There never was a formal synagogue in Cape Verde.) Some Jewish settlers also migrated to Boa Vista, trading in pelts and hides. Surnames of Jewish derivation can be found among the inhabitants of each of these islands.

7. António Carreira, *The People of the Cape Verde Islands: Exploitation and Emigration,* trans. and ed. Christopher Fyfe (Hamden, Conn.: Archon Books, 1982), pp. 22–24.

8. The term *creole* refers to a language that develops when two or more groups of people come into contact, develop a trade language called a pidgin, and that contact language becomes native, as when the children learn it as their first language. With the colonial domination by Western Europe of much of the rest of the world, many such creoles were developed: English-based creoles, as in Jamaica; French-based creoles, as in Haiti, and Portuguese-based creoles, as in the Cape Verde Islands, depending on which European power colonized the people.

9. *Crioulo* is the expressive instrument of the people, the language most suitable for sharing intimacy and feelings, for expressing the "soul" of the archipelago. It is the language for joking, singing, storytelling, or lovemaking.

10. Emilio Moran in "The Evolution of Cape Verde's Agriculture," *African Economic History,* 2 (1982): 63–86, convincingly argues this position.

11. It is likely that the earliest contact between Americans and Cape Verdeans occurred in the year 1643, which also marked the first slave voyage in New England history to be involved in the triangular trade. The event was recorded in Massachusetts colonist John Winthrop's journal. In this case a Yankee vessel returning from the African coast via Barbados in the West Indies arrived in Boston harbor carrying tobacco, sugar, salt, and wine. This commerce was conducted "in exchange for Africoes, which she carried from the Isle of Maio (Cape Verde Islands). Quoted in Bernard Bailyn, *The New England Merchants in the Seventeenth Century* (Cambridge, Mass.: Harvard University Press, 1955), p. 84.

One of the earliest official accounts of a Cape Verdean in the United States appears in the colonial Connecticut court records cited in Robert J. Taylor, *Colonial Connecticut: A History* (Millwood, N.Y.: KTO Press, 1979), p. 160, as follows: "In 1775, a native of the Cape Verde Islands named Jonah sought relief from a Justice of the Peace, who appealed to the General Assembly for a ruling. No record of its ruling has been found, however."

12. Briton Cooper Busch, "Cape Verdeans in the American Whaling and Sealing Industry, 1850–1900," *American Neptune* 45, no. 2 (Spring 1985): 104–16.

13. Other smaller Cape Verdean settlements exist in California, particularly in the Sacramento area, as well as in New Jersey, New York, Philadelphia, and Ohio.

14. Raymond Anthony Almeida, *Cape Verdeans in America: Our Story* (Boston: American Committee for Cape Verde, 1978), p. 31.

15. Two relevant works on the subject that are informative but limited in scope are David Tyack, "Cape Verdeans in the United States" (Honors thesis, Harvard University, 1952); Almeida, *Cape Verdeans in America.* Deirdre Meintel Machado's "Cape Verdean–Americans: Their Cultural and Historical Background" (Ph.D. diss., Brown University, 1978) is an excellent anthropological study which deals primarily with cultural patterns in Cape Verde itself rather than documenting the Cape Verdean American experience, as the title of her thesis might suggest.

16. Deirdre Meintel, *Race, Culture and Portuguese Colonialism in Cabo Verde* (Syracuse: Maxwell School of Citizenship and Public Affairs, Syracuse University, 1984), p. ix.

17. Ibid., p. 164.

18. Stanley Lieberson, *A Piece of the Pie: Blacks and White Immigrants since 1880* (Berkeley: University of California Press, 1980), p. 31.

19. Some of those who have come up against this problem in their research are Tyack, "Cape Verdeans in the United States"; Almeida, *Cape Verdeans in America;* Francis Rogers in *The Harvard Encyclopedia of*

American Ethnic Groups, ed. Stephen Thernstrom (Cambridge, Mass.: Belknap Press, 1980), pp. 198–200.

20. See, for example, John Bodnar, Michael Weber, and Roger Simon, "Migration, Kinship and Urban Adjustment: Blacks and Poles in Pittsburgh, 1900–1930," *Journal of American History* 66 (1979): 548–65; John Appel, Jr., "American Negro and Immigrant Experience: Similarities and Differences," *American Quarterly* 18 (Spring 1966): 95–103; Timothy L. Smith, "Native Blacks and Foreign Whites: Varying Responses to Educational Opportunity in America, 1880–1950," *Perspectives in American History* 6 (1972): 309–35; Oscar Handlin, *Boston's Immigrants 1790–1880: A Study in Acculturation* (Cambridge: Harvard University Press, 1959); Nathan Glazer, "Blacks and Ethnic Groups: The Difference and the Political Difference It Makes," *Social Problems* 8, no. 4 (Spring 1971): 441–61; Gilbert Osofsky, *Harlem: The Making of a Ghetto* (New York: Harper and Row, 1963); and Lieberson, *Piece of the Pie.*

21. Paul Cressey, "Population Succession in Chicago, 1898–1930," *American Journal of Sociology* 64 (July 1938); Edward Banfield, *The Unheavenly City* (Boston: Little Brown, 1974); Louis Wirth, *The Ghetto* (Chicago: University of Chicago Press, 1928); Oscar Handlin, *The Newcomers: Negroes and Puerto Ricans in a Changing Metropolis* (Garden City: Doubleday, 1962); Irving Kristol, "The Negro Today Is like the Immigrant of Yesterday," *New York Times Sunday Magazine,* 11 Sept. 1966, pp. 50–124.

22. Josef Barton, *Peasants and Strangers: Italians, Rumanians and Slovaks in an American City, 1890–1950* (Cambridge: Harvard University Press, 1975); Herbert Gutman, *The Black Family in Slavery and Freedom, 1750–1925* (New York: Pantheon, 1976); Judith Ellen Smith, *Family Connections: A History of Italian & Jewish Immigrant Lives in Providence, Rhode Island, 1900–1940* (Albany, N.Y.: SUNY Press, 1985); Elizabeth H. Pleck, "The Two-Parent Household: Black Family Structure in Late Nineteenth Century Boston," *Journal of Social History* 6, no. 2 (Fall 1972): 1–31; Virginia Yans-McLaughlin, *Family and Community: Italian Immigrants in Buffalo, 1880–1920* (Ithaca, N.Y.: Cornell University Press: 1977); John Briggs, *An Italian Passage: Immigrants in Three American Cities, 1890–1930* (New Haven: Yale University Press, 1978).

23. See especially, Elizabeth H. Pleck, *Black Migration and Poverty: Boston, 1865–1900* (New York: Academic Press, 1979); Stephen Thernstrom, *The Other Bostonians: Poverty and Progress in the American Metropolis, 1880–1970* (Cambridge: Harvard University Press, 1973), pp. 176–219; Lieberson, *Piece of the Pie;* National Advisory Commission on Civil Disorders. *Report of the National Advisory Commission on Civil Disorders* (Washington, D.C.: Government Printing Office, 1968), pp. 143–44; Theo-

dore Hershberg, et al., *Philadelphia: Work, Space, Family, and Group Experience in the 19th Century* (New York: Oxford University Press, 1981); Olivier Zunz, *The Changing Face of Inequality: Urbanization, Industrial Development and Immigrants in Detroit, 1880–1920* (Chicago: University of Chicago Press, 1982); John Bodnar, Roger Simon, and Michael P. Weber, *Lives of Their Own: Blacks, Italians and Poles in Pittsburgh, 1900–1960* (Urbana: University of Illinois Press, 1982) and William J. Wilson, *The Declining Significance of Race: Blacks and Changing American Institutions,* 2d ed. (Chicago: University of Chicago Press, 1980).

24. Lawrence Fuchs offers an extremely useful framework for understanding variations in racial and ethnic incorporation into American society in his recently published book *The American Kaleidoscope: Race, Ethnicity and the Civic Culture* (Hanover, N.H.: University Press of New England, 1990) by presenting several variations on American pluralism. The dominant form is *voluntary* pluralism—the sanctioning of individual rights and protection of ethnic group interests—which has operated best for European immigrants. Other types such as tribal pluralism—which describes the history of U.S. policy toward Native Americans; involuntary caste pluralism—the rationalization of Euro-American enslavement of Africans; and finally sojourner pluralism—the design for nonwhite immigrants regarded as temporary residents all fall under the larger category of *coercive* pluralisms.

25. Michael Omni and Howard Winant, *Racial Formation in the United States: From the 1960s to the 1980s* (Boston: Routledge & Kegan Paul, 1986), p. 23.

26. See, for example, Hans Kohn, *American Nationalism: An Interpretive Essay,* 1954. (New York: Macmillan, 1957), p. 168.

27. Ronald Takaki, *Strangers from a Different Shore: A History of Asian Americans* (Boston: Little Brown, 1989), p. 7

28. Maurice R. Davie, *A Constructive Immigration Policy* (New Haven: Yale University Press, 1923), pp. 6–7.

29. See, for example, such classic works as Oscar Handlin, *The Uprooted: The Epic Story of the Great Migrations that Made the American People,* 2d ed. (Boston: Little Brown, 1973); Milton Gordon, *Assimilation in American Life: The Role of Race, Religion and National Origins* (New York: Oxford University Press, 1964); Horace M. Kallen, *Culture and Democracy in the United States* (New York: Boni and Liveright, 1924); and John Higham, *Send These to Me: Jews and Other Immigrants in Urban America* (New York: Atheneum, 1975).

30. Barbara J. Fields, "Ideology and Race in American History," in *Region, Race and Reconstruction: Essays in Honor of C. Vann Woodward,* ed. J. Morgan Kousser and James M. McPherson (New York: Oxford

University Press, 1982), p. 146. See also her recent article, "Slavery, Race and Ideology in the United States of America," *New Left Review* 181 (May/June 1990): 95–118.

31. Richard Hakluyt, *The Principal Navigations, Voyages, Traffiques and Discoveries of the English Nation . . .* , 12 vols., 1598 ed. (Glasgow, 1903–05), 10:15 quoted in Winthrop D. Jordan, *White Over Black: American Attitudes toward the Negro, 1550–1812* (New York: W. W. Norton, 1977), p. 4.

32. Joan Wallach Scott, *Gender and the Politics of History* (New York, Columbia University Press, 1988).

33. Charles Wagley, "On the Concept of Social Race in the Americas," in *Contemporary Cultures and Societies of Latin America: A Reader in the Social Anthropology of Middle and South America and the Caribbean,* ed. Dwight B. Heath and Richard N. Adams (New York: Random House, 1959), p. 531. Or consider this epigraph from James W. Loewen's *The Mississippi Chinese: Between Black and White* (Cambridge: Harvard University Press, 1971):

> "You're either a white man or a nigger, here. Now,
> that's the whole story. When I first came to the
> Delta, the Chinese were classed as nigras."
>
> ["And now they are called whites?"]
>
> "That's right!"
> —Conversation with white Baptist
> minister, Clarksdale, Mississippi

34. Nancy Foner, *New Immigrants in New York* (New York: Columbia University Press, 1987), p. 202; Karen Blu, *The Lumbee Problem: The Making of an American People* (Harvard: Cambridge University Press, 1980), p. 211.

35. Omni and Winant, *Racial Formation in the United States,* p. 62.

36. Barry Glassner, "Cape Verdeans: A People without a Race," *Sepia* (Nov. 1975): 65–71.

37. "Cape Verdians: *Our World* Visits New Bedford," *Our World* 1, no. 5 (Sept. 1946).

38. Lucille Ramos, "Black, White or Portuguese: A Cape Verdean Dilemma," in *Spinner: People and Culture in Southeastern Massachusetts,* vol. 1. ed. Donna Huse (New Bedford, Mass.: Spinner Publications, 1981), pp. 34–37.

39. Carlos Guillermo Wilson, "The Chombo Odyssey" (Paper presented at the American Studies Association Annual Meeting, Miami, 1988); Heriberto Dixon, "Black Cubans and the U.S.: A Case of the Conflicts Between

Race and Ethnicity" (Paper presented at the American Studies Association Annual Meeting, Miami, 1988), p. 7; Dixon, "Who Ever Heard of a Black Cuban." *Afro-Hispanic Review* 1, no. 3 (Sept. 19): 10; Clara Rodriguez, *Puerto Ricans: Born in the U.S.A.* (Boston: Unwin Hyman, 1989); Susan Buchanan Stafford, "The Haitians: The Cultural Meaning of Race and Ethnicity," in Foner, *New Immigrants in New York,* pp. 131–58.

40. Roy Simon Bryce-LaPorte, "Black Immigrants: The Experience of Invisibility and Inequality." *Journal of Black Studies* (Sept. 1972): 31, 48.

41. W. E. B. Du Bois, *The Souls of Black Folk,* 1903. (New York: Vintage Books, 1990), pp. 8–9.

42. Ralph Ellison, *Invisible Man* (New York: Vintage Books, 1989), p. xv.

43. See, for example, the writings of Stephen Gould, particularly, *The Mismeasure of Man* (New York: W. W. Norton, 1981) and Margaret Mead et al., *Science and the Concept of Race* (New York: Columbia University Press, 1968).

44. Marlon Riggs, *Ethnic Notions,* California Newsreel, 1987.

45. Malcolm X, *The Autobiography of Malcolm X as told to Alex Haley,* 1965 (New York: Ballantine Books, 1990), pp. 333, 340–41.

46. Virginia Dominguez, *White by Definition: Social Classification in Creole Louisiana* (New Jersey: Rutgers University Press, 1986), pp. 262–63.

47. For discussion of the neglected role of women in the literature on migration, as well as their marginality within the scholarly fields that would seem the most obvious place for such work to be located, see Silvia Pedraza, "Women and Migration: The Social Consequences of Gender," *Annual Review of Sociology* 17 (1991): 303–25 and Donna Gabaccia, "Immigrant Women: Nowhere at Home?" *Journal of American Ethnic History* 10, no. 4 (Summer 1991): 61–87. Two bibliographies on immigrant women have appeared in the last five years documenting the growing interest in this subject. Francesco Cordasco, *The Immigrant Woman in North America: An Annotated Bibliography of Selected References* (Metuchen, N.J.: Scarecrow Press, 1985) and Donna Gabaccia, *Immigrant Women in the United States: A Multi-Disciplinary Bibliography* (Westport, Conn.: Greenwood Press, 1989). *Immigrant Women* is particularly comprehensive since it includes the very recent years when so much of this research was undertaken as well as listing dissertations from before 1989.

48. For examples of scholarship that models the intersection of gender with other social categories, see Sarah Deutsch, *No Separate Refuge: Culture, Class, and Gender on an Anglo-Hispanic Frontier in the American Southwest, 1880-1940* (New York: Oxford University Press, 1987); Evelyn Nakano Glenn, *Issei, Nisei, War Bride: Three Generations of Japanese*

American Women in Domestic Service (Philadelphia: Temple University Press, 1986); Susan A. Glenn, *Daughters of the Shtetl: Life and Labor in the Immigrant Generation* (Ithaca, N.Y.: Cornell University Press, 1990); Nancy A. Hewitt, "Building a 'Virile' Union: Latin Workers, Politics and the Community of Labor" (Paper presented at the Annual Meeting of the Organization of American Historians, St. Louis, 1989); Maria-Cristina Garcia, "Creating Little Havana: Cuban American Women and the Making of an Ethnic Community" (Paper presented at the American Studies Association Annual Meeting, Miami, 1988).

49. Special thanks to Sarah Deutsch for a conversation that helped point my analysis in this direction.

50. For treatments of southern black communities that encompassed both the rural and urban dimensions, see Robin D. G. Kelley, *Hammer and Hoe: Alabama Communists during the Great Depression* (Chapel Hill: University of North Carolina Press, 1990); Earl Lewis, *In Their Own Interests: Race, Class, and Power in Twentieth-Century Norfolk Virginia* (Berkeley: University of California Press, 1991).

51. The Custom House on Brava Island does hold archival material including ship lists and other documentation related to emigration. However, over the years of colonization, these records stored in gunny sacks or heaped in piles have been seriously damaged by worms and severe weather conditions. However, in order to arrest the steady deterioration of these files, a group of concerned individuals in New England has recently formed the Brava Custom House Project Committee whose purpose is to find ways to salvage these important documents.

52. In 1900, only two schooners sailed from Cape Verde to New Bedford, but neither was allowed entry because of a smallpox epidemic in the Islands. These packets were diverted to Boston so that no other information beyond the number of passengers on the two vessels (149) is available.

53. See especially Clifford Geertz, *The Interpretation of Cultures: Selected Essays* (New York: Basic Books, 1973).

54. Ronald Walters, "Signs of the Times: Clifford Geertz and Historians," *Social Research* 47, no. 3 (Autumn 1980): 556.

55. About the same time that I was completing the final revisions of this manuscript, I became aware of recent work on the uses of oral history, especially Virginia Yans-McLaughlin's provocative and illuminating essay, "Metaphors of Self: Subjectivity, Oral Narration and Immigration Studies," in *Immigration Reconsidered,* edited by Yans-McLaughlin (New York: Oxford University Press, 1990), pp. 254–90. Had it been available to me at an earlier stage of either my research or writing, this model of methodological possibilities would have led me to reformulate my interpretations

of this material. While I do attempt to make explicit the particular script I bring to the interviews, my tendency has been to use the historical data from the oral accounts much like any other kind of archival source. Yan-McLaughlin prompts a rethinking of this approach to subjective documents, suggesting possible ways that the tools of the ethnographer, textual analysis, and the hermeneutic method might further the oral history project by revealing the ways that the process of creating such documents itself may shape the narrative as well as illustrating what emergent patterns in the interview material might convey about historical context.

56. One such effort is by Joao Pires and John Hutchinson, *Disionarius Preliminariu Kriolu* (Preliminary Creole Dictionary), Cape Verdean/English, 1st ed. (Boston, 1983).

57. Roger Sanjek, *Fieldnotes: The Making of Anthropology* (Ithaca, N.Y.: Cornell University Press, 1990), p. xii.

58. Joseph Ramos quoted in Mark Vosburgh, "Old Whaler's Stories Are Harpoons that Pin Down Time," *Standard Times* 3 Mar. 1983, p. 5.

59. I especially want to thank Joaquim A. Custodio and Ron Barboza for their partnerships with me in the interviewing process. Yvonne Houtman also arranged for and accompanied me to an interview with her grandmother, and Carol Pimentel set up my interview with "Canja" Fortes.

60. In preparation for the oral histories I developed and continually modified a detailed questionnaire organized around major areas pertinent to the research topic, such as premigration culture, family history, employment, and social life. My style of inquiry was informal and open-ended, however, so that the questionnaire never served as more than a backdrop to each session. This approach not only allowed for greater spontaneity but it also made it possible for the respondent to at times take charge of the direction of the conversation. The systematic outline functioned best to focus the material being discussed and to minimize the amount of extraneous anecdotal information that was shared.

61. See especially, Maria Luisa Nunes, *A Portuguese Colonial in America: Belmira Nunes Lopes, The Autobiography of a Cape Verdean–American* (Pittsburgh: Latin American Literary Review Press, 1982); Lucillia Lima, "*Lembrança-Crioulo* Memories," in *Spinner: People and Culture in Southeastern Massachusetts,* vol. 1, ed. Donna Huse (New Bedford, Mass.: Spinner Publications, 1981), pp. 92–95; Lucille Ramos, "Black, White or Portuguese? A Cape Verdean Dilemma," in Spinner, 1:34–37; Joseph Ramos interviewed by Michael DeCicco in *Spinner,* 2:107–10; Quinton Degrasse interviewed by Jill Anderson in *Spinner,* 2: 98–102; Sam Beck and the members of local 1329, "From Cape Verde to Providence: The International Longshoremen's Association Local 1329," 1983; Dorothy Cottle

Poole, "Antone Fortes, Whaleman," *The Dukes County Intelligencer* 2, no. 4 (Edgartown: May 1970): 129–53.

62. Baltasar Lopes, *Chiquinho* (S. Vicente, Cabo Verde: "Claridade," 1947). Translation from Russell Hamilton, *Voices from an Empire: A History of Afro-Portuguese Literature* (Minneapolis: University of Minnesota Press, 1975), p. 324.

63. Translated in Stephen L. Cabral and Sam Beck, *Nha Distino: Cape Verdean Folk Arts* (Providence: Roger Williams Park Museum), Publication No. 5

Becoming Visible:
A Demographic Profile

1

In the section on Cape Verdeans in the *Harvard Encyclopedia of Ethnic Groups,* we are told that "it is virtually impossible to calculate the number of Cape Verdeans who have immigrated [to this country]."[1] This is not a very encouraging statement. The poor prognosis for ascertaining the demographic makeup of this group relates directly back to the problem of being caught between racial and ethnic social categories. Ambiguity of social identity touches all aspects of Cape Verdean's history, even to the point of seeming to erase them from the public record altogether. The complexities that make Cape Verdean Americans both noteworthy and difficult to analyze demographically stem from the mixture of African and Portuguese elements in a foreign population voluntarily emigrating to the United States.

Typically, population studies rely heavily for their data on the federal census or on United States Immigration figures. Yet, where the Cape Verdean American is concerned, neither of these tools has been of particular use. Not until the 1980 census did a category even exist for a possible response of "Cape Verdean" to the question of ancestry.[2] Since the Cape Verde Islands were a colony of Portugal until their independence in 1975, Cape Verdeans were simply lumped with the Portuguese group.

Similarly, the records of the United States Immigration Service fail to differentiate Cape Verdeans from Portuguese nationals. The Immigration Service brought further confusion to its figures by applying the customary American standards of "black" and "white" to the arriving Cape Verdeans. Those seeming to resemble the "white" European type were classified as Portuguese, while the remainder were grouped under the categories of "black Portuguese" or "African Portuguese." Other official classifications under which Cape Verdeans also were haphazardly listed were as "Bravas," meaning Cape Verdeans from the island of

Brava, and "Atlantic Islanders," which included the Azores and Madeira as well as, at times, the Spanish Canary Islands.

The documentation used by investigators thus far has had such severe limitations that researchers could only make rough estimates of the volume of the migration and only hazy generalizations concerning the demography of the Cape Verdean immigrants. Omni and Winant have stressed that such questions of statistical representation are not to be taken lightly:

> How one is categorized is far from a merely academic or even personal matter. Such matters as access to employment, housing or other publicly or privately valued goods, social program design and the disbursement of local, state, and federal funds, or the organization of elections (among many other issues) are directly affected by racial classification and the recognition of "legitimate" groups. The determination of racial categories is thus an intensely political process. Viewed as a whole, the census's racial classification reflects prevailing conceptions of race, establishes boundaries by which one's racial "identity" can be understood, determines the allocation of resources and frames diverse political issues and conflicts.[3]

Perhaps the most blatant instance of the political role of the U.S. Census in support of institutionalized racism and in violation of human rights occurred in California in the months leading up to the internment of the Japanese during World War II. While authorization to release the names of specific individuals was illegal, the Census Bureau's chief of statistical research was, nonetheless, flown in to assist officials in tabulating and consequently locating the Japanese inhabitants, thus facilitating the round-up.

For the Cape Verdeans, the method of distinguishing them from the moment of their arrival in this country on the basis of racial characteristics rather than their place of birth or last residence was the beginning of a pattern to which the newcomers would have to adjust over and over again in the course of their settlement here. "This early failure of the United States Immigration and Naturalization Service to institute procedures which would identify Cape Verdeans as a distinct ethnic cultural group and as a multi-racial people with a geographic 'land of origin' would form the basis for many problems they would have as a people in their new homeland,"[4] writes Raymond Almeida, formerly a staff member of the Cape Verde embassy in Washington, D.C.

Upon discovery of the existence of the passenger and crew lists of packet ships voyaging from the Cape Verde Islands to the shores of

New Bedford, Massachusetts, it became clear that the first step in making the Cape Verdean immigrants more visible was to utilize these records to create the supposedly "impossible" demographic profile. As with any statistical source of this kind, there are definite limitations to these records. However, the ship manifests provide an excellent alternative to census documentation, at times surpassing what the census could have potentially offered. Their value to immigration research is becoming increasingly recognized in the field, as a recent article in the *Journal of American Ethnic History* extolling the uses of passenger lists proclaims: "Given the high-powered technology now available, one can envision the day when tens of millions of arriving immigrants will be summoned like shades returning from the grave, to reappear at a moment's call on computer terminal screens. For immigration historians and genealogists, this will seem like nirvana. The very flesh and blood of the human cargo that poured across the Atlantic will be at our fingertips."[5]

Fortunately, given the scope of this project, the Cape Verdean numbers totaled in the tens of thousands rather than millions. Information on over 20,000 arrivals was culled from the packet ship records. Appendix 2 lists all the vessels manifested by year, from 1860 to 1940, showing the name of the packet and type (schooner, brig, or bark), name of captain, origin of the boat, date of arrival, and number of passengers.[6] Numbers range from a single passenger on a voyage to as many as 544 arriving on the *S.S. Insulano* from Fogo in 1914.

Records first appeared showing arrivals from the Islands to New Bedford in the year 1860.[7] The immigration started slowly, with an average of 28 people coming over annually between 1860–87. Only a couple of vessels made the journey each year. In some years, none arrived; in other years, there were three or four voyages. However, by 1889, between five and nine boats were coming into the port of New Bedford regularly from the Cape Verde Islands. Almost all of these embarked from the island of Brava. The average annual number of passengers increased substantially to 204.4 in the decade from 1889 to 1899. For the years of the mass migration, 1900–1921, the period that is the primary focus of this study, the figures climbed to an average of 896 Cape Verdeans who arrived annually. The number of packets sailing onto the shores of New Bedford in these years jumped to between nine and twenty-two voyages per year.

After 1921, the doors to immigration were practically closed to Cape Verdeans by the passage of stringent immigration laws in the United States Congress as well as by obstacles imposed by the Portuguese government.[8] Consequently, in the period 1921 to 1934, the average number of passengers arriving plummeted to 142.4 (see fig. 2). Almost all these individuals had been to the United States previously. What followed until the mid 1960s, when the doors opened up again, was a long period of dormancy that contributed heavily to the demise of the packet trade itself. The following graph shows the volume of Cape Verdean immigration to New Bedford by decade for the period 1860–1940.

The kind of information asked of the incoming passengers and recorded by the officials on the lists varied somewhat according to the forms that were required at different periods. Nonetheless, in all of the records, it is clear whether the arrival was from the Cape Verde Islands, so that there is absolutely no confusion about the individual's land of origin. My calculations are based on the question of last residence and place of birth rather than on the ambiguous and arbitrary categories of "white" and "black" Portuguese that have been used in the official Immigration Service reports.

In the nineteenth century, a shorter form was used, requesting only name, occupation, age, sex, last residence or place of birth, and condition of health. Usually the arrival would be asked if he or she had ever been to the United States before. From 1889 to 1893, the question

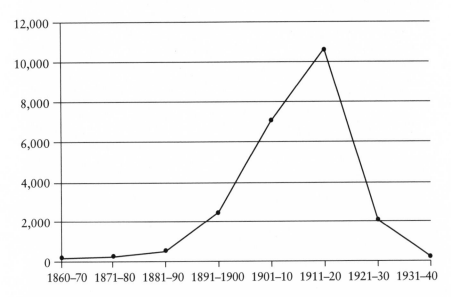

Figure 2. Cape Verdean Immigration to New Bedford, Massachusetts, 1860–1940.

of final destination in the United States was included from time to time. By 1894, a new, longer and more thorough register was introduced with over twenty different categories of information, such as marital status, literacy, and occupation and very specific questions, reflecting the social and political concerns of the time, for example, whether or not the individual was a polygamist or an anarchist. (Of course, all answered "no" to both questions.) By 1908, the form had again expanded to a two-page document with thirty different categories of questions.[9]

Accounts found in the New Bedford city newspapers of the time, the *Evening Standard* and the *Morning Mercury,* were also useful in compiling information on the packet boats. Typically on the day a packet ship arrived, an article would appear describing the voyage, its length, and the conditions it encountered at sea, as well as the total passengers on board, and often a breakdown of numbers of women and children. The name of the captain, the type of cargo, and the names of any returning arrivals who were well known to the community would all be published. Special circumstances such as an unusually long or difficult journey, the presence of stowaways, or problems with quarantine would also be detailed. For example, when the *Maria Luiza* came in from Brava on 17 April 1910, the *Evening Standard* provided this description the next day:

> The *Maria Luiza* has 166 passengers, 59 in her crew and one stowaway. She brought as freight 1050 barrels of sperm oil, the catch of the whaling brig *Sullivan,* which was landed there last fall when it could not be taken by the schooner sent out to the Azores.
>
> The immigrants were a healthy looking lot, the immigration physician Dr. Bullard, finding only one case which he deemed necessary to hold, that being of a man, Caezar Pina, whose general physical condition was poor, and who possibly has tuberculosis.
>
> Most of the immigrants were dressed very good, the women especially, several of them wearing light silk dresses of gaudy hues.
>
> The usual large crowd gathered on the dock wharf, where a rope had been stretched across half way from the head of the wharf to the immigration shed, and the greetings were very profuse and frequent when the immigrants began to go up the dock and crawl under the outstretched rope.[10]

What percentage, then, of the total volume of migration from the Cape Verde Islands to the United States during this seventy-five-year span, do the 23,168 entries represent? Evidence suggests that as many as 85 to 90 percent of those immigrating to this country came through

New Bedford's harbor. The evolution of the packet trade as the principal means of transport to the United States from Cape Verde early established New Bedford as the primary port of entry.

A perusal of the official Providence, Rhode Island passenger listings, the only other harbor involved in the packet trade, showed a mere sprinkling of Cape Verdean arrivals.[11] Although Providence was the intended destination for many of the emigrating Cape Verdeans, it was faster and easier to disembark at the pier in New Bedford and travel overland to Providence than it was to sail there directly. A train ran regularly between the two cities. In one study, almost all of the parents and grandparents of a group of Cape Verdeans interviewed in 1980 who were living in the Fox Point neighborhood of Providence came via New Bedford.[12] Steamship travel to the ports of Boston or New York was unavailable from the Cape Verde Islands until later years so that those traditional points of entry can be ruled out as significant in swelling the total figures on immigration.

However, the primary evidence to support the hypothesis that all but about 10 to 15 percent of those arriving came to New Bedford derives from the work of Antonio Carreira on Cape Verdean emigration.[13] Using official government bulletins, Carreira has tabulated the number of those exiting Cape Verde to the United States in the years 1900 to 1920. In table 1, I compare Carreira's data to my own findings. His figures are for all exits to the United States, while mine total only those entering the port of New Bedford.

The totals, 18,629 departures from Cape Verde and 18,122 arrivals to New Bedford, are almost identical. A Pearson Correlation analysis of the two sets of data calculated on a yearly basis resulted in a finding of .8365, an exceptionally high degree of agreement. This level of correlation between the two figures simply does not leave open the possibility that significant numbers of departing Cape Verdeans entered ports other than New Bedford's. Consequently, almost any analysis of the data gathered in this study of Cape Verdeans arriving in New Bedford is tantamount to an inquiry into the demographics of the entire Cape Verdean immigration to the United States during this period.

Discrepancies in departure and arrival totals may be attributed to the failure of both the Cape Verdean sources and the American records to show how many of those exiting Cape Verde or entering the United States, were doing so for the first time. Yet, reports confirm that many Cape Verdean immigrants traveled back to the islands and returned to the United States again. Finally, the number of clandestine departures and arrivals among the Cape Verdeans leaves a question about how many have settled here without a record of their having immigrated.

Table 1. Departures from the Cape Verde Islands and Arrivals to New Bedford, Massachusetts, 1900–1920

Year	Departures from the Cape Verde Islands (*Carreira*)	Arrivals to New Bedford (*Halter*)
1900	293	398
1901	245	149
1902	284	342
1903	542	1,311
1904	361	493
1905	317	356
1906	638	708
1907	560	596
1908	1,296	1,192
1909	695	703
1910	1,054	1,049
1911	1,474	1,555
1912	1,128	960
1913	1,691	1,307
1914	1,610	2,167
1915	784	833
1916	1,829	1,275
1917	1,508	1,209
1918	323	292
1919	491	226
1920	1,506	1,001
TOTALS	18,629	18,122

Sources: Carreira, *The People*, p. 201; *Passenger Lists of Vessels Arriving at New Bedford, Mass., 1902–1942*. Microcopy No. T-944. 8 rolls.

Carreira's data does show population emigrating by island, and once again the immigration and emigration breakdowns match up. Both sets of figures indicate that over half of the newcomers from Cape Verde originated from Brava and Fogo. In fact, the Sotavento group, or Leeward Islands, including Brava, Fogo, São Tiago, and Maio, yielded three-fourths of the emigrating population (and two-thirds of those arriving to New Bedford). Santo Antão, São Vicente, São Nicolau, Sal, and Boa Vista, the islands of the Barlavento group or Windward Islands, are less populated and have generally faced less acute hardship, so that they have contributed fewer numbers for emigration. Figure 3 shows immigration by island based on the compilations of New Bedford ship manifest data from 1860 to 1934, while table 2 presents a comparison of Carreira's emigration totals by island with my tabulations on immigration for the period 1900–1920.

My statistics are based on responses to the question of last residence. Differences between Carreira's figures and my own can be accounted for in large part by the fact that approximately 10 percent of those entering New Bedford listed as their place of last residence the United States, rather than one of the Cape Verde Islands. This group was part of the return migration traffic.

The only island showing a notable discrepancy in percentage of

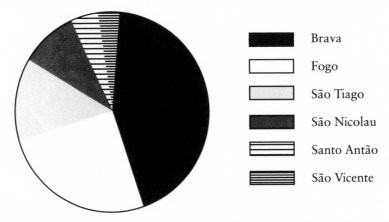

Note: The sparsely populated islands of Boa Vista, Sal, and Maio together make up only a small portion of the total volume of migration—between 2 and 4 percent.

Figure 3. Cape Verdean Immigration by Island, 1860–1934

Table 2. Emigration from the Cape Verde Islands/Immigration to New Bedford, Massachusetts, by Island, 1900–1920

Island of Origin	Emigrating from the Islands (%)	Immigrating to New Bedford (%)
Brava	32.6	28.6
Fogo	28.5	25.6
São Tiago	14.5	12.4
São Vicente	11.7	2.6
São Nicolau	9.2	8.6
Santo Antão	4.6	4.0

departures versus arrivals is São Vicente. The number of recorded exits is significantly higher than the entries. However, because of the lack of adequate harbors for large vessels on the islands of Santo Antão and São Nicolau, many of the residents of these islands had to embark from São Vicente to travel to the United States. Carreira points out that it is quite likely that many of those originating from the other Barlavento islands would have been listed as going from São Vicente.[14] Upon arrival in New Bedford, those entering were more exact in reporting their actual island of last residence.

Of interest here in terms of racial composition is that the island of São Tiago, which has always been by far the most populated of the Cape Verdes, provided only around 13 percent of the emigrants to the United States. At the same time, however, they have been the most likely to be conscripted into forced labor migrations to the cocoa and coffee plantations on the Portuguese controlled islands of São Tomé and Príncipe where conditions were notoriously wretched. Paul Barrows in his recently completed doctoral thesis on the political history of the Cape Verde Islands argues that it was the lighter-skinned mestizo population that had the option of voluntary migration while the more African in appearance were coerced into forced labor relocations.[15] The Cape Verdean American immigrant breakdown by island initially does seem to support this point, but the explanation is more complex than that. Virtually all of the pioneering emigrants to the United States came from the island of Brava, the direct result of the connections made in the nineteenth century through the whaling industry. While the inhabitants of Brava are characteristically the most Portuguese influenced and of lightest hue, it was the geographic features of the island that initially brought the whaling vessels to its ports. Once this link was solidified, the chain migration followed quite naturally and the Packet Trade boats continued to travel the same routes, docking at Brava. The island of Fogo, which provided the second largest flow of migrants to this country is a short distance away—you can easily see Brava from Fogo's western shores, and on a clear day it almost seems as if one could reach over and touch it—making the route of departure readily accessible to the Fogo population. Thus, it was a combination of social and topographical factors that resulted in the mestizo majority of Cape Verdean emigrants to the United States.

It should also be further noted here that many of the Cape Verdean newcomers did not at first identify themselves as hailing from the Cape Verde Islands. Rather, they were more likely to see themselves as native to their particular island of origin—as "Bravas" and "Fogos" just as, for example, the Italian immigrants initially defined themselves as being from a specific village or region of Italy, rather than as Italians.

Neither Carreira's findings nor my own show a positive correlation between periods of extreme drought in the archipelago and increased annual immigration totals. The nineteenth-century arrival figures do reveal a slight relationship between drought years and higher numbers of incoming passengers, but by the twentieth century, the tide of immigration rose to a steady momentum that was no longer dependent upon changes in the severity of island conditions. One of the most devastating periods of drought was well underway by 1918, but emigration was forestalled by the start of World War I, which had already reduced the number of packet ships that could safely navigate in Atlantic waters.

The amount calculated by the United States Immigration Service under the category of African Portuguese admitted to the country during the same period, 1900–1920, was only 13,367.[16] This amounts to less than 75 percent of my total, suggesting just how imperfect the record was. The numbers published by the Immigration Service of those emigrating from the Cape Verde Islands, however, do very closely resemble Carreira's findings. These figures are only available for the years 1912–20, but the total is listed as 10,476, as compared to Carreira's 10,870, for the same nine-year span.[17] There is also census data recorded for the years 1910 and 1920 on "non-whites of Portuguese birth." In 1910, 1,737 were counted; in 1920, 2,538. Such totals are even further off the mark.

One fairly accurate assessment of the volume of Cape Verdean immigration to New Bedford was made by an observer at the time. In a report dated 1911, it was estimated that between 1,200 and 1,500 newcomers from Cape Verde arrived annually.[18] According to my calculations, this figure would be a bit high. Averaging my yearly totals for the five years before this study amounts to approximately 1,000 arrivals a year.

Another way to approach the question of the size of the migration is to try to determine the percentage of Portuguese immigration that Cape Verdeans represent (see table 3). The *Harvard Encyclopedia of Ethnic Groups* suggests that a "reasonable guess might be 10–20% . . . or from 43,000 to 85,000 over the years 1820–1976, not including illegal immigrants."[19] These estimates, which are high, would have to be looked at as a maximum measurement, while my own tabulations would represent a minimum count, because they do not include Cape Verdeans who arrived at other ports (roughly 15 percent of the total). Still, it is

Table 3. Cape Verdean Percentages of Total Portuguese Immigration to the United States, 1860–1930

Years	Portuguese Immigrants to U.S.	Cape Verdean Immigrants to U.S.	Percentage of Cape Verdeans
1860–1870	2,658	124	4.6%
1871–1880	14,082	144	1.0%
1881–1890	16,978	571	3.3%
1891–1900	27,508	2,340	8.5%
1901–1910	69,149	6,899	9.9%
1911–1920	89,732	10,825	12.0%
1921–1930	29,994	1,999	6.6%

Sources: Calculated from U.S. Bureau of Immigration; U.S. Customs Service. Record Group 36. Records of the New Bedford Collector of Customs. *Inward Passenger lists, 1823–99.* National Archives Microfilm (3 rolls) in New Bedford Free Public Library, New Bedford, Massachusetts, and *Passenger Lists of Vessels Arriving at New Bedford, Mass., 1902–1942.* Microcopy No. T-944. 8 rolls.

only in the decade 1911–20 that the percentage of Cape Verdeans fell between the 10 and 20 percent figure, as can be seen in table 3.

The official counts of Portuguese immigration, as listed above, have their own limitations, in addition to the problems already discussed in this chapter concerning the records of the Immigration Service. At times, they included the Azores islands; at other times, not. Statistics on Madeira are not added in until 1925. The figures do not include Hawaii, and particularly in the years 1878–1910, they were numerically significant. And, finally, as with the data on Cape Verdeans, the issue of re-emigration was not taken into account.[20] Thus, these figures must be seen as simply the best estimates available to us.

If I were to add to my total of 23,168 Cape Verdean immigrants to New Bedford for the years 1860–1935, the official numbers through 1976[21] plus an estimated 500 to 1,000 coming in on whalers in the years 1820–1860, I would come up with roughly 35,000. This is considerably lower than the *Harvard Encyclopedia*'s estimate. However, the two appraisals give us a good minimum-maximum range to start from. The most accurate statement is that between 35,000 and 45,000 Cape Verdeans immigrated here in the years 1820–1976 and that in the peak years this figure comprised between 10 and 15 percent of the overall Portuguese arrivals. Since the independence of Cape Verde in 1975, emigration from the archipelago to the United States has increased again, with an annual average of 913.6 persons arriving between 1975–80.[22]

Like the bulk of the southern and eastern European newcomers in the years of mass immigration, the Cape Verdean sex ratio was heavily skewed toward male immigrants. The overall percentages of Cape Verdean arrivals from 1860–1934 were 83.4 percent males and 16.6 percent females. These figures roughly correspond to the Italian statistics on migration by gender in this period[23] but show a greater imbalance than the white Portuguese ratios. Males never constituted more than 70 percent of the Portuguese total, and in one year, 1917, the percentage of female arrivals was actually higher than the male entries.[24]

The Dillingham Commission report of 1911 on Cape Verdean cranberry workers corroborates that one-sixth to one-third of the pickers in the cranberry district were women and children.[25] The lower estimate is more accurate. Another survey conducted in the Providence area around 1930 found this same ratio between the sexes still holding among Cape Verdean immigrants residing there.[26] While collecting tales and riddles from Cape Verdean immigrants in the summers of 1916 and 1917 for her study *Folklore of the Cape Verde Islands* the anthropologist Elsie Clews Parsons commented, "as a rule the Island immigrants are married to their own country-women, of whom there are comparatively few, or they live celibate."[27]

Interestingly, the popular assumption that single men immigrated first and then were followed in subsequent years by the women and children is not borne out by my findings.[28] A close examination of the gender and age data reveals just the opposite trend. While unmarried males predominated throughout, a higher proportion of women and children were arriving in the late nineteenth century than in the years of the mass migration that followed. For example, the percentages in the period 1860–99 were 28.6 percent females and 71.3 percent males, while the figures for the years 1900–1919 showed 15.4 percent females and 84.6 percent males.

Greater numbers of children entered this country in the nineteenth century as well, with 10 percent listed as being under the age of 14 as compared to only 4.5 percent in the twentieth century.[29] The nineteenth-century adult population was also slightly older at the time of arrival. In terms of age structure, the most dramatic shift occurred in the 20–29 cohort, showing 20 percent more immigrants of that age group arriving in the years 1902–9.

Finally, the proportion of immigrant men who were married was higher in the earlier period than it was during large-scale migration. In the last decades of the nineteenth century, approximately 40 percent of the male arrivals were married, while only one out of four were married in the years 1900–1920. It appears that most of the women who were arriving in the 1880s and 1890s were voyaging alongside their husbands and that the phenomenon of entire families relocating was also more prevalent in these years.

With the exception of the Jewish immigrants in this period, who were forced out as whole families from their original homes, the most typical pattern of voluntary emigration with the intention of economic improvement was that the able-bodied men in their wage-earning years would embark on the journey to America first, accumulate some savings, perhaps establish a permanent residence, and then send for their wives and children. Why, then, do the figures from the ship manifest data seem to suggest a variation on this theme?

One factor that may have inflated the totals of single men arriving in the later years is the degree of transiency among them. Single men would be the most likely to have been counted more than once in the final tabulations of entries to the United States, with fewer having had the opportunity to make repeat trips that would then have a distorting effect on the nineteenth-century figures. Nevertheless, this does not entirely account for the absence of an increase in the proportion of women and children arriving as the immigration gained momentum. The continued low frequency of family migration is best explained by the tentative nature of Cape Verdean settlement in this country. By and large, the arrivals from Cape Verde did not intend to permanently relocate and, as a result, did not envision bringing their wives and children to join them in building a family life here. While this approach was characteristic of some other groups immigrating in this period — for example the Italian, Azorean, and Greek influx — the Cape Verdeans may have held on longer than other newcomers to the dream of eventual return to their islands. The temporary quality of their migration as well as the persistent ties to the old country will be discussed more fully in the following chapter.

Four years before the implementation of strict immigration quotas, the U.S. Immigration Service passed a literacy law that did not significantly change the numbers of entering aliens but that did have an effect on their composition. As of May 1917, adult and adolescent newcomers were required to demonstrate an ability to read and write by passing a literacy test administered to them by the immigration authorities upon arrival in this country.

In the years before enforcement of the literacy requirement, the Portuguese immigrants as a whole showed the highest rate of illiteracy of any nationality entering the United States, followed by the Turks and the southern Italians.[30] Leo Pap, in *The Portuguese-Americans,* suggests that of the various groupings encompassed by the Portuguese immigration, the Cape Verdeans exhibited the highest degree of literacy, even higher than the Continental Portuguese. Those from Madeira comprised the smallest proportion of literates.[31]

In explaining the use of *Crioulo* among Cape Verdeans, a New Bedford immigration inspector noted, "The literate Cape Verde islander will, however, understand as well as read Portuguese as taught in the schools, 'Royal Portuguese' he calls it, and probably speak it quite fluently. The Cape Verde islanders have impressed me as being better linguists than the average white Portuguese."[32]

My data on literacy does confirm that proportionally more Cape Verdean immigrants could read and write than the "white" Portuguese arrivals. The percentage of Portuguese illiterates in the years 1899–1910 was 68.2 percent, while the Cape Verdean illiteracy figure totals 45.9 percent. In the period 1911–17, the Portuguese rate dropped some to around 50 percent, while Cape Verdean illiteracy showed a slight increase to 48.5 percent so that in these years the levels became nearly the same.

The island with the highest proportion of emigrants who could read and write was São Nicolau. Over three-fourths of its entering population was literate. This is not surprising since for many years, this island featured the only *liceu* in Cape Verde, a seminary, founded in 1866. It was originally planned for location in Praia, São Tiago, but Governor Vasco Guedes de Carvalho e Menezes decided that the climate in São Nicolau was preferable.[33]

For several generations, this educational institution offered excellent formal instruction to its students, many of whom were from the poorer sectors of the society. When Archibald Lyall visited the Cape Verde Islands in the early 1930s he commented, "The urchins of San Nicolau are to be found begging not for food to put into their mouths but for ink and paper to take to school." He also discovered that the key to being accepted by the natives was to stress his literary training: "I soon found that describing myself as a *jornalista* was a surer passport to respect than if I had been a captain of industry."[34] The seminary produced missionaries, writers, teachers, and public servants but also included facilities such as a bindery, and carpentry and blacksmith shops for the training of skilled craftsmen. Not only was this the only facility of its type in the Cape Verde Islands but it was also unique to the Portuguese colonies as a whole. The resources of the São Nicolau seminary provided an oasis of intellectual and literary life in the overseas provinces while at the same time, giving those who were forced to leave the island a solid educational foundation upon which to make a new start.

By 1917, however, organizational problems and lack of financial support led to the demise of the seminary. At the same time, under the leadership of Governor Fontura da Costa, a secular *liceu* was established in São Vicente. His plan was to revise the primary school system, by increasing the number of primary level facilities in rural areas and by having teachers trained through the new *liceu*. The high levels of literacy among the emigrants to the United States from São Vicente (71.2 percent) and the nearby island of Santo Antão (74.7 percent) reflect the availability of instruction there. In table 4, I chart correlations of literacy by island of last residence.

Fontura de Costa's educational reforms fortuitously coincided with the passage of the literacy law in the United States, expanding the opportunities for potential emigrants to learn to read and write. For two years before the literacy ruling, as the government in Cape Verde began to get wind of the possibility that those who could not read and write might be excluded from the emigration process, an attempt was made to promote literacy among the youth of the archipelago.

The dependence on emigration to the United States both as a source of income through remittances to the islands and as an outlet for victims of famine caused the officials in Cape Verde to step up their literacy campaign. A 1917 government circular reiterated the urgency of obtaining some kind of educational instruction to keep the option of emigration open:

> It is advisable to undertake . . . diligent and persistent propaganda to make any natives who aspire to go and work in the dominions of that Nation understand that it is very convenient — or rather an absolute necessity — for them to acquire in the state or municipal

Table 4. Literacy Rate by Island of Last Residence

Island	Percentage
São Nicolau	77.3
Santo Antão	74.7
São Vicente	71.2
Brava	59.8
Boa Vista, Sal, Maio	59.7
Fogo	44.7
São Tiago	41.4

schools, or through private tuition, the rudimentary knowledge to enable them to obtain the primary examination diploma . . . as an indispensable requirement, since if they do not, they run the risk of seeing themselves forbidden entry to the United States, which would cause harm to a great number of families . . . and appreciable damage to the economy to which the proceeds of emigrant labour to North America make a very valuable contribution.[35]

From this side of the Atlantic, a different type of reaction to the literacy statute emerged. Arguments were made that, particularly since the United States was involved in World War I at that time, the need for immigrant labor was crucial to maintaining the economy on the home front and to producing necessary munitions. One letter to the editor in a New Bedford daily, entitled "Barring Cape Verde Labor," expressed it this way: "We must centralize, we must specialize, we must produce and produce and produce again, if we are to emerge from the great crisis a triumphant nation. We must accept healthy labor, it is our greatest asset, whether literate or illiterate does not prevent a man from making a shell, forging a cannon, a set of cards or spinning yarn, hoeing potatoes, or digging a sewer. We cannot afford to turn willing, healthy workers away from these shores."[36]

Despite this viewpoint, the law went into effect as planned. Before long the news of the United States literacy requirement had reached the general populace in Cape Verde. One observer in Fogo noted that the passage of the literacy law in America gave the young people on the island the impetus to learn to read and write.[37]

A few of the emigrants, however, got caught midstream as the policy on literacy changed. Some had departed already and were enroute to this country when the ruling went into effect, while others left the islands in the days following the passage of the law unaware of the new restrictions. These people arrived unprepared to take a literacy exam and those not able to read and write found themselves unexpectedly barred from admission to this country.

In the case of the brig *Santiago,* a delay due to heavy seas caused the packet to reach the port of New Bedford just days after enforcement of the literacy requirement. Scheduled for arrival before the cut-off date, the boat was shipwrecked on Block Island. At least half of the passengers aboard were illiterate: "Among the passengers held was one man, Joaquim Viera, who could talk English and who appeared to be a bright fellow. He said that he had been in this country and worked for three years in the rope works, and had a small sum of money in a savings bank in this city, but he had lost the book in the wreck. He is afraid he will be deported for he cannot read."[38]

By the second week of June 1917, the port at New Bedford harbored several boats from which approximately three hundred passengers had been taken into custody because of the literacy statute. An appeal was made by representatives of the *Gremio Social Caboverdeano,* a Cape Verdean community organization, and sent to the Department of Labor via the local Congressman, Joseph Walsh, asking that their fellow countrymen be allowed to stay in order to help the war effort as well as to prevent their being further endangered by sailing back in waters where enemy vessels might attack. The Labor department refused the request, but did propose temporary admission for the detainees to allow them to engage solely in agricultural activities.[39] The immigrants, however, declined the offer, contending that they had come to this country to work in the munitions factories at between $2.50 and $3.00 a day, not to do the low-paying farm work. As a result, they were deported.[40]

Packet owners also bore some of the brunt of the change in policy toward illiterates. Under the new law, the owners of the vessels were liable for all maintenance charges at the rate of 45 cents a day for each alien while under detention as well as being subject to fines of $200.00 for each person unable to pass the literacy test.

Captain Arthur Silva of the *Ambrose Snow,* a schooner that arrived just days after the requirement went into effect with fifteen passengers that could not pass the test, declared, "Had I known what a mess I was getting into. . . . I would have turned my vessel right around and sailed back to St. Vincent."[41] Similarly, the Captain of the *Emma and Helen,* with an even greater number of illiterate passengers detained in Boston, went so far as to request that the individuals who were already ordered deported be sent back to New Bedford while other cases were pending. He stated that it would be cheaper to take those passengers back to the Cape Verde Islands than to have them held in Boston at the expense of the schooner.[42] By the end of June 1917, most of the problems in enforcing the literacy law had been ironed out and the subsequent Cape Verdean arrivals were able, for the most part, to read and write.

One limitation on the accuracy of any calculations concerning the volume of migration between the Cape Verde Islands and the United States is the extent of clandestine traffic. From the very beginning of the migration there was always a steady flow of secret departures. The reason for this constant stream of illegal trafficking is not difficult to explain. Physical survival in Cape Verde had been so problematic that almost everyone in the society at one point or another had thought of fleeing the horrifying misery in search of better living conditions abroad. Furthermore, Portuguese government's forced emigration plan and the continual threat of being drafted to serve in the military in Guinea pushed the Cape Verdeans to seek more acceptable alternatives even if they lacked the necessary funds or faced other restrictions to official voluntary emigration. They simply would consider whatever means they deemed necessary, legal or not, to escape.

Yet it does not appear that the amount of clandestine emigration was ever very large, especially as compared to legal emigration. The small size of the vessels as well as the logistics of illegal embarkation kept the numbers limited. Leaving the Islands unofficially was much easier than gaining entry to the United States. The schemes for illegal embarkation on packet boats had been well established in the whaling era. Whaling vessels and the packet ships would put in at tiny secluded harbors along the isolated coast of Brava. Under cover of darkness, those wishing to leave clandestinely would make their way to the vessels. Inhabitants of Brava generally do not know how to swim, but the young boys who wanted to get away on the whalers would learn this skill, just to be able to reach the waiting boats.[43] An 1880 government memo on illegal sailings talks of the futility of trying to officially monitor this type of activity: "Nor are the members of the police reliable enforcement agents in this business; since there has been a case of their being the first to go on board, leaving their truncheons behind on the beach as a memento."[44] Examples such as these are indicative of the universality of the desperation to leave among the inhabitants as well as the crumbling of state control particularly during periods of widespread starvation.

For entry into the United States, several different tactics were employed. Just as vessels would stop at isolated spots in Cape Verde to pick up illegal emigrants, they could then put in at secluded harbors along the Cape Cod and Buzzard's Bay coastline to allow these passengers to disembark before sailing on to the port of New Bedford with the correct number of aliens aboard. One former whaler from the island of São Nicolau recalled that "they would take them ashore close to Colonel Green's mansion, a short distance along the coast from New Bedford's harbor, and then they would hide during the night in the nearby bushes."[45]

How frequently this occurred is difficult to determine but incidents of attempted clandestine journeying were newsworthy, hence offering up more detailed, and at times revealing information about packet boat traffic than the ship lists alone. As early as 1897, it was reported in the New Bedford daily that the captain of the ship *Zulmira* was fined for bringing in more passengers than the law allowed.[46] One well-publicized incident of this type of illegal entry was the case of the three-masted schooner, the *William H. Draper,* from Brava. At dawn the morning of 12 May 1922, thirty passengers and eleven crew members were smuggled ashore in Westport Harbor near the port of New Bedford and were last seen heading toward Cape Cod. At least three trips on a boat that could hold approximately fifteen passengers had to be made to get the group on land from the schooner, which was lying a half-mile off the coast. Originally bound for Bermuda with a cargo of whiskey and aguardiente (Portuguese whiskey), one of few Cape Verdean exports, the craft was driven off the shores there by strong head winds forcing the Captain to proceed north to try to make the port at New Bedford.

An extensive search was conducted for the missing passengers but none were ever found. Because this successful smuggling attempt occurred after the passage of more restrictive immigration laws and because it was also known that some of the passengers were illiterate, therefore, also in violation of the 1917 literacy statute, the federal authorities got involved in the *Draper* case, resolving to make an example of it. It is likely, too, that clandestine immigration had been on the rise at this time, as a result of a drought that brought on severe famine in Cape Verde in the years 1921–22. Authorities claimed that the *Draper* incident represented the largest number that ever entered the country illegally in the New England district.[47]

While this might be true for the New England area, another rather extraordinary episode of illegal entry of many more passengers occurred earlier in the century off the coast of North Carolina. Riddled with racial overtones, it is likely the earliest known report of contact between Cape Verdeans and southern whites and blacks. Bound for New Bedford, the vessel *Vera Cruz VII* sailing from Brava, encountered severe gale winds and went ashore at Ocracoke inlet ostensibly to obtain fresh water for the four hundred or so passengers on board.[48]

The sighting of a ship of this type in those waters took the North Carolina coastal lookout by surprise. More than that, the assembly of nonwhite passengers who were *also* non-English speaking aroused a mixture of chagrin and ridicule as one observer commented: "Never in their lives had Ocracoke pilots seen such a spectacle. What might have resembled a deck full of black-birds at a distance turned out to be Negroes. A hundred of them so it seemed, in a solid mass, some in the rigging, some on top the hatchways and cabins but most of them packed along the rails, shouting in some foreign language to those aboard the small motor boat."[49]

In fact, only 240 of the 400-odd passengers were actually manifested, with only 50 of those holding valid passports. The group included 23 women and several children. Most were from the island of Fogo. At least one child had been born during the voyage and one passenger died and was buried during the Ocracoke stopover. According to the inspector, 90 percent of the passengers had had smallpox. None carried money or valuables. Anything of value had been given over to the Captain, Julio Fernandes, for safekeeping.[50] Several of the passengers revealed that Captain Fernandes had promised them entry to America whether or not they had valid passports.

After having been beached at Ocracoke for a day or two, well supplied with food and water, and having traded quantities of choice Portuguese liquor, the vessel was then guided by the pilots through the inlet. But the ship ran aground near the town of Portsmouth. All accounts suggest that Captain Fernandes deliberately shipwrecked the *Vera Cruz VII*. When he went into the nearest town with a telegraph service to supposedly wire the agents in New Bedford for further instructions, he disappeared with the necessary papers and the passengers' cash and valuables. He must have, at some point, realized that he could never have eluded the authorities carrying so many illegal immigrants. Rumor had it that Fernandes, instead of telegraphing for help, bought a ticket aboard a train, headed to New Bedford, incognito, and was later smuggled out of the country himself, hidden aboard a whaler in an empty oil cask!

Claims were also made that for many days before the arrival of the *Vera Cruz,* an unusually large number of "down east" fishing boats had been sighted in the waters adjacent to Ocracoke Island and that it was assumed that these fishermen were waiting to rendezvous with the Cape Verdean bark in order to transport the passengers to New Bedford. The Captain, by arriving several days late, apparently failed to make the connection.

Once it became known that the Captain had disappeared, local rescue workers came to the aid of the stranded passengers. They only had one small life-saving surf boat available to transport all four hundred to Portsmouth, a tiny village that itself had less than a hundred inhabitants. Somehow, the abandoned group was fed and sheltered. One report states that a total of 1,248 meals were eaten and that it took 4½ barrels of flour to make enough bread for all of them.

The immigrants were later transferred to the larger town of New Bern, where arrangements were made to send most of the passengers to New Bedford. At one stopover heading north, the following scene was depicted.

> An amusing incident of the trip occurred during a stop at Goldsboro, N.C. The Negroes of that place, seeing such a party of men of their own color, crowded from all directions to greet them.
>
> When conversation was attempted by the American Negroes and the foreigners came back with Portuguese dialect, there was consternation among the men of Goldsboro. They were afraid of language they could not understand and thought of "conjer" men and "obeah" sent them scurrying away. After that they carefully avoided the people of *familiar shade but outlandish tongue* [italics mine].[51]

The white chronicler distances himself from the interchange by smugly describing it as though he were watching a spectator sport played for his own entertainment. The Negro men are portrayed in belittling and childlike terms as "afraid," "not [able to] understand" and "scurrying away." Yet, given the obvious consternation expressed earlier in the first glimpse of this group by the North Carolina Coast Guard, where they were compared to a flock of blackbirds, suggesting a swarm or undifferentiated, animal-like mass, perhaps the amusement of the reporter is a mask for his own bewilderment and fear of these darker-skinned strangers. In any case, the initial assessment of the immigrants as being at once "familiar" and "outlandish" captures the dilemma that the Cape Verdean settlers would so often reflect as they established themselves in this country.

A few of the stranded passengers were permitted entry into North Carolina, and it is said that some of them settled there in the backcountry. At least one immigrant, Charles Mendes, remained in the town of New Bern. Back in New Bedford, penniless and weary, the rest of the group received some help from the city until relatives and friends arrived to claim them. A feature story about shipwrecks along the Carolina coast, which appeared in a 1950 newspaper, tells us, "Until this day on Ocracoke Island some of the empty jugs and bottles once filled with fine liquors salvaged from the *Vera Cruz VII* may still be seen."[52]

Dr. Victor Safford, an immigration official in New Bedford during this period, suggested that the practice of smuggling in aliens was arranged in complicity with the cranberry growers to recruit migrant workers. The price of the ticket, plus fees to pay off the captain and packet owners, would put the destitute arrivals heavily in debt to the bog owners. In this way, their hard labor could be exploited until they were able to pay off what was owed.[53]

However, while there were examples of business dealings between bog owners and packet captains to transport workers from the islands, as was the case with Henrique Mendes, captain of the schooner *Ernestina*, these arrangements were literally "above board."[54] The evidence of the manipulative and dishonest type of recruitment has been sparse. Moreover, among the Cape Verdean immigrants as well as other ethnic groups in this period, ties of kinship and ethnicity became so effective that illegal arrangements, whether through middlemen or labor agents, quickly became unnecessary. An informal network of friends and relatives assisted in the procurement of willing laborers. In her autobiography, the Cape Verdean educator Belmira Nunes Lopes recalled that,

> The Cape Verdeans were never contracted from the Islands. They came to this country because at that time, before 1917, they could come in freely, and they came. The moment they started coming to this country around the last decade or two of the nineteenth century, Cape Verdeans followed each other to this country. Brothers would send for brothers, sisters would send for brothers, and friends would come because they knew other friends had come. They found employment here in the factories, in the bogs and on the boats cooking and doing odd jobs. My father was one of those men who was often sent by the owners of cranberry bogs such as L. B. R. Barker on Cape Cod to recruit other Cape Verdeans who were already in New Bedford, but they were never contracted to come here from the Islands by the Americans who owned the bogs.[55]

Dr. Safford himself notes that his official responsibilities related only to the medical inspection and detection of disease. It appears that most of the allegations concerning the extent of illegal entry, including Dr. Safford's, based their evidence on the story of the *Vera Cruz VII*, which received much publicity at the time, but was certainly an exceptional case in the history of the packet trade.[56]

Another more common way of smuggling in extra immigrants was to register them as members of the crew. In this way, regulations limiting the number of passengers per vessel could be circumvented. Those falsely listed as crew members would then be allowed to disembark with the rest of the group. Because the ship records do include crew as well as passenger listings, I am assuming that much of this particular type of clandestine activity is encompassed in my figures. In some cases, immigration inspectors would officially note on the passenger roster a change of status from crew to arriving alien. An example is this addendum to the ship manifest regarding four of the passengers on the

Bertha D. Nickerson sailing from Brava in 1916, "These aliens shipped for the round trip and before the time to return decided that as they could get employment at good wage, they would abandon their calling as seamen, and seek admission to the United States in the regular way as immigrant aliens." Furthermore, usually on the records of the official crew lists, it was indicated whether the seaman was staying on board or being discharged in New Bedford.[57] Padding the crew became so commonplace that by the later years of immigration, the newspapers would routinely report such occurrences without any apparent repercussions to the owner, captain, or the illegal passengers.

Finally, another practice that was not at all unusual was for a boat to land legally at the port of New Bedford but to be carrying a handful of stowaways aboard. The officials in Cape Verde usually did nothing to stop them from leaving, but when they arrived, United States immigration authorities proved to be more strict. Various strategies were developed, such as bribing immigration officers with money or, especially in Prohibition years, with cane brandy. An alternative scheme was that of contriving false linings in the holds where a stowaway could hide until the ship was inspected. Then, with the help of relatives already living here or the dock workers, often Cape Verdeans themselves, the clandestine passengers could be smuggled ashore. One account of a stowaway's journey over to America tells how a young man hid himself in a barrel of salt, becoming known from then on by the nickname Manny Salgado (Salty).[58]

At the end of a list of legal passengers, notations can sometimes be found that were written by the immigration authorities recording the presence of stowaways found on board. In all, I found only twenty-five officially listed as stowaways.

Particularly when an incident of clandestine entry had human interest appeal the newspapers would run a story. In one case, a young woman, Maria da Ramos, stowed away on the *Carlton Bell,* expecting that her fiance would claim her upon her arrival here. Her intended husband never showed up, however, despite a long distance courtship and promise of marriage. Another man, José Francisco Vera Cruz, aged sixty, came forward with an offer of marriage, but Ms. Ramos refused because of the difference in age. She was subsequently excluded from entry into this country.[59]

At about the same time a twelve-year-old stowaway, Isadore Soares, arrived here in a similar situation. He had hoped to join an uncle in New Bedford, but the man never claimed him. The young boy told officials that he hid away so that he could come here and make a large sum of money to send back to his impoverished family in São Vicente.

Just before being deported, he was given the chance to remain in this country when relatives made contact with the Boston authorities.[60]

A slight escalation in the amount of clandestine traffic did occur after May 1917, when the literacy law went into effect. Several incidents were reported, particularly in the following month of June, resulting from the time lapse in transporting the immigrants. Some packets had set sail from the Cape Verde Islands before the passage of the law or had embarked apparently unaware of the new restrictions and found that by the time of their arrival, the illiterate passengers would not be allowed entry.

Reports of immigrants dramatically evading customs and bribing the inspectors hit the local newspapers. The *Morning Mercury* reports that "Four of the detained Bravas who were to have been sent away yesterday didn't go, for they escaped from the immigration shed during the dark hours of the night and made a clean getaway and no trace of them has been found. From all appearances they must have been thrown a rope from the outside of the north end of the building and climbed down to the wharf and then made their escape."[61] The next day one could read the following: "Two Bravas escaped from the Bertha D. Nickerson Thursday afternoon as they were being placed on board from the shed. The Bravas were checked off as they were put on board, but two of them, climbing out on the bowsprit of the craft, which was on the south side of the state pier, jumped to the wharf and made a getaway."[62]

When illegal passengers were discovered by the officials, the owners of the boats became liable, with an average fine of $300.00 levied per passenger. Sometimes this could amount to a sizable expense and the eventual scrapping of the vessel, as was the case with the three-masted schooner *Fairhaven*. When the arrivals without papers skipped out during the night after being ordered to remain aboard, the owner was fined $22,000 for violating the law. The government then auctioned the ship off for $500. Similarly, several years later, the former whaling ship *Manta* had to be sold and the owner fined after eleven immigrants were found hiding below deck.[63]

Although the actual volume of clandestine traffic at no time amounted to a sizable proportion of the total migration and therefore does not significantly alter the figures based on the passenger list data, the variety and ingenuity that was demonstrated by the emigrants in their attempts to leave Cape Verde are testimony to the existence of a compelling need and desire to try to escape the miserable conditions regardless of the consequences.

As a result of the legacy of invisibility, determination of accurate population figures has been a recurrent and nagging issue of considerable significance for Cape Verdean Americans. It simply has not been possible to stand up and be counted by the usual means which has made speculation about the size of the community an ever present concern. One puzzle that my data on Cape Verdeans cannot really do much to solve is the question of the actual size of the Cape Verdean population in the United States, including immigrants and their descendants, at any given period in history. This problem has been a continuing challenge to those interested in defining the Cape Verdean American community, but without statistics on rates of fertility and mortality, it is still only possible to make broad generalizations concerning the total population.[64]

Even without the necessary quantitative information, however, some scholars have tried to estimate the total Cape Verdean American population. One study suggests that by 1921 there were between 10 and 15,000 Cape Verdeans living in the southeastern Massachusetts area.[65] Another 1911 report gives a figure of 4,000 Cape Verdeans living in New Bedford and lists the "Bravas" as the third largest ethnic group, after the French Canadians and the Portuguese.[66] It is generally thought that the number of Cape Verdeans living in the United States today is between 250,000 and 300,000, with 15,000 located in the city of New Bedford, still the hub of the Cape Verdean American community, although Pawtucket, Rhode Island and the areas around the cities of Brockton and Scituate, Massachusetts, have drawn larger numbers of new immigrants. The 1980 population figure for the Cape Verde islands was 295,703 or roughly the same number as the total of those Cape Verdeans and their descendants who are currently residing in the United States.

Calculations from the ship manifest records have shown that a demographic outline of the Cape Verdean immigrants has not been an impossibility after all. Yet the sense of being a statistical nonentity has still been a persistent theme in the development of a Cape Verdean American identity. Perhaps in counterbalance to this quantitative anonymity, the following chapter explores how the contours of the packet boat trade served to personalize the actual transplantation process for many of the Cape Verdean arrivals to their new land.

NOTES

1. Stephen Thernstrom, ed. *Harvard Encyclopedia of American Ethnic Groups* (Cambridge, Mass.: Belknap Press, 1980), p. 198.

2. Even with the 1980 inclusion of a category for Cape Verdean descent,

calculations were not accurate since many Cape Verdean Americans still defined themselves as Portuguese Americans or American blacks.

3. Michael Omi and Howard Winant, *Racial Formation in the United States from the 1960s to the 1980s* (New York: Routledge & Kegan Paul, 1986), pp. 3–4.

4. Ray Anthony Almeida, *Cape Verdeans in America: Our Story* (Boston: American Committee for Cape Verde, 1978), p. 51.

5. Robert P. Swiegenga, "List Upon List: The Ship Passenger Records and Immigration Research" *Journal of American Ethnic History* 10, no. 3 (Spring 1991), p. 50.

6. This catalog is already being made use of by Cape Verdeans interested in tracing their family histories. Scraps of information that have been passed down can be plugged into the chart to reveal a more complete picture.

7. Since compiling the data, the original manifest from the Brig *Lucy Atwood* arriving in New Bedford on 6 June 1856 from São Tiago has been recovered. On it are listed two passengers, a man, aged twenty-four, who is not named and a woman, Mary de Souza also twenty-four years of age, who was likely the first Cape Verdean female arrival to this country. The first official listing of departing passengers from the Cape Verdes to the United States appear in the Brava records for the year 1864. See Deirdre Meintel Machado, "Cape Verdean–Americans: Their Culture and Historical Background" (Ph.D. diss., Brown University, 1978), p. 239, for a discussion of the unreliability of the nineteenth-century figures on Cape Verdean emigration.

8. During the 1914–18 war, decrees were proclaimed by the Portuguese government restricting the movement of men liable for military service. These regulations were renewed after the war as well. However, in 1920, a crisis was declared due to severe food shortages on the islands, which prompted local authorities to take measures easing emigration to the United States. See, António Carreira, *The People of the Cape Verde Islands: Exploitation and Emigration,* trans. and ed. Christopher Fyfe (Hamden, Conn.: Archon Books, 1982, pp. 64–68, for a detailed discussion of this period of emigration.

9. In compiling the data from the passenger manifests, I chose to record only those categories that afforded some variety in response and which were workable for a statistical program. Thus, a question like "whether or not a polygamist" was skipped over since all answered in the negative. Similarly, responses to "occupation," although potentially of significance, were not entered because almost all forms simply listed "laborer," "seaman," or nothing at all. Since the bulk of the immigration from Cape

Verde was composed of impoverished subsistence farmers whose land could no longer feed them, the question of occupation was moot.

Names and addresses of close relatives and friends in the Islands or those who the newcomer was joining here were too unwieldy and in many cases too illegible to catalog. The nine areas that I chose to quantify for statistical analysis are age, sex, marital status, literacy, last permanent residence, final destination, whether ever before in the United States, place of birth, and year of arrival.

10. "Immigrants Arrive," *The Evening Standard* (New Bedford), 18 Apr. 1910, p. 4.

11. Unfortunately, records are not available before 1911. Those from 1911 until the doors were closed showed only about two hundred Cape Verdean entries.

12. Sam Beck, "Manny Almeida's Ringside Lounge—The Cape Verdean Struggle for Their Neighborhood" (Ms., 1981), p. 78.

13. Carreira, *People of the Cape Verde Islands;* Carreira, *Migraçoes Nas Ilhas De Cabo Verde,* 2d ed. (Instituto Cabo-Verdeano de Livro, 1983).

14. Carreira, *People of the Cape Verde Islands,* p. 53.

15. Paul W. Barrows, "The Historical Roots of Cape Verdean Dependency, 1460–1990" (Ph.D. diss., University of Minnesota, 1990), p. 123

16. Walter Wilcox, *International Migrations: Statistics,* vol. 1 (New York: National Bureau of Economic Research, 1929), p. 460.

17. Ibid., 1079.

18. "Immigrants in New Bedford" (Ms., New Bedford Free Public Library, 1911).

19. Thernstrom, *Harvard Encyclopedia,* p. 198.

20. Leo Pap, *The Portuguese-Americans* (Boston: Twayne, 1981), pp. 35–36.

21. Carreira, *Migraçoes,* p. 125, and unpublished data courtesy of Roger Kramer, Immigration and Naturalization Service, United States Department of Justice, Washington, D.C., cited in World Bank Report No. 5446-CV, 2, p. 62.

22. World Bank Report, No. 5446-CV, 2.

22. Thomas Kessner, *The Golden Door: Italian and Jewish Immigrant Mobility in New York City, 1880–1915* (New York: Oxford University Press, 1977), p. 30.

24. Pap, *Portuguese-Americans,* p. 106

25. William P. Dillingham, "Cape Cod, Massachusetts: Bravas, or Black Portuguese, Cranberry Pickers," chapter 7 in *Immigrants in Industries, Report of the Immigration Commission, Recent Immigrants in Agriculture,* vol. 22 (1911), p. 540.

26. "A Survey of the Foreign Communities of Providence," Report (Providence: International Institute, July 1935).

27. Elsie Clews Parsons, *Folk-Lore from the Cape Verde Islands,* 2 vols. (Cambridge, Mass.: The American Folk-Lore Society, 1923), p. xi.

28. Machado, "Cape Verdean–Americans," p. 247; David Tyack, "Cape Verdean Immigration to the United States" (Honors thesis, Harvard University), p. 23.

29. The percentages averaged by decade of those arriving under the age of 14: 1880–89, .093; 1890–99, .106; 1902–09, .048; 1910–1919, .044.

30. Pap, *Portuguese-Americans,* p. 116.

31. Ibid., p. 117.

32. Dr. Victor Safford, "Cape Cod Africans," *Falmouth Enterprise,* 25 Aug., 1944.

33. Norman Araujo, *A Study of Cape Verdean Literature* (Boston: Boston College Press, 1966), p. 12.

34. Archibald Lyall, *Black and White Makes Brown: An Account of a Journey to the Cape Verde Islands and Portuguese Guinea* (London: W. Herman, 1938), p. 70.

35. *Boletim Oficial de Cabo Verde* 18 (15 May 1917).

36. "Barring Cape Verde Labor," *Morning Mercury,* 1 June 1917, p. 7.

37. Tyack, "Cape Verdean Immigration," p. 29.

38. "Wrecked Immigrants Landed at this Port," *Morning Mercury,* 11 June 1917, p. 8.

39. Ibid.

40. "Declined by Bravas," *Morning Mercury,* 18 June 1917, p. 1; "Cape Verders Are Ordered Deported," *Morning Mercury,* 20 June 1917, p. 8.

41. "Fifty-Six More Passengers Held," *Morning Mercury,* 1 June 1917, p. 12.

42. "May Admit Illiterate Bravas Temporarily," *Morning Mercury,* 9 June 1917, p. 8.

43. Machado, "Cape Verdean–Americans," p. 233.

44. *Boletim Oficial de Cabo Verde* 40 (2 Sept. 1880), p. 254.

45. Interview with Jose Flore Livramento, videotaped by Ron Barboza, June 1984.

46. "*Zulmira* Captain Fined," *Morning Mercury,* 20 May 1897, p. 8.

47. From the *New Bedford Evening Standard:* "Cape Verders Reported Smuggled Ashore at Dawn Today in Westport Harbor," 12 May 1922, pp. 1, 2; "Master of *Draper* Will Search Cape for 41 Runaways," 13 May 1922, pp. 1, 2; "Plan Probe of *Draper* Case," 16 May 1922, p. 2. From the *Morning Mercury:* "Clew (sic) Reported in Search for the Missing Aliens," 15 May 1922, p. 10; "Two Merchants Are Held on the Schooner *Draper,*" 17 May 1922, p. 4.

48. Aycock Brown, "The Mystery of the Vera Cruz," *The News and Observer* (Raleigh, N.C.), 9 Dec. 1934; Aycock Brown, "The Vera Cruz: Her Death at Ocracoke Inlet," *Durham Morning Herald,* 11 Mar., 1951; Aycock Brown, "50th Anniversary of Coastal Shipwreck Passes Unnoticed," *The Citizen* (Ashville, N.C.) 15 May 1953; and in *The Morning Mercury,* "Vera Cruz Total Loss," 11 May 1903, p. 8; "Emigrants Face Want," 12 May 1903, p. 8; "Vera Cruz's Free List," 15 May 1903, p. 8; "Bread Riot in City," 20 May 1903, p. 10; "Bravas Removed from City Hall," 21 May 1903, p. 5.

49. Brown, "Mystery of the Vera Cruz."

50. This fact was specified on the lists with the notation, "Capt. Has," written next to the amount in the possession of each passenger.

51. "Bread Riot in City," *Morning Mercury,* 20 May 1903, p. 10.

52. Brown, "Vera Cruz."

53. Safford, "Cape Cod Africans," p. 5.

54. Almeida, *Cape Verdeans in America,* p. 38.

55. Maria Luisa Nunes, *A Portuguese Colonial in America: Belmira Nunes Lopes, the Autobiography of a Cape Verdean–American* (Pittsburgh: Latin American Literary Review Press, 1982), pp. 33–34.

56. Safford, "Cape Cod Africans," p. 11; Cooper Gaw, "The Cape Verde Islands and Cape Verdean Immigrants," *Evening Standard* 29 July 1905, p. 3; Machado, "Cape Verdean–Americans," p. 250, Tyack, "Cape Verdean Immigration," pp. 25–26.

57. In at least one case, at a time when Portuguese authorities had begun to crack down on the practice of padding the crew, the individuals illegally listed as crew members were not allowed entry into this country and the shipowners who were responsible were subsequently fined. A government bulletin dated 3 Nov. 1920 contains the following report of the incident:

It is customary for ships which leave the ports of this archipelago for North America to register a large number of people who are paying their own passages but purport to be crew members, hoping to elude and deceive the authorities by landing clandestinely in the United States, evading the requirements of the law. Such proceedings only serve to cause difficulties for those who make use of these irregular methods, since the deception is easily discovered, and does harm to Portuguese commerce and brings our government into disrepute. Repeated incidents have proved that the main object that ships leaving this colony have, is to carry emigrants clandestinely into that country. In order to warn the unwary, it is hereby announced that the government has recently been informed that the following individuals have been forced to leave North America, having landed illegally from the ships mentioned below, whose owners are reported to have had to pay 100 to 200 dollars for each passenger:

From the barque *Lima*—Aníbal Lopes Monteiro, Isidro da Cruz e Silva, Pascoal da Costa Brito, Teotónio Lopes Correira, Joao Sequeira, Sebastiao Rodrigues Pires and Francisco Rocha. From the schooner *Fannie Belle Atwood*—Alfredo da Pina Correia, Belmiro Tavares, and Floréncio José Lopes. From the schooner *Agnes*—Virgínia Silva. *Boletim Oficial de Cabo Verde*, p. 48 cited in Carreira, *People of the Cape Verde Islands*, pp. 98–99.

58. Machado, "Cape Verdean–Americans," p. 249.

59. "Fiance Fails to Come for Stowaway," *Morning Mercury*, 20 May 1921, p. 5.

60. "Boy Stowaway Aboard Packet," *Morning Mercury*, 18 May and "Fiance Fails," *Morning Mercury*, 20 May 1921.

61. "Says He Paid $75 for Woman's Escape," *Morning Mercury*, 29 June 1917, p. 8.

62. "Few Illiterates on the Carleton Bell," *Morning Mercury*, 30 June 1917.

63. Almeida, *Cape Verdeans in America*, pp. 32, 35.

Except for occasional cases of aguardiente, illegal trafficking appears to have been restricted to passengers rather than goods. In only two cases did I find record of cargo systematically smuggled into this country from the Cape Verde Islands. In 1917, seven men were arrested in New Bedford by the federal authorities and charged with smuggling tobacco on the *A. E. Whyland* and the *Bertha D. Nickerson*. "Accused of Smuggling Tobacco from Island," *Morning Mercury*, 15 June 1917, p. 6.

Several years later, in 1923, cocaine was found by the Cuttyhunk coast guard hidden in a shipment of salt on the packet *Eugenia Emilia* sailing from the islands. "St. Pierre Britisher and Bark with Cocaine Come to Harbor," *Evening Standard*, 5 Feb. 1923, p. 1.

64. Some beginning research on the life expectancy of Cape Verdeans is, however, currently in progress. The project is based on a data analysis of 777 obituaries that appeared in two Cape Verdean newspapers, the *Cape Verde News* and *The Cape Verdean*, during the period 1973–1983. Of the 230 in the sample who were born in the Cape Verde Islands, the mean life expectancy was 82.1 years (79.9—males; 82.8—females). These figures are contrasted with the much lower figures of 48.3 years for males and 51.7 years for females who stayed in the islands. However, the report does point out that there are limitations on the immigrant subsample, which account, in part, for the high average of life expectancy. It is skewed

both by having eliminated the cohorts with high infant mortality and by self-selection of the young, presumably healthy, males who make up such a large part of the immigration here. Nevertheless, the preliminary findings do point to a considerable level of longevity among the Cape Verdean immigrants. Richard Lobban, Waltraud Coli, and Robert J. Tidwell, "Cape Verdean Life Expectancy" (Ms., 1985).

Certainly, the oral histories gathered for this dissertation provided me with many examples of individuals who lived exceptionally long and active lives. These numerous instances of longevity clearly are a source of pride among Cape Verdeans and are often presented as evidence of the vitality of the immigrants.

Statistics on mortality are not available for the Portuguese population either, but, similarly, it is thought that Portuguese islanders have a greater life expectancy than the American population at large. The Portuguese immigrant press would frequently feature stories of island immigrants who lived a hundred years or more.

Even less is known about birth rates either for the Portuguese group as a whole or for the Cape Verdeans. Portugal itself has been a country with a high birth rate as compared to the rest of Europe and to the United States. Whether or not this also holds true for the emigrating population is a matter of conjecture. While a high proportion of the immigrants were of childbearing age, those age brackets of greater fecundity were also heavily skewed toward males. Cases of parents with many children appear again and again in the narrations of Cape Verdean family life, but it is not possible to come up with even an estimated birth rate on the basis of individual examples of prolific families alone.

65. Herbert D. Bliss, "Feeling on Cape Is Not Inimical to Cape Verdeans," *New Bedford Sunday Standard*, 28 August 1921, p. 5.

66. "Immigrants in New Bedford," p. 3

From Archipelago to America: A Sentimental Geography

2

When letters arrived from America, I was called to read them. My reputation as a good student at the Seminary made me the inevitable confidant of the emigrants' intimacies. In that way I came to know the Creole nostalgia of the islands' sons. The letters were varied, but they all revealed the archipelago's voice beckoning the emigrants to the corner of the world they had left behind. Letters to parents and legal proxies asking them to buy the piece of land on which to build a house with the red tile roof of Marseille, decorated with portraits and oil paintings of President Wilson, and the American flag with the 48 little stars gathered in the corner; letters to godparents of children left in their care at God's mercy and the godparents' expense; letters to girlfriends, enclosing the sign of love that carried the hope of marriage for the following year, the much anticipated news. There were also photographs to decorate the walls and the American end tables. They showed groups of fashionable Creole men wearing cashmere suits, heavy rings on their fingers, and watch chains dangling over their vests. A sentimental geography which placed America very near me. It no longer seemed a faraway land. America was at the reach of my hand. The distances became almost meaningless because of the intimacy those letters established with the island. To go to America was a natural step for the children of the islands to take so they could wear good suits, have watches and shoes, and earn dollars to buy a plot of land and a resistant mule.

In this way, little by little, distance became a part of my life. A distance that was hardly mysterious, so full of intimacy, it seemed to me that my island did not end at Ponta de Vermelharia, but instead continued beyond the sea, until it covered all of America, transposed, in the Creole feeling, to the street where each home prepared the familiar comfort of its coziness.

The sea was also going to be my way out.

—From Baltasar Lopes, *Chiquinho*

Like many of the other new arrivals to the Northeast in the late nineteenth and early twentieth centuries, the Cape Verdean settlers followed a pattern of chain migration based primarily on kinship ties.[1] The oral histories are dotted with numerous examples of how relatives, friends and fellow islanders drew others to join them and assisted in the transition to this new land. Perhaps Jose Centeio from Providence, Rhode Island, best summarized the connection as he described "growing up in Cape Verde when there was not much for a young man to do except listen to stories about relatives in the United States—chiefly New Bedford—who had made it."[2]

Emigration was a deliberate strategy for survival that very much depended on the resources of family networks, particularly those links on the America end of the chain. Reliance on kin to provide information about job availability and to obtain employment once arrived was also crucial to this process. The passage from *Chiquinho* quoted above expresses the reflections of the main character of the title's name articulated just before his own emigration to the United States. His is a classic example of chain migration. As the story is told, Chiquinho's father, Antonio Manuel, first left São Nicolau for America in 1915 because of the severe drought conditions. His letters home, his words of encouragement to his son and finally his having arranged work for him in New Bedford bring Chiquinho to leave his beloved Cape Verde and follow in his father's footsteps.

The Cape Verdean chain of movement was similar to both European immigration and black relocation from South to North during this period. "Kinfolk were the invisible links that extended from the Tidewater to Wheeler Street, substantially the same kind of chains as those that connected Sicily with Little Italy," writes Elizabeth Pleck in her Boston study of black migration and poverty,[3] while Bodnar, Weber, and Simon found that occupational networking through the connections of family and friends was characteristic of both newly arrived black workers and the white ethnic employees of Pittsburgh's mills and plants.[4]

Typically, chain migration begins with single men relocating. The Cape Verdeans are no exception to this pattern. In this instance, it was the whalers who had initiated the process at the close of the nineteenth century. Joseph Ramos, who at the time of his interview was one of the oldest living former whalemen, remembered well his decision to become part of a crew and thereby find a way to join his father, already in the United States. "When I went whaling, my mother was crying, but I was going to become a man. She didn't want me to go, but my father was here in the United States. He was sick. I was to join him, make some money and help support our family. There was no choice but to take a chance. When I signed on, the captain demanded $5 right away to overlook my age. I had just turned eighteen and crewmen were supposed to be twenty-one."[5] Joseph Andrade at age ninety-seven, another of a handful of whalers still alive at this writing, recalled that his link to the United States was a sibling: "My oldest brother had shipped out from New Bedford on a whaling boat. When I heard he was coming to the Cape Verde Islands, I was on the lookout for him. I was eighteen years old. When he arrived I asked him to ask the captain to give me a chance and he did. They took two of us."[6]

In the case of the Cape Verdean migration, once the packet trade got under way, their transatlantic system of support was greatly facilitated by the particular mode of transportation that carried the newcomers to the United States. While there certainly were instances of hazardous voyaging on the packet boats, that they were owned and operated by the Cape Verdeans themselves served to further strengthen the chain between the islands and the American settlement. To compensate for the risks of travel on these aged vessels, which have been described both as "floating shipwrecks"[7] and as "a cross between a caravel of Columbus and Huck Finn's raft,"[8] the Cape Verdeans were surrounded by their own compatriots. On the crossing, they could hear the familiar sounds of their native language and of the *mornas* and *coladeiras* played by passengers carrying their musical instruments. They could also continue eating their traditional *Crioulo* foods.

Belmira Nunes described how her half-sister Maria Luisa passed the time on the month-long voyage from Brava aboard the *Maria Luisa,* a vessel coincidentally bearing her same name. "The trip had been a hazardous one, but sometimes the ocean was calm. The passengers, anxious to reach America, grew impatient. . . . Then the amateur musicians, always a violinist and a guitar player, occasionally a mandolin or a *violao* strummer, would play the sweet, nostalgic *mornas*. Possibly, the slow-paced sentimental *morna* would be replaced by a fast waltz. Not that there was much room for dancing, since the miniscule lounge barely held a dozen people."[9]

In the packet trade it was customary to bring fresh meat from the islands "on the leg" and to kill the animals as needed on board. The local newspaper provided this vivid account of the scene on deck when one of the packet boats pulled into the New Bedford pier in the summer of 1909:

> There was the usual menagerie effect about the deck of the boat as she lay at the dock. A black pig that had survived the voyage had

wisely selected the port side, where the sun in the west shone agreeably upon him. There he slept peacefully, unmindful of the efforts of one of the passengers to "sick" two cheerful puppies upon him.

On the other side of the house, a small family of goats wandered about, with an air of blasé indifference to the stir about them, and here and there strolled an occasional chicken.

A number of goat skins and cowhide, which were spread out on the dock, drying, served as a remembrance of the animals that had formed part of the menu during the voyage from Brava.[10]

Those who were fortunate enough to travel on the three-hundred-foot "luxury liner" *Coriolanus*, an acquisition of lawyer Roy Texeira that could carry two hundred passengers and crew, were even treated to a paid orchestra as well as a busy schedule of entertainment on deck, including the "christening" of the crew's pet monkey.[11] Moreover, the route was direct from the small harbors of the Islands, following a mild current to the Gulf Stream and north to the port of New Bedford, keeping to warm latitudes with no uneasy layovers in foreign lands. Emigration became a much more likely choice for men and women of all ages while communication between southeastern Massachusetts and the old country flowed steadily via the back and forth movement of the packet trade.[12] As one Cape Verdean American educator has commented, "There have always been the boats, that's the lifeline that binds us."[13]

Control over the means of passage not only eased the transition on the journey itself but in conjunction with the social dynamics of chain migration it also meant that the initial experience of relocation was far less jarring or bewildering to the newly arrived than was the characteristic first encounter for the vast majority of immigrants to America at this time. At its height as many as five thousand immigrants passed through Ellis Island daily during this period, which meant that even if the processing went smoothly, usually lasting only a few hours if there were no complications, it was, nonetheless, primarily a bureaucratic event. Furthermore, for others, it proved to be a most traumatic encounter. Some were detained, while others were separated from their families and, to their horror, sent back. Over the course of its operation, as many as three thousand people committed suicide at Ellis Island.[14] Once processed, the exhausted and confused arrivals had to deal with swindlers of all kinds, preying on the naiveté of the "greenhorns." Such was the depiction of the main character's arrival in Abraham Cahan's classic novel of immigration, *The Rise of David Levinsky*, (1917):

The harsh manner of the immigration officers was a grievous surprise to me. . . . These unfriendly voices flavored all America with a spirit of icy inhospitality that sent a chill through my very soul. . . . Gitelson, who like myself had no friends in New York never left my side. . . . I led the way out of the big Immigrant Station. As we reached the park outside we were pounced down upon by two evil-looking men, representatives of boarding-houses for immigrants. They pulled us so roughly and their general appearance and manner were so uninviting that we struggled and protested until they let us go—not without some parting curses.[15]

Yet it was not simply a matter of fewer numbers to handle that gave Cape Verdean newcomers to New Bedford such a positive start. Even immigrants arriving to less crowded points of disembarkation could experience the same kind of painful disorientation of those at Ellis Island. Consider the memory as recounted in Hilda Satt Polacheck's autobiography of her arrival to the port of Montreal in 1892: "The ship docked at Montreal on a bright morning in June. By this time I had recovered from my illness, but I was still a little unsteady on my feet. The whole family was a sorry bedraggled-looking group. . . . In addition to being hungry and dirty, there was no friendly face to greet us. We were taken to a sort of detention camp, with many other migrants, men, women and children who were herded into one enormous room and told to wait."[16]

By contrast, the newly arrived emigrants from the Cape Verde Islands typically received a warm, helpful, and enthusiastic reception from familiar faces that began even before they disembarked. A 1911 report on immigrants in New Bedford included this explanation, "To the Bravas, New Bedford is not as a strange land. Practically all who come have relatives or friends or persons they know about. There appears, therefore, to be no need of protection or direction at the docks. This is done by kinsmen or friends."[17] The arrival of a packet was always cause for celebration, as friends and relatives flocked down to the wharf to welcome the newcomers, eager for news from the islands and the assurance that the voyage had been completed safely. Some would hop aboard to join in on the festivities, with much embracing, dancing, and drinking of *grog* (whiskey).

A general depiction of the scene at the pier, including both those arriving and the crowd gathered to greet them often completed the newspaper accounts of incoming packet boats. When the barkentine *Savoia* approached New Bedford's harbor in 1914, this was the scene:

> During the afternoon the *Savoia* attracted attention from all the pleasure craft out for the day and as many as a hundred sailed around

her, many containing persons who had made the trip down the bay especially to see who was on board from the islands. The *Savoia* is the only craft that is coming from the islands this fall and those who were expecting friends knew that they would come on the barkentine if they came at all. Many of the boats found their friends had come, and there were exchanges of conversation and energetic waving of handkerchiefs for hours.[18]

Or consider this account of the docking of the *Maria Luiza* in 1910: "The usual large crowd gathered on the dock wharf, where a rope had been stretched across half way from the head of the wharf to the immigration shed, and the greetings were very profuse and frequent when the immigrants began to go up the dock and crawl under the outstretched rope."[19]

The arrival of a packet boat was such an anticipated event that some who came in greeting simply could not wait until the passengers got off the vessel to make contact, "Since the *Carlton* tied up Saturday, soon a large crowd waited outside the shed where the examinations progressed. The waiting arrivals leaned out of windows while their friends held up oranges and packages to them on long wires."[20]

Those gathered at the wharf not only looked forward to reconnecting with compatriots and kin, they also might find themselves recipients of special items brought to them by the incoming passengers. While goods were shipped primarily from the United States to Cape Verde, there was also a flow of gifts coming in from the other direction. Packages containing sugar cane, papayas, manioc, guava paste, aguardiente, and special desserts were commonly sent on the boats arriving from Cape Verde. Belmira Nunes recalled that:

> Whenever a ship came in, my mother always got her share of edibles sent to her by her mother. For example, we used to get *camoca.* *Camoca* is a sweet powdered concoction made from roast corn that has been pounded to a powderlike consistency and had sugar added to it. I don't know what else they added to it, but we ate that oftentimes as a dessert. Father sometimes used to add *camoca* to his coffee. . . . We also used to get what they called *pira. Pira* is really *mandioca perles. Mandioca* is the root of the tapioca plant . . . probably more similar to a potato than any other vegetable. . . . Sometimes my mother's people would send her beans that grow in the Islands but not in the States. They had, for example, a bean that they used to call, *fija pedra.* They called it "stone bean" because it's a very hard bean.[21]

Retired longshoreman Antonio "Tote" Cabral reminisced with obvious delight about running down to the New Bedford pier as a boy to greet his father on an incoming ship and finding that a young goat had been transported aboard as a present to him!

> Everybody went down to the wharf. And the funniest part, every time you go down there, if they stopped in the Cape Verde Islands, they sent something. They called it *encomenda* (a gift package). They sent puddings and desserts, all stacked in boxes. They even sent me a nanny goat. Just like "Mary had a little lamb." He would follow me all around. Then my parents killed the goat and I didn't know it. They cooked him and they had a big party—the old people. They had a name for it. I kept asking "where's my goat?" They said they had put him somewhere else to graze him. I kept harping on it. Then some other kid told me what really happened.[22]

Despite the accessibility of transportation during the packet era, the cost of the passage, between twenty and fifty dollars, could still be prohibitive to the average peasant family in Cape Verde. Resources would then have to be pooled to enable one family member, usually a young man in his late teens or early twenties, to make the voyage. He would then work in this country to earn money enough so that other relatives could follow. Consequently family members migrated at different times rather than as whole families, a process that disrupted family life and caused both grief and anguish over the necessary separations.

One way that the inevitable pain of saying good-bye was made more bearable was through the belief that the leave-taking would be only temporary. Few initially planned to settle permanently in this country. The intention was to accumulate wealth abroad and return home with sufficient savings to ensure a secure life on their native islands. However, while there were some who did, in fact, repatriate, the reality was that most stayed in the United States, establishing themselves as permanent residents here.

By the height of the packet trade, three varying patterns of migration had emerged. One scenario, as mentioned, was that of temporary residence in the United States, where the original intention to return to Cape Verde was realized. After several years working in America, the visitor goes back to his island of origin, hoping to live out the remainder of his days in prosperity. The following refrain from a Brava *morna* speaks to the returning *Americano* with both admiration and a bit of chiding: *Americano tem dolar, / Tem dolar coma burro!* (The *Americano* has dollars / He has dollars to burn!).[23]

One such repatriate was Francisco Benholiel Silva, "Chucala," a native of Sal Rei, Boa Vista, who lived in the United States for over fifty years, during which time he became an American citizen and a veteran of both World Wars I and II. Despite his long tenure in this country plus travel to many other parts of the world, Silva's longing to return to Cape Verde, the *saudade,* never left him and in 1956 at age sixty-eight he retired to the very spot where he had grown up as a boy in Boa Vista. There in Sal Rei, he became an institution and could be found at any time of the day sitting on his doorstep, cane in hand and sporting his felt "Mussolini hat" worn smooth, a memento from his stay in Italy during the war. At the time of his interview, he was ninety-seven years of age, was being supported by American Social Security checks, had outlived three wives, and had children ranging from twelve to seventy years old.[24]

The celebrated writer Eugenio Tavares, himself a return migrant who came to the United States early in this century, having been exiled by the government for political reasons, stated in 1913 that "the Cape Verdean who emigrates never puts down roots in the lands where he goes to work."[25] And later, in a letter dated June 1918, from Brava, while extolling the virtues of emigration to America, Tavares declared, "When the Cape Verdean returns (for he who loves his family and the land of his birth always returns), he brings not only dollars but enlightenment."[26] For Tavares, emigration was assumed to be temporary, a sojourn with the purpose of reaping all that one can from the abundance of America and bringing it back to the ailing archipelago.

Another common pattern was to make at least one return trip to Cape Verde, perhaps to marry a girl from home or to arrange to bring other family members back to New England. The emigrant then returns to the United States having made a more conscious decision to permanently relocate. One young woman who emigrated from São Nicolau in 1894 was married in New Bedford to a man who had also come from her island. Two years later, however, when she became pregnant with her first child, she arranged to voyage back to Cape Verde just so that her baby would be born on her native island. After the birth of her son, she returned to her home in New Bedford and never again went back to the islands. The son, Antonio "Tote" Cabral, explained why his mother decided to go back to São Nicolau for his birth: "At that time they thought so much of their country (Cape Verde). They wanted you to be 'real Portuguese.' "[27]

Another instance of return migration involving one trip back to the islands is the story of Benjamin Varella, from São Tiago. After a year working in Rochester, Massachusetts, for the owner of a sawmill,

Varella returned to his island in 1902 in order to bring his family with him to this country. During Varella's absence the sawmill owner's wife died, leaving her alcoholic husband alone and failing in his ability to handle the business. Upon his arrival back here, Varella headed directly to his former workplace with his family. Within months, the owner offered to sell his property to Varella and arranged a sponsor for the immigrant. In this way, Varella became the first Cape Verdean to permanently settle in the town of Rochester.[28]

Finally, there did exist a certain amount of shuttling back and forth, particularly among cranberry and maritime workers. The packet trade enabled seasonal cranberry pickers who would finish the harvest in late fall to return on the last boats out of New Bedford in November so that they could then spend the winters in Cape Verde. Weddings and baptisms would take place in these winter months while the men were home. In the spring, the voyages back to the United States would commence again, giving the workers the option of remigrating to the cranberry bogs for the next season of picking.

For those working in whaling and related maritime pursuits, the pattern of trafficking back and forth had been established early in the immigration process. Throughout the second half of the nineteenth century, whaling vessels sailing from the harbor in New Bedford would routinely bring crew members back to their native islands of Brava and Fogo, for a visit with their families and to bring home their hard-earned cash. For those who continued to be engaged in seafaring and dockside occupations, the possibilities for return trips were many.

The journey took approximately six weeks so that those who embarked on such an expedition twice a year must certainly have felt that the cost of the voyage and the subsequent monetary reward in this country were worth the risks and time spent at sea. There is a way that these seasonal transatlantic migrants must have viewed the trip of 3,545 miles much like today's seasonal farm and garment workers, despite the extraordinary geographic distance.

The connection between the Cape Verdean American community and the Cape Verdes was so strong and transportation back and forth so accessible that the typical emigrant, upon leaving for the United States, was not required to make a final commitment to resettlement. This not only eased the anguish of separation but it also slowed the process of setting down roots in this country.

In 1921, the town clerk in an area of Cape Cod where quite a few Cape Verdeans had title to their own homes, estimated that only 1 percent of the Cape Verdean population was on the town's voting lists. This number indicates a very low rate of naturalization and signifies the still-tenuous nature of the intention to remain in this country, even among home owners.[29] The tapering off in numbers of women and children immigrating, a pattern detailed in the earlier discussion of demography, demonstrates the hesitancy with which lasting plans were made. Learning the language, establishing a permanent residence, setting up a business, or getting involved in ventures that might require a more long-term investment were all put on hold.

This level of mobility changed dramatically, however, with the passage of the new immigration laws of 1921 and 1924, which were particularly stringent toward groups of non-European origin. No longer was the Cape Verdean emigrant able to freely sail back home. For most, plans to return to Cape Verde were abandoned. Forced to make an abrupt decision that would likely be irreversible, most opted for American residence. The following "close call" described by Albertina Fernandes, long-standing cranberry grower from Carver, Massachusetts, conveys the uncertainty and risk involved in trying to insure family reunification in these years:

> My father made three trips back to Fogo before he decided in 1922 that he was going to send for us. I think they were married about eight or nine years and he would send the money back. My mother would buy more land. . . . We got here just in time. When we arrived, the new immigration law had just gone into effect. The owner that my father worked for was instrumental in keeping us here. In fact, a lot of the people that came on that ship had to go back. . . . We got to Carver in the fall because we had to stay on the ship for quite awhile. The State Rep from Carver, Frank Barros, had to intercede for us and the man my father was working for had to set up bond before we could get off the ship. The law had passed and no more were to be admitted. My mother said a lot of them jumped off the ship and swam ashore because they didn't want to go back.[30]

Another incident that occurred in the transitional months of limiting quotas was the case of ten-year-old Mary Baptiste, who came here from Fogo in 1921 to join her father and stepmother. Her mother had died several years earlier on the island. Although her father, a cranberry worker, owned a home and was permanently settled in Wareham, Massachusetts, he had never taken out citizenship papers. Official citizenship would have entitled his daughter, who had arrived after the month's quota had been filled, to automatic admission to this country. The case received much publicity in the local papers with photographs of the heartbroken little girl and a public appeal was launched to try to have the deportation orders reversed.[31]

Beginning in the year 1908, official counts of re-emigration were maintained by the United States Immigration Service. Once again, however, there were no separate listings for Cape Verdeans, their numbers having been subsumed under the Portuguese category. Nevertheless, although these records cannot help to determine the Cape Verdean rate of return, they do, at least, provide a basis for drawing comparisons with other ethnic groups on the issue of transiency after 1907.

While the information entered in the ship manifests do not enable us to exactly calculate the extent of re-migration, the answers to "Ever Before in the United States," a standard question on the registers, do begin to shed some light on the frequency of transoceanic travel, beyond individual case histories. This category also makes it possible to come up with common characteristics of the type of emigrant who was likely to make repeat trips.

During the years 1900 to 1920, one out of three answered "yes" to having been in the United States before.[32] What cannot be determined from the records, however, is how many of those 33 percent who have been here before were coming back for the first time. The manifests do not distinguish those who may have journeyed back and forth two, three, or more times during this period from those who are making their first and only return trip. In other words, a smaller number of individuals may have made several voyages as opposed to one out of every three arrivals being a returnee.[33] In several of the oral accounts, a history of having made as many as seven trips back to the islands was noted.

The 1911 New Bedford report on immigration did suggest that five hundred or more Cape Verdean immigrants would return each year to the islands.[34] This estimate appears to have been too high, since an average of the numbers of those who had been to the United States before, the group that most strongly indicates mobility, is 415.4 annually in the five years leading up to the 1911 observation.

Cross tabulations of the ship manifest data indicate that the prototypical re-emigrant was a literate (73 percent) male (91.4 percent) in his twenties (40.6 percent) who was probably shuttling between Brava (41 percent) and New Bedford (31.1 percent). The returnee was just as likely to be single as married so that marital status was not a significant factor in connection with transiency.

How does this picture of the Cape Verdean re-emigrant and the rate of return compare to the patterns of other newcomers arriving during the early twentieth century? Of the other Portuguese immigrants, the

Azoreans were the most likely to repatriate and to view their settlement in the United States as temporary. By the end of World War I, most of the inhabitants on some of the Azores Islands, had already been in the United States at least once.[35] Yet, while it is difficult to make an accurate comparison between Cape Verdean and Azorean transiency because of the limitations of the statistical information available, one authority on Portuguese immigration has suggested, from impressionistic evidence, that the Cape Verdean reflux was more pervasive.[36]

Repatriation was also a central feature of Italian immigration. Although the Italian and American compilations are somewhat conflicting on this point, in some years during the first decade of this century, the United States records show as many as one out of two Italian arrivals returning to Italy. The Italian figures are lower.[37] A commentator on the Italian-American experience has astutely pointed out that the well-known photograph of "The Steerage" by Alfred Stieglitz depicts immigrants *leaving* America.[38] Just as in the case of the Cape Verdeans, the transient Italians were primarily men between the ages of 14 and 44.[39] Greek immigrants show similar patterns of remigration.[40]

Functioning as a kind of international labor market, males in their wage-earning years came to this country, not to relocate, but to seek more lucrative short-term employment. This phenomenon was generally much more characteristic of the "New" immigrants than the "Old." The English, Irish, and Germans who arrived in the earlier period came to stay. One notable exception to the transiency of the newer immigrant groups were the Jews. Having only been granted visitors status in the countries from which they originated, the typical Jewish immigrant was likely to be fleeing persecution and would not be welcomed back in any case. Statistics on the Eastern Jewish immigrants bear this out. While the average repatriation for all newcomers in the years 1908–1912 was 42 percent, the Russion Jewish rate was only 7 percent, demonstrating a striking degree of permanence. The ratio between the sexes was also fairly balanced as opposed to the dominance of males in other ethnic groups. Moreover, data on age cohorts reaffirms that the Jewish immigration was a movement of families, as many more children were involved.[41]

Information on the issue of transiency among southern United States blacks who have moved to the North during this period is sketchy. But W. E. B. DuBois has described the migration from the Upper South to Philadelphia in terms much like that of Cape Verdeans and other seasonal immigrant workers, "Every spring the tide of immigration sets in, consisting of brickmakers, teamsters, asphalt workers, common laborers, etc, who work during the summer in the city and return to the cheaper living of Virginia and Maryland for the winter."[42] These transplanted workers would board in temporary lodgings, leaving their families back at home. A more recent study of black migration to Pittsburgh in the early decades of this century confirms the trend of short-term movement among the male population who were departing from their southern farms in search of supplemental wages in the Steel City.[43]

Pleck, in her book on black migration to Boston during the late nineteenth century, though concentrating on a different time period, confirms that return migration to the south was probably quite common.[44] Another study of black islanders from St. Helena, South Carolina, who migrated to Harlem in the 1930s, show patterns of temporary settlement quite similar to Cape Verde Islanders, with return trips home made yearly and important ritual events being scheduled for the time when the sojourner would come back again.[45]

Clearly, the scope of Cape Verdean remigration contains features common to other immigrant groups in this period as well as to the migratory patterns of descendants of slaves from the American South. What does appear to be distinctive is the extent to which the Cape Verdean immigrants continued to regard Cape Verde as their home and the tenacity with which they retained the notion of eventual repatriation particularly during the years of the packet trade.

However, despite the numerous individual cases of returnees to Cape Verde, the overwhelming majority of emigrants ended up settling permanently in the United States. Their choices were few given the natural difficulties of life in the archipelago—intolerable conditions resulting from colonial negligence, economic crisis, drought, famine, and lack of rewarding employment. Moreover, there was little or no acceptance by the European countries at that time of foreign workers without sufficient professional qualifications. Emigration to the United States and to southeastern New England in particular became the most sought after option for the general populace.

Whether or not an emigrant actually made a return visit to Cape Verde, the frequency of communication, the Islanders' dependence upon remittances and supplies sent from the United States, and the shortage of Cape Verdean women of marriageable age in this country all contributed to a persistent and compelling tie to the old country that was maintained throughout the years of the mass migration.

If the first generation of emigrants could not accomplish this dream of return, they would encourage their offspring to obtain a good education in the United States and to take their skills back to the Cape Verdean homeland. Albertina Fernandes recounted how her parents attempted to inculcate the idea of return as she was growing up, "I was supposed to go to college to become a teacher and to teach in the old country [*laughter*]. I used to hear that all the time coming up. 'Go teach in the old country.' But I wasn't too keen on going to the old country because, though I'd love to go now, at that time this was my country."[46]

Also quite common was the practice of sending extra earnings saved back to the islands to purchase land on which to live once they repatriated. In 1972, at the time of Machado's field work in Brava there were one thousand emigrants who still held land there. In addition to absentee ownership, she found that "hundreds of houses abandoned by emigrants gave certain parts of the island a rather ghostly air. Most are small stone cottages, but there are also sombre, decrepit *sobrados* [three-story frame houses] in the *vila,* boarded up for decades by families who expected to return one day."[47]

In explaining the reason why there was not widespread Cape Verdean ownership of cranberry bogs, Albertina Fernandes went on to suggest that the Cape Verdeans didn't have their minds set on living in this country. That's why they bought a lot of land in the old country because they were going to make the money and go back there to live. Even in my time, when I was growing up. Most of the folks of my parents' age, that's what their big thing was. They all bought land there and some went back and built homes, like my father."[48]

It was not unusual for the cargo of a packet boat arriving in Cape Verde to include American furnishings, from frying pans to bedding, sent over to the wives and female relatives of the primarily male emigrants. One older woman from Brava interviewed by Machado explained, "The ambition of young men was to go to America, for women it was to set up an American house with American furniture."[49] From seeing the kind of furnishings that return migrants brought back to the islands with them, the character Chiquinho was able to precisely envision the type of house in which he would live once he settled in the United States:

> In America, I would build for me and Nuninha the house that I had planned at the top of Horta Nova. Only America would enable me to build a good home to welcome Nuninha. A good home for Nuninha. I knew very pretty names of houses where people lived when they left the islands. . . . Nha Maria Lai had returned recently from such a house. They probably had very pretty things inside, judging from what Nh Maria Lai had brought. Spring mattress beds, a gramophone, a pianola, a chest of drawers, fine China, a ton of

things. The islands gave none of that to its slaves. A slave deserves no more than a straw bed, a box of goiaba tree wood, Boa Vista porcelain, and a pot in the corner of the house. I could not imagine Nuninha living that way. Chiquinho spending his life waiting for a vacancy as a temporary post teacher, in exchange for meager pay and the rest of the year spent staring at the rocks and asking the sky when it would rain. The grog awaiting me, like a narcotic. To subject Nuninha to such a trial would be to destroy her life.[50]

The phenomenon of the *casa mercana* (American house) is further evidence of the cohesiveness of the Cape Verdean American bond. Other common items shipped to the islands especially during times of drought were corn, beans, beef, and lard as well as petroleum, stoves, roof tiles, and dishes.

The packet trade also made possible a constant line of communication between those who had departed and those who remained on the islands. With each trip, not only were there passengers to transport but also letters and packages to be delivered to friends and kin on both sides. An important part of this connection was the custom of sending *mantenhas* (from the Portuguese, "to keep up" or "maintain"), verbal greetings that were essential to "maintaining" the bonds between those who have been geographically separated.[51] A trusted friend or family member would be selected to pass on a specific message overseas. Since *Crioulo* has traditionally been a spoken language, any letters that were written were likely penned in Portuguese, a language unfamiliar to most. Hence, the *mantenhas* took primacy over written correspondence as the vehicle for news, gossip, and general good tidings. Delivery of these oral greetings was not a casual request or a message to be taken lightly, but a serious responsibility assumed by the traveler. The tradition of sustaining contact through the transmission of *mantenhas* probably has its origins in the need Cape Verdeans have always had of finding ways to ensure interisland communication within the archipelago. To this day, transportation between the islands can be problematic and difficult to negotiate.

The pattern of keeping up community ties beyond specific locale has been transplanted to the Cape Verdean American settlements as well. The network of communal relationships in this country are not restricted by geographic proximity. News can travel as quickly from Wareham, Massachusetts, to Providence, Rhode Island, and on to Bridgeport, Connecticut, as it can among Cape Verdeans living in differing neighborhoods within the same city.

Even when I, a non–Cape Verdean without intimate personal connection to the islands, made my first trip to Cape Verde in 1984, by the time of my departure, I had to add to my luggage an extra suitcase of gifts and letters for loved ones on the islands as well as a head full of *mantenhas*. Two days before I left, I was occupied with phone calls and friends dropping in with messages for their kin in Cape Verde. Furthermore, ever since I made the journey myself, when others have made subsequent visits, I am, in turn, treated to greetings they have conveyed to me from the new friends I made during my own trips to the archipelago.

Some of the importance attached to the established custom of maintaining strong links between Cape Verdeans and Cape Verdean Americans stems from the islands' extreme dependence on remittances from the United States. Early in the emigration experience, it became clear that not only would the newcomers themselves benefit from the opportunities that they found in America, but their savings could mean the difference between survival and starvation for family back at home.

The short-term migrants were likely to save larger amounts of disposable income by minimizing living expenses while in the United States. Their earnings were accumulated for consumption upon return or were used to support relatives left behind. Permanent emigrants, as they established roots, were less prone to save and more likely to expend a greater proportion of their income in this country. Still, whatever could be spared would be sent back to Cape Verde.

The influx of American dollars into the islands meant a difference at the subsistence level, and its effect fueled the Cape Verdean economy as a whole. Many merchants depended on American capital to start businesses and to stock the stores, while some sharecroppers, with the help of remittances from the United States, were able to become owners of the land on which they had worked. In some instances, particularly on the island of Brava, even the continued celebration of traditional religious *festas* was only made possible by contributions from relatives living in the United States or from returned *Americanos*.

The postmaster of Brava stated in a 1920 report that "not a single letter arrives from an emigrant for his family that does not contain a remittance of some amount up to twenty dollars."[52] There is even a colloquial expression in Brava for correspondence that arrives without money enclosed—*carta seca,* "dry letter."[53] As the plot develops in the novel *Chiquinho,* the father, who has obtained a job in a cotton mill in New Bedford, regularly sends home gifts of money that make it possible for the relatives in São Nicolau to improve their standard of living beyond mere survival.

When the level of unemployment in New Bedford began to rise in the early 1920s due to cutbacks in the mills, the repercussions were strongly felt in Cape Verde. The joblessness in New England coincided with famine on the islands, causing officials to panic at the prospect of losing this crucial resource. A government bulletin issued in 1921 declared:

> Maize, which is virtually the chief and only food of the people, is being sold at prices which makes it almost inaccessible to them, since their resources are already exhausted. To make things worse, even dollar remittances from the United States of North America have dwindled, through lack of work in that Great Republic, and often the shipping slows down the arrival of the small amount that is sent, which does enormous damage, since it is well known that in these districts (São Tiago and Santo Antão) they make up the most important resource.[54]

By the time of the Great Depression, there was far less money to spare for sending over to the islands. In 1927, remittances from America amounted to over a million and a half dollars. By 1933, the total had slipped to a quarter of a million.[55] Despite the ups and downs of the United States economy, however, the practice among Cape Verdean American immigrants of sending cash and clothing—and, in times of drought, food—back to the "old country" has been constant throughout the years of their settlement here. To this day, the people of the Cape Verde Islands rely on this economic support. On the island of Santo Antão, the special ritual of slaughtering a pig was reserved for only two occasions—when it rained and when a boat came in from America.[56] Until independence, there were very few of the archipelago's inhabitants, particularly on Brava whose livelihood did not depend in some way on the flow of emigration to the United States. Even in more recent years when the direction has been toward greater self-sufficiency the Cape Verdean government reported that "the importance of emigrant remittances to the Cape Verdean economy cannot be overstated. Between 1978 and 1982 remittances accounted for more than 40% of GDP, over 50% of private consumption, and for nearly 50 percent of the total value of imports, exclusive of foreign aid."[57] Although these figures refer to monies coming in from all emigrants, not just the Cape Verdean Americans, the United States leads the list of the five countries that represent 86 percent of the total remittances to Cape Verde as of 1982.[58] The early commitment of the Cape Verdean American immigrants to the continued growth of Cape Verde has kept the bond between the two groups constant and vital over the generations. Today even those Cape Verdeans born in the United States who no longer have family connections left in Cape Verde participate in sending money or barrels of goods on ships back to the republic.

According to Lucillia Lima, an American-born Cape Verdean who has never been to the islands, "As long as I can remember, my grandmother was sending money home. When her mother died years ago, she sent money to bury her. And it got there just in time to pay for the burial. Then last year my aunt and I sent some money to help pay for my great aunt's burial, my grandmother's sister. . . . And I said to my aunt, 'I can never remember a time when we weren't sending money over there.' But that was the case with most of us."[59]

Finally, the disproportion between the sexes among Cape Verdean emigrants to the United States further reinforced a close association with the homeland. Because of the preponderance of single males as well as the value placed on endogamy within the Cape Verdean American community, the likely place to find an acceptable marriage partner was back in the Cape Verde Islands. Marriage to an American black at that time often meant social isolation from family and friends. Spouses of Portuguese or other "white" background were more tolerated, particularly if it was the woman who was Portuguese, but the existing ethnic divisions made this type of intermarriage infrequent. "Tote" Cabral confirmed that this was precisely the pattern that he perceived during the prewar years: "Sometimes Cape Verdean men married Azorean women. The women would be assimilated. After a while you'd forget they were from the Azores. They were accepted. But rarely were there marriages between an Azorean man and a Cape Verdean woman."[60]

Returning to his native island was how Joseph Andrade, a whaler who immigrated from São Nicolau in 1914, met his wife: "I went to the islands after the War . . . after everything settled down. At that time all the Cape Verdean men that were here had the custom of going back to the old country and marry a Cape Verdean woman and bring her back here. . . . My sister-in-law was the one that arranged the marriage. My brother was the captain of the ship *Brunhilde*. His wife was here and she arranged for me to go back and marry her sister. I had never met her but I saw a picture of her."[61]

At this point, Andrade's daughter interjected, "There were several women who wanted to marry him. He left a lot of women jealous over there because he brought my mother over." Picture brides were a variation on the custom of arranged marriages in the Cape Verde Islands. This pattern of courtship was how the parents of Lydia (Freitas) Gomes were united:

My father was quite young when he came here around 1905, when he started whaling. His father was from the Azores and he went to the Cape Verde Islands and was made head of the whaling industry in São Nicolau. In the meantime, my uncle came over here and my father saw this picture of my mother that he showed him and fell in love with my mother through this picture. And so when they had this vessel, the *Charles W. Morgan* that went back to the old country, to São Nicolau, my father went back and they were married. They delayed the voyage two weeks so they could have all their festivities. And so my father continued his voyage for two years and in the meantime, my mother and her family came here to New Bedford. After two years, when my father was finished with the voyage and came here, that was when Papa saw my little sister for the first time. She was two years old.[62]

Meanwhile, as would be expected, the demographics on the archipelago reflected the opposite imbalance with an excess of unmarried females. In 1920, in Brava, for example, the ratio of women to men was 187.9 to 100.[63] In 1924, the popular literary figure Eugenio Tavares commented on this aspect of Cape Verdean life by composing a satirical sonnet:

There are nine thousand healthy people living on our island. More than six thousand are women, only the remaining three thousand males. Of these three thousand only two thousand can 'celebrate'—which means that there are not nearly enough men to carry out the Biblical duties of multiplying and suchlike. . . .
A Brava ballroom! More than five thousand ladies sitting round, drawn to the dance, hearts aflame. If each lady keeps her partner (as law and custom demand) three thousand are going to have to do without dancing![64]

It is said that Tavares himself tried his best to compensate for the lack of partners, spending many an evening on the dance floor with untempered enthusiasm. Antonia Enos, who migrated from Brava when she was a young woman, remembered him well: "Eugenio Tavares was a wonderful man. He performed and danced like nobody's business. One time he asked me to dance but I didn't like his way of dancing, so I refused him!"[65]

When I was in Brava, I began to notice that it was quite common to see tatoos on both the men and women. One of the local inhabitants pointed out that it was distinctively Bravan to have a tatoo on one's arm. The men displayed traditional designs but the women often have the name of their husband or boyfriend and the date that he left permanently engraved on their bodies. These markings are graphic reminders of how profoundly the phenomenon of emigration has permeated the culture.

For many single Cape Verdean women, their only hope of marriage as well as an escape from the impoverished conditions was to attract an emigrant. Through the *mantenhas* and letters, some with photographs included, the long-range courtships would take place. On a trip home to the islands, a romance would be rekindled, a wedding celebrated and, in some instances, the new wife would join her husband for the return voyage to America.

In the case of one Cape Verdean American who went back to the islands in 1921 to get married, an attempt to live with his new wife in the United States failed, and she soon went back to her native Brava. Although for almost all of their sixty years of marriage they have not seen one another, they have had two children and have never thought of ending the marriage: "She is a good woman and in Cape Verde, if you have a good woman, you don't get a divorce or leave your wife," explained the husband.[66] In other instances, the emigrant would sail again after the wedding without his spouse, leaving her with a future unknown. Some women in this situation would then don black clothes and were referred to as "Americans' widows."[67] This phenomenon became even more pronounced during the long hiatus that followed the closing of the doors to immigration in the early 1920s. Many more women were permanently left behind because of the departure of their spouses to the United States.

I met one such "widow" during my stay in Fogo. In 1920 Amalia and Manuel Gonsalves were wed. After thirty-one days of marriage, Manuel left for the United States and never returned. He would, however, regularly send home money to his wife. Always dressed in black, pictures of her husband and his relatives in America adorning her bureau, she waited, never remarrying.

Her reunion with Richard Gonsalves, an American of Cape Verdean descent who was her nephew by marriage to Manuel, was the first time that she had seen anyone of her husband's family in sixty-odd years. Yet, through frequent transatlantic communication, news of the American relatives had steadily reached Amalia's remote village so that she was familiar with the lives of people in the United States whom she had never personally known. She greeted "Ricardo from America" with tears of joy and cried out, "I asked God every day to send me someone from the family." The emotional intensity of the meeting moved all of the villagers who witnessed the event. Amalia had become a widow in the true sense of the word in 1958 when Manuel died. Some fifteen years later, at the time of my visit, she was still receiving pension payments from his years of employment on the Buzzards Bay railroad.

The experience of migration has been such a universal in the history of the Cape Verdean islanders that the literature is imbued with themes of separation as well as nostalgia for the archipelago. A close reading of the lyrics of *Crioulo* poetry, songs, and prose, however, reveals gendered meanings in the emotional attachment felt for the homeland. In the passage from *Chiquinho* concerning the impact of emigration that opens this chapter, Baltasar Lopes speaks of the nostalgia of the islands' *sons*. The letters home are to girlfriends; the photographs of emigrés to the United States depict well-dressed young men. Similarly, the *mornas* and poetry typically phrase the wrenching separation from the native soil in female metaphors. The land is symbolized through images of melancholic longings for a mother or lover. In a sense, the *mornas* become love songs to the homeland, a place and idea that has been constructed as female. In some instances what is longed for in missing the land is the motherly nurturance that it represents. Consider this poem written in the genre of emigration literature by Teobaldo Virginio, a native of the island of Santo Antão and currently the director of the cultural review *Arquipélago*. Filled with maternal imagery, the displacement is at once from the land and from the breast of the mother.

> *Letter*
> Such nostalgia do I have for you
> beloved Country.
> Just like you in the sea
> seeking a way of life
> from the other side of the sea of life
> thinking of you.
> What destiny is this
> that separates a child from his mother?
> Your generous people
> your loving people
> your sweet land
> Call to me anywhere I am in the world.
> Just like your proofs of love
> I put in this letter
> A little branch of a big mango tree
> so that you can smell the aroma of my nostalgia!

When will the ship appear
that will make me disembark
on my mother's breast?

On your river banks
in your seaports
You work, you strive, you sweat
so that one day God will bless you.
In the sea waiting to be able to live
from the other side of the sea
to think about you![68]

The contemporary Cape Verdean American immigrant writer Donaldo Macedo has beautifully crafted the following poem of *saudade:*

Absence
I walk along a foreign road
all covered with snow
       cold
       white
       uncaring
away from the familiar alley
warmed by the tropical sun
away from the coffeetree, rocking
in the melancholic beat of Brava's breeze.

I walk along a foreign road
covered with patches of clouds
where the azure lay hidden
       bitter
       unfeeling
       strange
away from the ardent land
of radiant palm trees:

a land which lay alone
abandoned in the aching groan
of the unending beat of the pestle.[69]

The powerful image that closes this piece and symbolizes the anguish of separation is the sound of the traditional Cape Verdean woman at work, grinding corn with her pylon. In this sense, as with all the literature of *saudade* the emigrant is an assumed male figure. He journeys, crosses borders, makes changes, and experiences melancholia while the woman stays behind, static, firmly planted in the native soil, presumably with a different set of longings. In *Nha Destino,* the *morna* that concludes the introductory chapter of this book, the lyrics tell of simultaneously forsaking one's country and one's mother. The last stanza reads, "It is a Cape Verdean destiny to go far away from *his* land [italics mine]." By implication, what is being left is female. Caroline Brettell has succinctly captured this gendered phenomenon in titling her community study of emigration, marriage, and fertility patterns in northern Portugal, *Men Who Migrate, Women Who Wait.*[70]

Since almost without exception the published literature of both Cape Verdeans and Cape Verdean Americans has been written by male authors, it is impossible to know through these texts how the women may have experienced the inevitable separation that comes with such a highly mobile population. However, the oral histories do reflect a difference based on gender concerning the extent to which peoples' lives were oriented toward return migration more by the absences than by what is actually articulated. Nowhere is there evidence of the unabated desire to return in the voices of Cape Verdean women while the men often organize their biographies around the possibility or actuality of remigration.

Demographically, the social reality supports the gendered literary symbolism. For typically the women are not on the journey. *He* plaintively yearns to come back while *she,* rooted at home, may be hoping to be rescued from the miserable conditions of the drought-stricken archipelago either by being able to join her spouse or sons in America or by being transformed from Cape Verdean to Cape Verdean American via the transference of consumer goods to the archipelago — the *casa mercana* representing the material recreation of cultural change brought about by the migration to the United States.

In the first case her desire is to *leave* the homeland not to get back to it. In the second, the classic pattern of utilizing modernizing consumer products to assuage the pain of relocation, which was often the case for immigrant women on this side of the Atlantic, takes on a new twist. In *Immigrant Women in the Land of Dollars,* Elizabeth Ewen's study of Italian and Jewish female newcomers to New York's Lower East Side at the turn of the century, the oral accounts convey repeated instances of women adjusting to their new situations by making certain trade-offs. For example, the fulfilling aspects of old-country communal wash days, soaking up fresh air by the river and enjoying pleasant conversation, might well be replaced by the satisfaction of material wants in this country, such as the conveniences of running water, household labor-saving devices, or access to commercial laundries. Material gratification, thus, becomes as a substitute for emotional fulfillment. Similarly, while still remaining on the islands, Cape Verdean women left behind were perhaps better able to bear the absence of loved ones by receiving American-made products or remittances to improve their material circumstances.[71]

Not only has the literature of *saudade* not been authored by women, the social gatherings that spawned much of this artistic expression were male events. On the islands, a typical evening's leisure-time activity for the men was to meet in a small café or on someone's porch under the stars, drinking grog with your *cumpads*. Inevitably someone would begin to play a fiddle or guitar or both and the *mornas* would soulfully spill forth. Women may hover on the edges of these get-togethers as appreciative audiences, but the communing as well as the literary and musical creativity sprung from male participation. This was not women's place.

Some preliminary findings concerning attitudes toward return migration among recent immigrant populations in the United States are showing that while the men may hold more of a sojourner outlook, orienting their stay in the United States with an eye to returning, the women do not want to go back. For as difficult as it may be to adjust to the new environment, circumstances back at home would be worse for them, particularly concerning issues of individual autonomy. Many of the most recent arrivals are coming from highly patriarchal societies where the roles for women were rigidly circumscribed in subservience to men. Once they achieve even a small modicum of independence in the United States, the women are extremely reluctant to ever return to a situation of such complete male dominance. The men, on the other hand, may have lost some power and control through migration to this country, and part of their longing to return is a nostalgia for a time when, if in no other part of their lives, they at least ruled the family and household and were catered to by the female members.[72]

Historically in the Cape Verde Islands, the combined legacy of slavery and colonialism, a culture of *machismo*, and the teachings of the Catholic church has resulted in extreme gender inequality. The dire poverty, the environmental disaster, and the absence of men due to emigration left women to fend for themselves with little or no resources. However, the pattern was for women to bear many children, at times, to replace the devastation to the population of recurrent famine but also as a measure of status that it would give to the father. The nuclear family configuration was not typical in colonial Cape Verdean society. Rather, in part because of the shortage of men, the males would sire children from several different women and, commonly, many children from each partner. Belmira Nunes Lopes spoke of this phenomenon in her autobiography: "My grandmother had eleven children. Apart from the first, the others grew up with their own mother, my maternal grandmother. This second family was not an unusual custom. Polygamy was the rule with the Moors and many nations of Africa. It has been true all over Latin America just as it was true in all the Portuguese possessions. These men have a wife and several other women who bear them children. Their relationship was not any kind of a temporary affair. . . . Generally, men who had so many different wives looked after the children of these women. If they recognized a child, she or he was legally his daughter or son."[73] Juvenal Cabral, father of Amilcar Cabral, the leader of the movement for Cape Verdean independence, exemplified this pattern to the extreme. It is popularly known that Amilcar was one of over sixty-five children fathered by Juvenal. Since the achievement of Cape Verdean independence in 1975, the second-class status of women is being addressed at the national level. However, these changes are extremely slow to be realized, and the position of Cape Verdean women today is still very poor.

The point being raised here is that, as with other aspects of expressive culture, the concept of nostalgia too, can be examined for variation in meaning rather than assuming it to have universal connotations. How immigrants construct their relationship to their place of origin may well differ by gender and ethnicity. Cape Verdean women may have yearned for their husbands' return, but they did not appear to experience *saudade* in the same way as their male counterparts. In the Cape Verdean case, the *saudade* is a romantic male construction of distance and loss. Nostalgia, as an emotion, speaks to a sense of something missing. It keeps the individual from being completely in the present, whole, and accepting of the current situation. One has to have known some sense of fulfillment or belonging in the past to feel nostalgic for it. In some ways, nostalgia is a dreamy luxury that most Cape Verdean women never achieved. Would the freed slave have nostalgia for the good old days of plantation life? It was the southern whites, the former masters, who constructed the idea of the Sambo out of sentimental desires just as that way of life began to pass. Once living out of a patriarchy does a woman long to return? Does she think wistfully of bearing children nonstop, of not having enough food or water to sustain those children once born, of absentee spouses, of back-breaking labor in the fields, daily carrying water great distances or moving rocks to build roads, of political dependency and an absence of individual rights?

A recent unpublished study of Azorean immigrant women who arrived since 1965 does show that they typically expressed some longings for the homeland. While none of the respondents would want to go back because of the value they now placed on the individual autonomy that they have realized in the United States, their nostalgia had to do with sensual yearnings related to the land. Memories of the sweet smells of the lush countryside or the colors of the vegetation would recur in the oral accounts.[74] Again, because of the parched soils and unproductive landscape of the archipelago, Cape Verdean women have rarely expressed these kinds of sentiments about the natural elements. In some ways their experience more resembled that of the nineteenth-century female Irish immigrants fleeing their land of death and famine who had nothing to go back to than it does other Portuguese immigrant women in this period.

The connections detailed in this chapter have served to maintain the unusually extensive amount of contact between the Cape Verde Islands and the United States. In fact, the Cape Verdean American community has been dubbed a suburb of Cape Verde as well as having been referred to as "another island of the archipelago—bigger than our largest islands, São Tiago."[75] The emotional and material links between the two locales have been so complete that it appears to have had a shrinking effect on the actual physical distance involved.

As has been shown to be the case with other transplanted populations of this era, the family played a major role in maintaining cultural continuity for Cape Verdean immigrants. While ties of ethnicity and kinship were the essential ingredients in promoting the actual process of migration, they were also critical in shaping job distribution among the new arrivals. Cape Verdeans were concentrated in a handful of manual occupations in this country, with almost exclusive participation in two areas of employment—the cranberry industry in the rural areas and maritime-related work in the port cities, particularly as longshoremen. In broad terms, their premigration skills were being logically implemented in the new society. Most of the cranberry workers were peasants from the islands of Fogo and Brava where, when not plagued by drought, small-scale farming was the foundation of the economy. And while seafaring was not part of the earlier tradition of the archipelago, once whaling became the most viable escape from island poverty, dockside occupations on this side of the Atlantic reasonably followed.

The crucial links of family and island affiliation combined with the premigration experiences in channeling the immigrants into these few occupational clusters. Cape Verdean owners and captains of the packet boats fulfilled the demand for agricultural labor on the cranberry bogs by transporting their willing compatriots to the region at a time when the growers were having difficulty recruiting other workers. The bog owners had even resorted to trucking in Italians from Boston before the influx of Cape Verdean labor.[76] Similarly, earning a living as a stevedore depended on whether or not the arrival had kinship associations with the existing dock workers. Here, the integral place of fictive kin within the Cape Verdean family structure was carried over into the occupational realm. For example, godparents, or *cumpadre,* traditionally played a prominent role in family life, bestowing affection and offering guidance to their godchildren. Similarly, certain longshoremen became the *cumpads* of the workplace. They were the leaders of work groups for loading and unloading the ships and it was with their influence that a newcomer could procure employment.[77] Like other European immigrants in this period, Cape Verdean arrivals found limited job dispersion based on ethnicity and kinship.[78]

The clustering of workers into a small range of occupations cannot be viewed as solely the result of the interrelationship of premigration skills and ties of kinship, however. Also functioning to keep the Cape Verdean immigrants in certain employment categories was the ceiling placed on job advancement, as well as clear-cut segregation at the same level of occupational entry, due to institutional racism. The fishing industry in New Bedford offers an example of how this operated. During the 1920s, when whaling had come to a halt and commercial fishing began to become important to the city's economy, the able Cape Verdean seamen provided an obvious labor pool. However, the fisheries quickly came under the domain of the "white" immigrant groups, particularly the Azoreans, who systematically excluded Cape Verdeans. To this day, they are not represented in New Bedford's fleet, which annually brings in the highest revenues in fish in the country. The racial barriers that Cape Verdeans came up against from the start of their settlement in this country may well have reinforced the tendency, particularly among the male immigrants, to hold on to the dream of return.

As strong as bonds of kinship were, a larger force was also at work in defining the Cape Verdean American ethnic community. The boundaries of the ethnic neighborhood reached beyond residential contiguity alone, forming an immigrant enclave that encompassed a complex network of work and family associations. This socioeconomic web provided an institutional infrastructure for the immigrant workers, manifested in the formation of ethnic parishes, mutual aid societies, schools, fraternal clubs, and newspapers as well as the less tangible resources of occupational reciprocity and emotional support. While the ethnic neighborhood is typically residentially amorphous, it can, nonetheless, be encapsulated by invisible barriers resulting in isolation from the wider society.[79]

The Cape Verdean American experience exemplifies the enclave phenomenon with its intricate fabric of associations that functioned to preserve cultural belongings, and in some respects, which also helped to facilitate a positive adaptation to this society. As the multifaceted aspects of their complicated background began to sort themselves out, the Cape Verdeans accommodated to their new situation by setting themselves apart from the African American community while at the same time shrugging off the "white" Portuguese exclusionary strategy. They established their own parallel social and religious groups, maintained their *Crioulo* traditions, spoke their own language, clustered in the same neighborhoods and were essentially endogamous. Furthermore, their family and occupational networks often extended beyond the specific geographic concentration in southeastern Massachusetts to include other small communities of Cape Verdean settlers scattered along the Northeast coast and in California, as well as stretching back across the Atlantic to incorporate the remaining island inhabitants, with the packet trade making possible this exceptionally enduring tie to the old country. As outlined above, the circumstances of their adaptation to American society gave the Cape Verdean ethnic neighborhood an even more sharply circumscribed quality than even the most provincial of the immigrant enclaves. The ethnic neighborhood became a world within a world and the Cape Verdean enclave represented a minority among minorities in the United States.

NOTES

1. John S. MacDonald and Leatrice D. MacDonald, "Chain Migration, Ethnic Neighborhood Formation and Social Networks," *Milbank Memorial Fund Quarterly* 42, no. 1 (Jan. 1964): 82–97; Judith Ellen Smith, *Family Connections: A History of Italian & Jewish Immigrant Lives in Providence, Rhode Island, 1900–1940* (Albany, N.Y.: SUNY Press, 1985), pp. 139–43; John Bodnar, *Workers' World: Kinship, Community and Protest in an Industrial Society, 1900–1940* (Baltimore: Johns Hopkins University Press, 1982), pp. 171–72; John Bodnar, Michael Weber, and Roger Simon, "Migration, Kinship and Urban Adjustment: Blacks and Poles in Pittsburgh, 1900–1930," *Journal of American History* 66 (1979): 552–54; Thomas Kessner, *The Golden Door: Italian and Jewish Immigrant Mobility in New York City, 1880–1915* (New York: Oxford University Press), chap. 2; Virginia Yans-McLaughlin, *Family and Community: Italian Immigrants in Buffalo, 1880–1930* (Ithaca, N.Y.: Cornell University Press, 1977), chap.

2; Elizabeth H. Pleck, *Black Migration and Poverty: Boston, 1865–1900* (New York: Academic Press, 1979), pp. 64, 66–67.

2. Jose Centeio quoted in "Home Is Here, but Roots, Wife Are Elsewhere," *Evening Bulletin* (Providence), 1 Feb. 1979.

3. Pleck, *Black Migration and Poverty*, p. 64.

4. Bodnar, Weber, and Simon, "Migration, Kinship and Urban Adjustment," pp. 553–54.

5. Joseph Ramos quoted in *Spinner* 2:17.

6. Interview with Joseph R. Andrade, 10 Oct. 1983.

7. "Cape Verdeans Expert Sailors," *Evening Bulletin* (Providence), 29 May, 1929.

8. *The Providence Sunday Journal*, 6 Nov. 1949, p. 4.

9. Maria Luisa Nunes, *A Portuguese Colonial in America: Belmira Nunes Lopes, The Autobiography of a Cape Verdean–American* (Pittsburgh: Latin American Literary Review Press, 1982), pp. 47–48.

10. "Maria Luiza In," *Evening Standard* (New Bedford), 12 June 1909.

11. Raymond Anthony Almeida, *Cape Verdeans in America: Our Story* (Boston: American Committee for Cape Verde, 1978), p. 35.

12. For colorful sketches of the voyages of individual packet boats, see Almeida, *Cape Verdeans in America*, pp. 31–45.

13. Virginia Gonsalves quoted in Colin Nickerson, "Cape Verde — country of their hearts," *Boston Globe*, 29 Sept. 1983, p. 16.

14. Thomas J. Archdeacon, *Becoming American: An Ethnic History* (New York: Free Press, 1983), p. 146.

15. Abraham Cahan, *The Rise of David Levinsky*, 1917 (New York: Harper and Row, 1960), p. 89.

16. Hilda Satt Polacheck, *I Came a Stranger: The Story of a Hull-House Girl* (Urbana: University of Illinois, 1989), p. 25.

17. "Immigrants in New Bedford" (Ms., New Bedford Free Public Library, 1911), p. 4.

18. "*Savoia* Arrives," *New Bedford Sunday Standard*, 4 Oct. 1914.

19. "Immigrants Arrive," *Evening Standard* (New Bedford), 18 Apr. 1910, p. 4.

20. "The *Carlton Bell* Brings 114 Passengers," *Morning Mercury* (New Bedford), 18 June 1917.

21. Nunes, *A Portuguese Colonial in America*, pp. 43–44.

22. Interview with Antone "Tote" Cabral, 4 Jan. 1985.

23. T. Bentley Duncan, *The Atlantic Islands: Madeira, the Azores and the Cape Verdes in Seventeenth-Century Commerce and Navigation* (Chicago: University of Chicago Press, 1971), p. 249.

24. Videotaped interview by Ron Barboza, 1983.

25. Machado, "Cape Verdean–Americans: Their Culture and Historical Background" (Ph.D. diss., Brown University, 1978), pp. 246, 333.

26. As stated in a letter from Brava dated 10 June 1918 and quoted in Antonio Carreira, *The People of the Cape Verde Islands: Exploitation and Emigration*, trans. and ed. Christopher Fyfe (Hamden, Conn.: Archon Books, 1982), p. 62.

27. Interview with Antone "Tote" Cabral, 4 Jan. 1985.

28. Interview with Flora Monteiro, 30 Nov. 1983.

29. Josiah Folsom, *Farm Labor in Massachusetts, 1921*, U.S. Department of Agriculture Bulletin No. 1220 (Washington, D.C.: Apr. 1924), p. 7.

30. Interview with Albertina Alves Fernandes, 5 Dec. 1983

31. Minna Littman, "Only Appeal from Kind Hearts Can Save Father His Daughter," *Sunday Standard* (New Bedford), 23 Oct. 1921, p. 1.

32. The overall frequency percentages were 36.9 percent — "Yes"; 58.4 percent — "No"; 4.7 percent — missing, for the years 1884–1934.

33. The only way to further clarify this 33 percent figure would be to trace and record entries by individual name through the years, a task left to future research on the subject.

34. "Immigrants in New Bedford," p. 4.

35. Leo Pap, *The Portuguese-Americans* (Boston: Twayne, 1981), p. 48.

36. Ibid.

37. Kessner, *The Golden Door*, p. 28.

38. Andrew Rolle, *Troubled Roots* (New York: Free Press, 1980), p. 47.

39. Kessner, *The Golden Door*, p. 30.

40. Theodore Saloutos, "Causes and Patterns of Greek Emigration to the United States," in *Dislocation and Emigration — The Social Background of American Immigration*, vol. 3 of *Perspectives in American History*, ed. Donald Fleming and Bernard Bailyn (Cambridge, Mass.: Charles Warren Center for Studies in American History, Harvard University, 1973), pp. 381–437.

41. Kessner, *The Golden Door*, pp. 30–32.

42. W. E. Burghardt DuBois, *The Philadelphia Negro — A Social Study 1899* (New York: Benjamin Blum, 1967), p. 135.

43. Bodnar, Weber, and Simon, "Migration, Kinship and Urban Adjustment," p. 552.

44. Pleck, *Black Migration and Poverty*, p. 66.

45. Clyde Vernon Kiser, *Sea Island to City: A Study of St. Helena Islanders in Harlem and Other Urban Centers* (New York: AMS Press, 1967), pp. 83–83, 210.

46. Interview with Albertina Alves Fernandes, 5 Dec. 1983.

47. Machado, "Cape Verdean–Americans," p. 286.

48. Interview with Albertina Alves Fernandes, 5 Dec. 1983.

49. Machado, "Cape Verdean-Americans," p. 247.

50. Lopes, *Chiquinho*, p. 89.

51. Ibid., p. 251; Almeida, *Cape Verdeans in America*, p. 48.

52. "Portuguese Possessions," *Peace Handbooks*, 19, no. 117, Cape Verde Islands (London, 1920; Wilmington, Delaware, 1973), p. 21.

53. Machado, "Cape Verdean-Americans," p. 285.

54. *Boletim Oficial de Cabo Verde* 11 (15 Mar. 1922).

55. Archibald Lyall, *Black and White Makes Brown: An Account of the Journey to the Cape Verde Islands and Portuguese Guinea* (London: Heinemann, 1938), p. 127.

56. Conversation with Ron Barboza.

57. *World Bank Report*, no. 5446-CV, II, p. 29.

58. The other four countries are the Netherlands, Portugal, France, and Angola.

59. Interview with Lucillia Lima, 25 Jan. 1984.

60. Interview with Antone "Tote" Cabral, 16 Oct. 1985.

61. Interview with Joseph R. Andrade, 10 Oct. 1983.

62. Interview with Lydia (Freitas) Gomes, 30 May 1986.

63. Carreira, *People of the Cape Verde Islands*, p. 50.

64. From the newspaper, *Manduco*, 30 Jan. 1924 as quoted in Ibid., p. 51.

65. Interview with Antonia Enos, 3 Jan. 1985.

66. Jose Centeio in *The Evening Bulletin*, 1 Feb. 1979.

67. Carreira, *People of the Cape Verde Islands*, p. 50.

68. Telbaldo Virgíno, in *Viagen Para Lá De Fronteira*, p. 49, quoted in Ellen, *Across the Atlantic*, p. 165.

69. Donaldo P. Macedo, in *Cabo Verde no Coraçáo*, p. 19, quoted in M. Ellen, *Across the Atlantic*, p. 164.

70. Caroline Brettell, *Men Who Migrate, Women Who Wait: Population and History in a Portuguese Parish* (Princeton: Princeton University Press, 1986).

71. Elizabeth Ewen, *Immigrant Women in the Land of Dollars: Life and Culture on the Lower East Side, 1890-1925* (New York: Monthly Review Press, 1985).

72. See, for example, Patricia Pessar, "Dominicans: Women in the Household and the Garment Industry," in *New Immigrants in New York*, ed. Nancy Foner (New York: Columbia University Press, 1987), pp. 103-29; research in progress by Kyeyoung Park, Asian/American Center, Queens College CUNY, New York.

73. Nunes, *A Portuguese Colonial in America*, p. 23.

74. Thanks to Donna Huse for showing me the working draft of her

paper, "Saudade: Memory and Identity," co-authored with Bela Feldman-Bianco.

75. Talk given by M. Silva, representative, Cape Verdean Consulate at the Cape Verdean Ultramarine Band Club, June 1985.

76. Christian John Bannick, *Portuguese Immigration to the United States: Its Distribution and Status* (Berkeley: University of California Press, 1971), p. 65.

77. Sam Beck, "Manny Almeida's Ringside Lounge — The Cape Verdean Struggle for Their Neighborhood" Ms., 1981.

78. See, for example, John Bodnar, *Workers' World*; Caroline Golab, *Immigrant Destinations* (Philadelphia: Temple University Press, 1977); John Modell, *The Economics and Politics of Racial Accommodation* (Urbana: University of Illinois Press, 1977); Bodnar, Weber, and Simon, "Migration, Kinship and Urban Adjustment"; Stephen Thernstrom, *The Other Bostonians: Poverty and Progress in the American Metropolis, 1880–1970* (Cambridge, Mass.: Harvard University Press, 1978); Yans-McLaughlin, *Family and Community.*

79. For an excellent definition of the ethnic neighborhood, see Golab, *Immigrant Destinations,* pp. 111–56; For discussion of the concept of the immigrant enclave, see Bodnar, *Workers World,* pp. 63–118.

Immigrants on the *Savoia,* arriving 5 October 1914, from Fogo Island to New Bedford, 155 passengers, 28 crew. *New Bedford Whaling Museum.*

PARA CABO VERDE

(Fogo-Brava-Praia e Ilhas de Barlavento)

BARCA "CORIOLANUS"

A SAIR DE NEW BEDFORD A 20 DE OUTUBRO

Recebendo passageiros e carga para todas as Ilhas do arquipélago de Cabo Verde.
O navio irá directamente à Ilha do Fogo, onde o vapor "INFANTE D. HENRIQUE" receberá os passageiros que se destinam à Ilha Brava, sem mais despezas.

Barca "CORIOLANUS" no porto de Furna (Brava), em Fevereiro e Março de 1925

E' garantia do bom tratamento dos passageiros, os nomes já bastante conhecidos dos seus actuais proprietarios—ABILIO MONTEIRO DE MACEDO e ALBERTINO JOSE DE SENA (capitão)—que seguem viagem na barca "CORIOLANUS".

PREÇOS DAS PASSAGENS

Primeira Classe $80.00—Terceira Classe $50.00

O navio começará a receber carga e encomendas no dia 1 do próximo mês de Agosto, das 8 da manhã às 6 da tarde.

TABELA DE FRETES

Broadside advertising passage on the "luxury liner" packet ship *Coriolanus,* 1928. *New Bedford Whaling Museum.*

The wharfside labor force of the bark *Sunbeam*. Photograph by Clifford W. Ashley, 1904. *New Bedford Whaling Museum.*

Wanderer deck view on sailing day, 1924. Captain Antone T. Edwards and some of the crew. J. A. Gomes, first mate, is in the foreground. Photograph by Albert Cook Church. *New Bedford Whaling Museum.*

Port of Furna, Brava Island, at the height of the packet trade, 1908. *New Bedford Public Library, courtesy of Spinner Publications.*

"Crowded two-family tenement occupied by cranberry pickers ("Bravas") or black Portuguese." Wareham, Massachusetts, September 1911. Photograph and caption by Lewis Hine. *Library of Congress, courtesy of Spinner Publications.*

"Group of workers on Smart's Bog. The manager, a veritable slave driver, was an old sea captain who threatened the workers or 'you'll go ashore.'" South Carver, Massachusetts, September 1911. Photograph and caption by Lewis Hine. *Library of Congress, courtesy of Spinner Publications.*

"Walter Silva. Said ten years old. Picks three or four pails a day." Eldridge Bog, Rochester, Massachusetts, September 1911. Photograph and caption by Lewis Hine. *Library of Congress, courtesy of Spinner Publications.*

"Cecilia Perry (*right*), a young picker living in Rochester, Massachusetts."
Eldridge Bog, September 1911. Photograph and caption by Lewis Hine.
Library of Congress, courtesy of Spinner Publications.

Working the Bogs   **3**

The wild cranberry has the distinction of being one of only three fruits native to the United States, along with the Concord grape and the blueberry. Cranberries were originally found on the borders of the shallow ponds of Cape Cod. The surface of the Cape, with its numerous lakes and ponds formed by glacial action and its extensive swamps, provides natural conditions highly favorable to the growth of the fruit. Since about 1850, when large areas of swamp were cleared, drained and made into cranberry bogs, the cranberry crop has increased in importance.

Contrary to the popular image of local Yankee families embarking on a Sunday's outing of cranberry picking, the cranberry industry early began to require a large and intensive agricultural work force, particularly during the six or so weeks of the autumn cranberry harvest. The Italians, Poles, and Finns all provided the necessary labor in turn, but by 1910, the Cape Verdean immigrants completely dominated the harvest:

In 1924, anthropologist Albert Jenks explained,

> Cape Verders have been working in cranberry bogs for about thirty-five years and today they harvest nine-tenths of the Cape Cod cranberry crop. Consequently, if at a holiday dinner we think of any one group of people as having contributed most of the cranberry part of our repast, the Cape Verder is the one to have in mind. Over and over again, and without contradiction, owners and overseers of cranberry bogs pronounce the Cape Verder, whether he picks by hand, scoop or snap, the very best harvester of cranberries and spreader of sand with the wheelbarrow on the Cape Cod bogs.[1]

Approximately one-quarter of the total arriving immigrants from Cape Verde listed Plymouth County, the heart of the cranberry district, as their intended destination. Reports from the oral histories claim that the cranberry pickers came primarily from the island of Fogo. The statistical information gathered from the ship records confirms this point. Of all those whose destination was cited as being Plymouth County, the majority listed their last residence as Fogo. The Plymouth area had, by far, the largest concentration of Fogo islanders, the remainder having scattered themselves fairly uniformly throughout other locations in southeastern Massachusetts. Barnstable County on Cape Cod also shows a large number of settlers from Fogo but is followed closely by immigrants from Brava. (See tables 5 and 6, where I break down Cape Verdean arrivals to Plymouth and Barnstable counties by island of origin.)

The former whaleman and bog worker Joseph Ramos recalled that after several years of whaling, he came ashore and was in the country for about ten weeks when he first heard the word "cranberry" mentioned at a dance. "What does this mean—'cranberry?'" he asked his friends.[2] Although none of the Cape Verdean immigrants had ever seen a cranberry before coming to this country, the agricultural economy

Table 5. Destination Plymouth County, by Island of Last Residence

Island	Immigrants
São Vicente	28
São Nicolau	28
Santo Antão	88
Boa Vista, Sal, Maio	128
São Tiago	294
Brava	651
Fogo	3,176

Table 6. Destination Barnstable County, by Island of Last Residence

Island	Immigrants
São Vicente	4
Boa Vista, Sal Maio	4
São Nicolau	5
Santo Antão	7
São Tiago	16
Brava	226
Fogo	282

on the island of Fogo most resembled rural life in the cranberry region. When adequate rainfalls made possible cultivation of the land, Fogo islanders have maintained themselves as subsistence farmers. Because of its active volcano, the soil on Fogo is rich and arable allowing its inhabitants to be less dependent on the sea than those living on other islands. Coffee beans have been grown successfully on the island as well as sugar, tobacco, indigo, and millet. Because of the absence of good natural harbors, the food produced on Fogo has been for the residents themselves, rather than being shipped elsewhere.

The solid agrarian base of Fogo contrasted to the other islands that furnished the bulk of the Cape Verdean emigration to the United States. The economy of Brava had traditionally been much more tied up with the whaling industry. Furthermore, farming on this island has been severely curtailed by the method of land division. The *minifundia* system provided for subdivision of land tracts among one's offspring, both sons and daughters equally. Over the generations this has resulted in ownership of minute pieces of property on an island with a high population density. In 1924, there were 418 persons to the square mile. This figure was 2½ times greater than any of the other islands at that time.[3] Cultivation of such small bits of land has made subsistence difficult at best.

While São Nicolau has had more of an agricultural foundation, a greater urban presence could also be found on this island with its established port towns and the location of the seminary in the main city of Ribeira Brava. São Nicolau was also often hardest hit by drought that crippled the farming community. The island of São Vicente has never had a rural base. Its focus of development has been the bustling port city of Mindelo. And while the agricultural organization of São Tiago has most resembled that of Fogo, with the historical use of slaves to cultivate larger plantations, those peasants who have left São Tiago to work have traditionally been a part of the forced migrations to the islands of São Tomé and Príncipe rather than having the opportunity to come to the cranberry bogs of southeastern Massachusetts.

The people of Fogo are known as rugged farmers and they transferred this robust aptitude and passion for the land to their work in the cranberry bogs. Yet, while the economic success of the cranberry industry became completely dependent on the labors of all the Cape Verdean immigrants who were a part of it, very few themselves became owners of these productive bogs. For the most part, the bog workers remained seasonal laborers, residing off-season in urban areas, primarily New Bedford and Providence. By late August, they would drift back again into the cranberry district. In a local newspaper article from the year 1900, the reporter characterized the seasonal movement of Cape Verdean immigrants in this way: "By the end of the summer . . . they have folded their tents like the Arabs and silently stolen away to Cape Cod's cranberry bogs."[4]

There were exceptions to this pattern, however. A few of the Cape Verde Islanders were able to purchase wetlands and convert them into cranberry bogs. Those immigrants who did manage to become property owners in the cranberry region come closest, in many ways, to realizing the possibilities of the American dream while still maintaining the continuity of rural life that is their heritage.

For the rest, the cranberry-picking chapter in their lives may bring up pleasant memories of bonfires and dewy mornings, or of storytelling and record-breaking scooping. But more likely, it is a reminder of backbreaking toil for low pay, of ruthless overseers, of poor health and inadequate housing that gave a minimum of shelter and a maximum of profits to the bog owners. The late Tony Jesus, former whaler and cranberry foreman for the Fuller-Hammond Cranberry Company described it:

> The hardest job I've run across is picking cranberries. Of course, construction is hard but there's money in it so you don't feel it. Long as you make the money, you don't care. But you take a man, go out and wheel sand nine hours for $1.80, 20 cents an hour, and you have got to do it. If you stand around, if you don't put a big load, the boss says, "What's the matter? You going to travel? You left a place for a suitcase?" . . . Today, you don't work like years ago. Years ago we had to pick 'em, cart them to the screen house, then screen them through the machine, get 'em all clean and then box them up put labels, and ship them. And you have to have a man to take care of that when they sell it for you. Today, you don't do that. You just raise them and take them to Ocean Spray.

Late in his life Mr. Jesus's foot became infected, the infection spread to his leg, and his condition could only be treated by amputating the limb. He attributed the disease to the poisonous pesticides and herbicides to which he was repeatedly exposed during his many years on the bogs.[5] The retired longshoreman, "Tote" Cabral agreed, "Now cranberry picking—that was hard work. I'd rather do pick and shovel work than that."[6] Flora Monteiro, for years bed-ridden with arthritis, attributed the severity of her illness to having labored so long on the bogs, "I know what I did and what effort I put into it. That's why I'm in bed today, is the result of it, because you sweat—you sweat up a storm. Then, after a while, your clothes dry up on you and that's no good for you."[7]

According to former picker Cecilia Perry Vieira (for a picture of Cecilia as a young girl, see photo section) of West Wareham, she "can't bear" to eat cranberries today owing to the harsh memories of the work, "I can look at them, yes, but not eat them. It was so hard on your hands. It tore the skin off and got under your fingernails. And it hurt your knees to kneel there in the bogs for so long."[8] During an interview with centenarian Mary Da Rosa Barros, she pointed to her left shoulder and declared, "This arm here did a lot of picking . . . Sometimes I have this awful pain in my shoulder. I say, 'It's from pickin.' "[9]

All the hardships characteristics of migrant labor were experienced by the Cape Verdean bog workers. Yet, in comparison to adaptation to factory work, to congested city life, to unemployment and discrimination in employment, the weeks of the cranberry harvest were a welcome change for many. Not only were these former peasants able to work the land again, but the wages that one could accumulate during a good season would be sufficient to take them through the cold winter months with extra to send back to the old country or, in some cases, to make the return trip themselves. The money would also be used to bring other family members here to the United States. For those whose entry into this country came via the whaling industry, cranberry picking was an immediate way to begin to earn some hard cash. The former whaler Joseph Ramos recalled: "Whaling was dirty work, a nasty job. We didn't make any money whaling because they discounted everything—food, clothing. . . . it was a form of passport. So three days after I got off the ship, I was picking cranberries. On the *Wanderer,* I made fourteen dollars for one year. Then, on the *Margarett,* with the same crew, I made sixteen dollars for six months. In the cranberry bogs, I made $130 for six weeks. I paid $30 for board and came to New Bedford with $100."[10]

The pickers were frugal with a disposition to save. A count made in 1908 at one bank in the cranberry district showed five hundred Cape Verdean depositors, with savings averaging from two to three hundred dollars. Some amounts were as high as eight hundred, a thousand, and fifteen hundred. At the end of the cranberry harvest, the bank paid out over twenty thousand dollars in savings to Cape Verdeans.[11] Workers were paid once at the end of the season and had to live on credit in the meantime. One of the main reasons that Cape Verdeans were able to save this much, however, was that their standard of living was so low. A study of farm labor in Massachusetts made in 1921 found that cranberry growers, as compared to dairy and tobacco farmers as well as market gardeners, furnished the least to their workers in terms of living accommodations.[12]

Single men stayed in shacks or "shanties," as they were called, which were cheap, shedlike structures typically only ten by twelve feet and six feet high, overcrowded, with barely enough room to stretch out on straw or sleep on flimsy mattresses. Workers were expected to gather their own deadwood for heat and cooking and provide their own food and utensils.[13]

Some of the owners of more or less isolated cranberry bogs did provide cottages for foremen near the bogs. Increasingly, though, Cape Verdeans who had the savings and had given up on the notion of returning to the islands would buy cheap lots and erect cottages or buy land for small farms. In the early 1920s, one town clerk estimated that 80 percent of the Cape Verdean resident families had title to their homes in comparison with 50 percent of native families.[14]

On the plus side, those immigrants who moved to the Cape and Plymouth County as year-round residents were able to re-create their traditional habits more freely in a rural setting. Many of the oral histories describe the family garden, canning and preserving the produce and preparing *Crioulo* recipes from homegrown food. Most popular of the staple dishes were *manchupa,* or *cachup,* a hearty stew made with samp (a coarse corn meal) as its base and cooked with potatoes, squash, and linguica or other meat, as well as *jagacida,* the *Crioulo* version of rice and beans. Some even continued the use of the large wooden mortar and pestle, or *pilon,* imported from the islands to grind corn in the traditional manner. Belmira Nunes Lopes detailed her mother's activities in growing and preparing customary foods for the family.

> Since she liked working out in the fields [my mother] would work with a baby tied to her back very much the way Indian women tied their papooses to their backs when they worked or went anywhere. She raised corn, beans, turnips, squash, peas, potatoes, and, in the fall, since she had a number of apple trees, we used to pack the apples in barrels and put them in the cellar to use during the winter. She used to salt a pig or two that were always killed in the fall and make *linguica,* pork meat that has been cut up and well seasoned with vinegar and salt. . . . Mother had a large, wooden mortar that was sent to her from Brava that we call the *pilo.* Since it was a custom in the Cape Verde Islands to make corn grits by pounding the corn in this large mortar with a heavy pestle, she wanted to do the same

thing here, so that her mother sent a *pilo* upon her request. She used to make one of the principal dishes of our diet from this process when I was child, *manchupa,* as we called it, *cachupa,* as some Cape Verdeans from other islands call it.[15]

Flora Monteiro recounted how the autumn harvest enabled her family to eat during the months that followed, "Picking cranberries was our main thing for the winter to pay bills and do whats-so-ever. Buy your food by the sack and put it in the house, sugar by the hundred pound, butter by the five pound tub, rice, beans. We had plenty of beans from the garden. We had our meat from the pig and chickens and eggs. We made our own home butter sometimes. We lived."[16]

Since cranberries were unknown to the Cape Verdeans on the islands, the newcomers had to learn how best to eat the berries that were collected for their own personal use: "Nobody knew how to make the cranberry juice. That's a fairly new product and so are the pastries. My mother used to make the sauce and jelly and we used to have it on all the holidays. All the owners allowed us to have a few cranberries if we wanted them. Either that or we'd hand pick the underberries, because when you scoop you lose a lot, so the underberries are left there."[17]

Tony Jesus remembered his wife saying, "'Bring home a couple of quarts of cranberries today and I would bring them home from the bogs and she would make something good. They didn't care if we took some cranberries from the bogs because there were so many.[18]

Growing up in a family of cranberry pickers meant beginning to harvest the berries at an early age. At the same time, harvesting cranberries has never been restricted to the young only. Older men and women, out of necessity, have worked the bogs since the industry began. Young children amused themselves alongside their working parents and older siblings, but as soon as it was profitable, the children would pick the underberries by hand, filling up pails and delivering them to the adults. Some growers even devised smaller scoops for the children's use.

Usually it meant that school-age children would not start the school year until mid-October, at the end of the cranberry season. In Falmouth, on 5 November 1927, four parents were brought into court, charged with keeping their minor children out of school. As defense, they produced permits that had been issued from the Superintendent of Schools allowing their children to labor as cranberry pickers.[19] Other children would have to leave school early, before the term was up in the spring in order to assist in the June gathering of strawberries, a common off-season activity for families that worked the bogs.

Belmira Nunes Lopes told of how growing up in Harwich and East Wareham, her school schedule was adjusted according to the needs of the cranberry harvest:

> During my high school years, I didn't always start school on time. As a matter of fact, I don't believe I ever started school at the beginning of the school year in September when the other students did because my parents were itinerant agricultural workers. They picked cranberries in the fall, and sometimes, when the cranberry season was over in one bog, it might still be going on in another, and they'd move from one bog to another to help pick cranberries, screen them, and box them. I almost always started school sometime in October when the cranberry season was over.[20]

Belmira also described how her cousin George Leighton never was able to finish grammar school because he worked the bogs: "He was a very bright young man but never had the chance because his people were on the bogs early in the spring, and his father was there late in the fall, and because he missed so much school, he never was able to get beyond the sixth grade."[21] Despite the obstacles, Leighton continued to study on his own, attending Works Progress Administration classes at night. With an undaunted determination to receive a higher education, he completed law school and became an attorney. He is currently a United States District Judge in Chicago, Illinois, and serves on the Harvard University Board of Overseers.

Lewis Hine, the noted photographer who documented child labor practices in industrial America during the early part of this century, included as part of his study a series of photographs of children working on the cranberry bogs. Employed by the National Child Labor Committee between 1906 and 1918, he came to the Massachusetts cranberry district in the autumn of 1911. In his notes from that visit, Hine mentions one little girl, Amelia, aged twelve and in the third grade, who reported that the Superintendent of Schools had come to her bog that day and said that the children had one more week to pick, although school was already in session. He also recorded the following conversation that was overheard at the Hollow Brook Bog. The boss there was characterized by Hine as a "veritable slave driver."

> A tousled headed boy about 10 years old comes up with a box of cranberries balanced on his head, struggling with both hands to keep it up.

The checker is very profane. (The boss on the field is worse.) "Put it in there, god damn it. Hold on, god damn it, go back and fill it up." (The box is heaping but not quite heaping enough.) The checker has told me that the boxes are supposed to hold two measures (12 quarts) but really hold 13½ quarts.

"There ain't no need of cursing," someone says.

"Well, I ain't cursing, god damn it, but go back and fill it up."

A little boy of 12 is picking vines from the barrels and hears the checker say—"Take the vines out. Throw 'em to hell overboard." The checker keeps up a running fire of this "speeding-up" sweatshop talk.

He calls across the field to a boy half-way in with his box. "Go back and fill it up or god damn it, you'll go home."[22]

For the children, cranberry harvesting did have its special moments, however. Lucillia Lima spoke nostalgically of picking with her grandmother, Maria Gamboa, of the songs she sang and the stories she told, "I liked to be with my grandmother when she picked. The work was so hard, but she talked to us and told jokes. She'd sing old Cape Verdean songs, the one about the sea of the full moon, rolling on the beach and playing in the sand. . . . I remember the phrase in one: "What killed him was the tongue of the world." Grandpa Cy always sang 'Bye Bye Blackbird,' sang it wherever he went." She also reminisced about the delights of storytelling for amusement in the evening hours during the cranberry season:

> We always looked forward to Saturday nights. The neighbors' children would all come over, and we would have hot bread with cranberry jam and hot cocoa. . . . Yho Lalla was a great story teller. He was much older and had a white mustache and smoked a pipe. He told us stories of *Yho Lobo,* the wolf. *Yho Lobo* was always the bad guy and some other animal was always the goodie two-shoes. The stories recounted all the terrible things that happened to the wolf, how he fell into the hot fire or had nothing to eat in winter. The moral was to mind mother and never be lazy.[23]

Belmira Nunes Lopes and Albertina Fernandes also had fond memories of storytelling and socializing after work. Belmira remembered:

> My mother used to entertain us with stories at night. Almost every night she would gather us around her and tell us the story of *"Ti"* *Lobo* and *Chibinha,* a kind of Br'er Rabbit. . . . There were many, many stories. My youngest Uncle, Manuel, after his arrival in the

United States, was especially famous for telling stories about *"Ti"*
Lobo and *Chibinha.*

Other than the storytelling, our amusements were attending christ-
enings. When all of the neighbors from near and far were invited to
the christening, we had a dance and we'd serve *canja* at night, a thick
chicken soup, crackers, and anything else my mother could prepare,
and we'd dance from night until morning. Even the young children,
not too young of course but those who were ten years old or so,
would be allowed to stay up as late as they could stay awake.[24]

Like Belmira, Albertina "used to hear stories of everything from
fairy tales to factual things about the family. They told stories for
hours. That was the pastime with no television or radio. They told
our generation, the younger ones, about their trips and experiences.
So that's how I learned—from my parents and relatives."[25]

Others described the flirtations and courting that occurred in their
adolescent years on the bogs. Lucillia Lima said that she remembers
when her aunt was "in her teens, she'd go ice skating with her boyfriend
on the bog just behind the house. I was the chaperone. I had to go
along. And they would go skating along the edge of the bog where
the blueberry bushes would overhang and they would kiss. I'd say, 'I'll
tell Mama.' "[26]

Two of the women interviewed, Mary Barboza and Mary Da Rosa
Barros, met their future husbands while picking cranberries. Mary
Barboza tells her story.

Pa worked at Sabrino's grocery store. They would take orders and
then in the afternoon they'd deliver it to the bogs. He'd come in a
horse and buggy with canned milk, rice, sugar, beans. We noticed
each other right away. We were attracted to each other.[27]

Mary Da Rosa Barros tells of a similar encounter.

I picked cranberries and my mother picked. My father stayed home
and worked in Norwich, Connecticut, on a coal barge. My brother
picked too, and my husband had a little grocery store. We bought
groceries from him when I was a girl. He used to deliver to the little
places where were were picking. That's how I met him. In 1905, we
got married.[28]

The women usually continued to pick after marrying, bringing their
little ones with them to the bog. It is estimated that females made up
one-fourth to one-third of the labor force.[29] Of the three methods for
picking cranberries—by hand, with a scoop, or with a snap machine—

women and children were said to hand pick more rapidly than men and strong-handed women were known to be the best snappers. However, Hine noted that women were not generally hired as scoopers because the overseers thought of it as a technique that only the men could handle. All of the larger bogs that he visited in 1911 used male scoopers almost entirely. It was not until the 1930s that women were routinely given the opportunity to scoop. They quickly proved to be at least as efficient as the men.

Lucillia Lima noted that her grandmother was undaunted by the prohibition on women using the scoop:

> My grandmother was basically a liberated lady and my grandfather learned a lot from her. She was a very big woman. She was six feet. At first she picked by hand. They used to pick by the measure and the men would pick with the scoops. They would make more money because they could scoop up more than you could pick by hand. So she said she wanted to pick with the scoop and the men didn't go for it too much because she picked very well, more than many of them . . . so they had to put her in her own section. And she'd be way ahead, often finishing her section before they finished theirs. She'd tie her head and she'd sing her *Crioulo* numbers, her Cape Verdean songs, and she'd push ahead.[30]

Like the peasants on the islands, women in the rural areas retained the customs of wrapping their hair in scarves and carrying heavy loads on their heads. It was not uncommon to see a female bog worker hoisting a crate of cranberries onto her covered head as she transported the full boxes to the tallykeeper for a count. Belmira Nunes Lopes "wondered if her [mother] carrying herself so straight and in such a queenly manner was not because, when she was in Brava, she used to go to get water from remote areas where there was a spring. They used to carry these buckets of water on their heads through the hilly roads of Brava for miles without spilling a drop."[31]

These traditions were more quickly abandoned in the city, where typically women would only put on scarves inside the house or in the yard. Similarly, the women in the cranberry district held on longer to the island practice of smoking a pipe and would smoke in public, while their urban counterparts gave up smoking soon after arriving in this country or they would only smoke in the privacy of their own homes.[32]

Several of the women interviewed expressed pride in their swift harvesting ability and vividly recalled incidents of outstanding production. The stress of working at a "piecework" rate, combined with the pressure of competing for this privilege with men, prodded them to become superior pickers. Flora Monteiro told of one memorable day of harvesting: "We went picking one Sunday to this place. My nephews went and when it was 2 o'clock, I asked the fella, 'How many boxes have I got?' He say, '72.' I say, 'Lord, 72! I'm going to make it 100.' And I grabbed my scoop and boxes on both sides. I went over and found a plot and when I got through with that plot, I had 24 more boxes. Lord, I thought, I'm going to make it to 100. I made it to 100 and said, 'That's it!' "

Her reputation for speed and efficiency with the scoop became renowned throughout the area in which she worked:

> I picked cranberries for Makepeace Company. One time, the boss — he was an Italian fellow — he says, "Flora, I want you to come pick cranberries over here to a section that I got here. I don't want to put all the crowd in there. I want you alone. Come with me." That place was just like you took a bucket of cranberries and emptied it down on the ground. I didn't see him but he told me afterwards that, while I was picking, he took out his watch and timed me. He says, "Flora, every minute you had a box. You were filling those boxes so fast that I had to time you."[33]

Filling a hundred boxes in a day was a challenge to Albertina Fernandes as well:

> When I picked, I picked by the box. I did piece work. A lot of the women didn't want to do piece work. I never liked hourly work. To me, it was too slow. I could make three times more an hour picking by the box than I could by just the hourly rate. With the hourly rate, you go on your knees and scooped one scoop at a time. I just couldn't pick at that pace. . . . The most I can remember picking in one day is 88 boxes. There's supposed to be a picture of me and my brother — my brother is quite the picker — taken on a day that I supposedly picked 100 boxes. I don't remember that — 100 boxes![34]

While cranberry picking was seen to be less desirable employment than laboring in the textile mills, work on the bogs did facilitate child-rearing and family-centered role expectations. In 1913, a federally-sponsored field study of infant mortality rates based on births for that year was conducted in New Bedford, which sheds some light on the problem as it concerns the Cape Verdean immigrant population. The survey showed that the foreign-born "white" Portuguese had an infant mortality rate of 201 per 1,000, which was twice as high as other ethnic groups in the city, including French-Canadians, the English, the Poles and the "Portuguese Negroes" or Cape Verdeans.[35]

Another report on infant mortality in Fall River, Massachusetts, completed in 1908 found a causal connection between high numbers of infant deaths and artificial feeding, including the early introduction of solid food as well as cow's milk.[36] Other studies in this period also concluded that babies who were breast-fed were more likely to survive beyond the first year of life.[37]

For the Portuguese immigrant woman, working in the textile factories of New Bedford and Fall River provided the primary means by which she could earn a wage that would make it possible for her family to survive in the new land. She would have to leave her infant children to the care of others. The pressure to feed the child solid food too early or to wean the child to cow's milk was very great.

The Cape Verdean women, on the other hand, faced discrimination in hiring in the mills, due to racism. Never employed in large numbers in the cotton industry, they were also the first to be laid off when business was slow. Hence, their heavy participation as migrant laborers in the cranberry bogs and strawberry fields of the surrounding rural areas, or as domestic help in the wealthier homes in New Bedford. Harvesting cranberries involved the whole family. Children accompanied their mothers and fathers to the bogs, beginning to pick the underberries when they were old enough to make it profitable. But the very young children would play along the bogs' edges while the infants lay in baskets near their mothers. This enabled the women to breast-feed while working and it meant that the babies could receive this essential nourishment until the age when they were actually ready to digest solid food. Numerous accounts, both oral and photographic, depict the scene of an infant resting alongside its mother as she picked the vines on the bogs.

When harvesting the strawberries during the off-season, an activity that was almost entirely dominated by female labor, once again, nursing mothers could have close access to their babies. Domestic labor, as well, allowed for arrangements that would enable a woman to continue breast-feeding longer than if she worked in the factories. The neighborhoods of the mill-owning and professional families that employed the Cape Verdean immigrants in domestic service were contiguous to the Cape Verdean residential area in New Bedford. If the infant could not stay with its mother all day, babies were brought by their caretakers to their mothers for feeding time, or the woman working as a domestic could adapt her working hours to make possible trips home to nurse.

The irony here is that denial of the better paying textile jobs to Cape Verdean women because of racial prejudice meant the greater possibility of survival for her children. The choice to board her infant in order to earn higher wages was not hers to make. Consequently, the young Cape Verdean child received the necessary sustenance to survive that important first year of life and the overall infant mortality rate was lowered. By the early 1920s, an economic recession had resulted in cutbacks in production at area mills forcing many women out of the workplace. According to the 1924 New Bedford Board of Health Annual Report, the increase in the number of unemployed mothers corresponded to a drop in infant mortality among the white Portuguese population.[38]

This aspect of the Cape Verdean woman's accommodation to the labor market, the ways that her family and work responsibilities converged as she found strategies to support family survival, exemplifies the necessity of including all of the social factors in the discussion of migration patterns. In their capacity as workers, the female Cape Verdean immigrants' labor market incorporation was most similar to that of African American women in this time period. Factory work offered white immigrant and native-born working-class women options in the industrializing nation while domestic service and other types of "women's work" continued to lose standing. However, black women were barred from employment in the factories of the burgeoning urban centers of the north and therefore turned to domestic service to earn a wage. In this case, the white ethnic women competed successfully with the native-born women of color for the better paying jobs. Factors of race and gender were in operation, creating a system of stratification that inevitably resulted in the worst jobs being reserved for women and racial minorities. Rather than solely being the consequence of choice, the fact that Cape Verdean immigrant women labored primarily as cranberry pickers or as domestic help in the urban areas fits the standard pattern for racial-ethnic women who migrated at this particular time. For these individuals, there were few options other than agricultural work or domestic service that were open to them. Within these constraints, the Cape Verdean working mothers found ways to maximize the possibilities for simultaneously fulfilling the demands of both her child-rearing and bread-winning roles.

In addition to harvesting the cranberries, the women did the work of setting vines in the spring. The vines were all hand set. During the growing season, women could also be employed as weeders bringing their baskets to tend the young cranberry plants. However, year-round employment on the bogs was restricted to the men only. The full-time male workers engaged in all aspects of the cranberry industry — building bogs, planting, draining, wood-cutting, flooding, sanding, weeding, fertilizing, grading, sorting, packing, storing, and shipping. Only males were made foremen.

Tony Jesus told the following story of how he had to persuade his wife to move to the country so that he could accept a year-round position as foreman of a bog:

> In 1919, I drove team. When we got through picking in October, it got kind of chilly one day. My wife was there. My oldest boy was a year old. I got through and I told Mr. Hammond, "Mr. Hammond, you want to get ready to pay because I've got to go back to my winter job." "Oh, no, no, no," he said, "I'm going to make you foreman in Carver because the foreman there is going back to Finland and not coming back again."... So Mr. Hammond wanted to get me. I used to jump around like a monkey. Course I was young and I liked that. So I asked my wife. She didn't want to. She said, "I don't want to live in the woods." So all right, we pack up and we go to New Bedford. . . . I went back to the mill, a cotton mill. Then I beg. I beg until she decides it's all right. In 1920, I call the old man first week in April. He said, "Come right along." I became a year-round man. I put in about 15 years in the Carver bog.[39]

During the off season, many of the women picked strawberries in and around the Falmouth area. Cape Verdean immigrants were responsible for introducing the strawberry to Cape Cod at the end of the nineteenth century. As was the case with the cranberries, natural conditions were very favorable to growing a high quality berry. The sandy soil was easily worked but heavy enough to withstand drought. A mild winter climate did not subject the plants to excessive cold.

While the development of the strawberry crop was slow at first, by 1910 it became a thriving industry, dominated by the Cape Verdean growers. Unlike the cranberry bogs, not only did the island immigrants labor in the strawberry fields, but the land was often owned by them as well. These tracts were usually not larger than an acre, but careful cultivation could produce high yields. The strawberries were then transported by freight to the Boston markets, although some were also sold in New Bedford. After three or four years of successful strawberry harvests, poor marketing conditions caused profits to begin to dwindle. The farmers responded by forming the Cape Cod Strawberry Growers' Association in 1915. By working together, buying and selling as one unit, they were able to turn the situation around and garner decent returns again.[40] For about four weeks in June and early July, laborers were needed to pick the strawberries. Women usually did this work and then moved on to harvest blueberries in the woods of Plymouth

County later in the summer. By the time the blueberries were finished, it was September and time to go back to the cranberry bogs again.

Harvesting blueberries, like strawberry and cranberry picking was a family affair. Lucillia Lima had pleasant recollections of this activity as well.

> Grandma took the whole family with her and knew where all the wild blueberries were. We'd fill those big zinc pails, a couple of gallons a pail, with berries. She had a little blanket for me and Bennie in case we got tired. Of course we had our dog, *Ny Pianga*—Miss Peggy. . . . Then we would take the full pails of berries out to Howland Station at the end of Howland Road and head toward New Bedford. The train would stop there to pick up passengers. We took the train to Fall River and sold our berries at better restaurants. The owner of one restaurant always gave me a bowl of ice cream.[41]

Other types of jobs that were done by part-time seasonal pickers during the rest of the year were chopping cord wood to sell, cutting ice from ponds that would be insulated with sawdust in blocks for use in summer ice boxes, gardening, construction work on the roads and railways, factory and maritime employment in New Bedford and Providence, and gathering the mayflower in the spring. These flowers, also called trailing arbutus, were arranged in bunches and sold to Boston buyers who would travel to the Cape by train. A bouquet could bring in between 5 and 75 cents, depending on its size. In her autobiography, Belmira Nunes Lopes chronicled the shifts in seasonal work in her family of itinerant pickers.

> One of the things we used to do was to pick mayflowers in the spring and sell them to people who came in on the trains. The white people traveling appreciated having these wild flowers sold to them. They bought them because they smelled very sweet, and they were beautiful. . . . That was something in which the men very seldom indulged.
>
> The real season for working out of doors began with strawberry picking. Oftentimes we'd go to a place like Falmouth and other sections of the Cape where some large fields of strawberries had been planted. We would pick strawberries from about four o'clock in the morning until about eleven o'clock or so, generally before noon, because at that time when the sun is high and hot, the strawberries tend to crush easily. . . . Generally, we had all the strawberries we wanted to eat, and our fare consisted oftentimes very largely of strawberries with sugar on them and crackers.

Summer was for picking blueberries. The woods on the way to the cranberry bogs abounded in them. The berries were sold to the boarding houses and to neighbors who did not care to indulge in such backbreaking activities. Or they were taken to the center and sold to the more affluent homes. The money wasn't much but it helped to keep body and soul together until cranberry-picking time. . . . wherever we thought there was a good crop of blueberries in the woods, we moved into that area. We sometimes went to live in shanties; other times, some very good, friendly Cape Verdean would allow us to use some of the rooms in his house during that season. . . . we would start picking as soon as we could see the berries. I remember my mother used to say *terral dja risca* (there were traces of light in the sky . . .) The journey was not altogether unpleasant, and during that time we had a horse. We would all get into our buggy. . . . We had to straddle the pails full of blueberries as well as we could on the return home.[42]

An additional source of income for women was to put up preserves from the harvested fruits and have their canned goods sold to S. S. Pierce. Unfortunately, with the cranberry bosses as middlemen, the women were never paid adequately for these fine products. An attempt to exploit the canning talents of Lucillia Lima's grandmother occurred over one winter season:

One of the things that I found unfair was that my grandmother was very good at making conserves. Mr. Bullock, who owned the bogs, chose her to make jellies and jams for S. S. Pierce. She'd get like $25 a week. This extra money helped during the winter. She worked all these crazy hours putting up stuff for S. S. Pierce. . . .

The boss had a contract with the company to make certain kinds of preserves people preferred. He worked her and pushed her and pushed her to try and make the lemon jelly. Lemon was a very difficult fruit to make into jelly. She worked on it and I can remember how tired she got. She just couldn't master that particular flavor. He kept pushing and she'd work on it until late in the night. . . . Then my Uncle Joe came home from the Navy and had a big fight with the owner. He told him, "My mother is not going to stand there over those hot stoves. She can't get it, so that's it."[43]

For those who worked the bogs on Nantucket, many remained on the island throughout the entire year. During the summer, they were employed as porters, chambermaids, waiters, and waitresses in the numerous hotels and boarding houses.

In part because of the seasonal nature of their work, it was difficult for the cranberry pickers to organize. But that did not mean that they were happy with the status quo. The earliest account of labor unrest occurred in 1900 when a riot at a bog in North Carver was reported. Worker dissatisfaction with the low wages led to fist fighting and arson on the bogs.[44]

By the Depression years, a more organized effort took place. In September 1933, fifteen hundred workers went out on strike, demanding an increase in wages, guaranteed employment until the end of the season, and recognition of their right to unionize. Assisted by labor organizer J. J. McIntosh, who was authorized by another local leader, Abraham Binns of New Bedford's Central Labor Union, The Cape Cod Cranberry Pickers Union, Local No. 1 was formed. The union set up its headquarters in Onset and agreed that the following wage scale should be met by the growers:

Men scooping: 80¢/hour
Women scooping: 70¢/hour
Handpicking: 15¢ per 6 quart measure
Women screening: 40¢/hour
Men weeding and sanding: 50¢/hour for a five day, 40 hour week

In addition to demanding a new schedule of wages, the union members specified a series of conditions that they wanted immediately implemented including the formation of a workers' committee to routinely inspect the living and working conditions on the bogs and a shift to payment at two-week intervals rather than only once at the end of the season. During the two weeks between paychecks, credit slips would be accepted at the local stores and banks. Prohibitions against children laboring on the bogs were also at issue.[45]

Workers claimed that some owners were unfairly paying the workers by the box when berries were sparse and by the hour when the crop was abundant. One picker said that he was paid thirty cents for harvesting thirty-two quarts when only a few others were on the bogs, but this was cut to eighteen cents when more laborers showed up. Allegations were also made that some workers were illegally fired for joining the union. According to James Bento, a Cape Verdean judge who was an attorney at the time, the strike was initially organized by outsiders but the pickers, after a generation of poor working conditions, readily took part in hopes of improving their situation. Others supported the strike out of solidarity or fear of reprisal.[46]

The work stoppage spread to some forty bogs throughout the Carver, Onset, and Wareham region. Strikers demonstrated their growing militancy by donning arm bands with the words "Picket" on them and driving trucks with signs such as "We Want A Living Wage" through the area. Meanwhile, the cranberry growers attempted to break the strike by the posting of lands to make it possible to arrest the strikers for trespassing. They also deputized approximately one hundred foremen "and other reliable whites" from Plymouth and Wareham to "protect the workers" and "drive agitators out of the cranberry bogs."[47]

The ever proud and feisty Flora Monteiro remembered well how she dealt with the sudden appearance of the instant deputies:

> At that time they had hired cops because of strikes going on at different bogs and they had the hired men dressed as cops. And I was strong. The hired man said, "What do you think you are?" I said, "I know what I am. I'm a cranberry picker for Makepeace, but I want what I picked *marked down*. I ain't making the boss no present." And the cop came to me and says, "Lady, you got to keep quiet or else I'll take ya." I said, "You won't *dare* put your hands on me." I called him all kind of names. . . . After the season was over, the hired cops became the workers and they were working right along with my husband. So I said to my husband. "Where did he leave his uniform, in the sand bank?"[48]

The labor dispute escalated to the point that on 14 September violence erupted. A local bog owner and chairman of the Carver Selectmen shot a Cape Verdean worker, Alfred Gomes of Onset, wounding him in the hand. Gomes had allegedly tried to wrest the shotgun from the owner and it went off. State police quickly arrived on the scene. They fired shots that wounded several people and arrested sixty-four pickers for assault or attempted assault. The Wareham selectmen filed a request for martial law, and word came from Boston that Governor Ely was watching the situation closely.[49]

The most complete account of the strike comes from the files of the *Wareham Courier*, which was consistently biased against the organizing efforts of the pickers, as expressed in both the editorial content and the news coverage of the events. Because of the emotionally charged nature of the events, as well as the skewed perspective of the *Courier*, which consistently downplayed the purpose of the strike, it is difficult to reconstruct what actually happened in the end. What is clear is that outside workers were brought in by the growers to pick the already rotting berries. Organizers McIntosh and Fred Woods were then arrested on what appeared to be trumped up charges of falsely representing themselves to the workers in their signature campaign. They were convicted and given two-month sentences.

Perhaps the most significant factor in dissipating the momentum of the strike was several days of particularly heavy rains that fell during the third week of September, at the near height of the harvesting season.[50] With the bogs flooded and the ceaseless downpour, picking had to come to a halt, regardless of the tactic of organized work stoppages. There were no benefits for striking laborers, which meant no harvest wages to carry them through the long, cold winter. Many workers had continued to pick after the first few days of the strike, in any case, admitting that although they supported the strike in principle, they could not afford to hold out for their demands. At this point, the union drive began to dwindle. The strikers, hungry and desperate, gradually went back to work under police surveillance.

Although strike efforts did not result in a general wage increase or unionization, in some cases settlements were made for higher wages on individual bogs. More importantly, this was the first strike by agricultural workers in the history of Massachusetts, as well as the only labor dispute that involved primarily Cape Verdean immigrants. By the time the scabs were brought in, the strikers had generated enough local support to elicit from the Onset Cape Verdean Advancement Association a resolution of solidarity with their efforts to unionize. The statement also chastised one of the members of the Association for his involvement in hiring outsiders.[51] At least one grower has stated in a recent interview that in retrospect, he believed that the pickers' monetary demands were not unreasonable: "The pickers were entitled to more. It was the only time of the year they could get it [money]— to get a little extra for the winter. Harvesting rates probably should've been higher than the other jobs. It was harder work. They looked forward to picking season, just as we did."[52]

In addition to the organized efforts of the cranberry pickers, examples of individual acts of protest against the working conditions abound in the oral histories. Always outspoken, Flora Monteiro stood up to the overseer when he tried to cheat her:

> One time I picked four boxes in a half an hour. That time you had to take them to shore. And I was right near the edge so all I did was just jump and put them on the shore. And the tallykeeper says, "You picked four boxes right now? What do you think you are, a machine?" . . . He didn't put the four boxes down, you know, he put three. He put three just to be mean. And I was tired. I opened my lunchbox. I couldn't eat because I was so hot and sweaty and tired. And I said, "You better put four boxes down." So Tosy, the boss, heard me arguing with the tallykeeper. He says to the tallykeeper, "If

she told you she picked four, she picked four. Whatever she tells you. I know her long enough."

When it came time to quit around 5 o'clock, my husband says, "I have three boxes out there. Come help me with one and I'll bring two." So before I went to help, I asked the tallykeeper how many boxes my husband had. He had 27 on the tally sheet. So we went and got the three. When we came back, I says, "Yup, that makes 30. He said. "Oh, no, 29." Then I really cussed him out. I say, "27 and 3 is what, 29? What school did you go to? Tosy, you better get this guy out of here because he's going to run into trouble." And so he put the right number down.[53]

As foreman, Tony Jesus recalled how he and his workers forced their boss into paying higher wages on their bog:

By 10 o'clock it's dry enough to pick. We're ready to scoop but I can't take the gang out until we find out about our wages. I tell them to wait right there. Then the old man, Mr. Hammond, put in and says, "What's the matter?" . . . I say, "Wait a minute, Mr. Hammond, for one thing, you're paying two prices. You offer 75 cents but we got a man here who only gets 30 cents an hour and I've got another man here who only gets 20 cents an hour. . . . I had a smart fellow working who jumped right in and he said, "Mr. Hammond, I'm going to speak for the whole gang. We'll settle this strike right here, if you cooperate with us."

Mr. Hammond says, "Sure." He's a big, pot-bellied man, understand. So he wants to take our slips and go down to the office and take care of it. But this smart fellow turned around and said, "No, I'll come with you. I want to make sure that we get our 75 cents an hour and that no mistakes are made. And you bring me back here." . . . Mr. Hammond said "O.K., get in." He had a Model T coupe. The fellow did come back with the pay they wanted. I started the gang back up again around 2 o'clock.[54]

Another bold example of resistance to the authority of the bog owners is the following episode:

My grandfather and Mr. Bullock would lock horns every now and then. Mr. Bullock would hide in the trees and watch the pickers from his perch. One day my grandfather started chopping the tree down. Yes, Bullock hid in the trees and my grandfather said he'd fix him. He took the axe and started cutting the tree down. Mr. Bullock couldn't get down fast enough. . . . My grandfather says, "Are you going to watch us again?" He said, "Oh, I was just looking beyond section so and so and this, that and the other thing." My grandfather says, "You're not spying on the men anymore."[55]

As the Cape Verdeans began to settle with more permanence in Plymouth County and along the Cape, they encountered increasing racial prejudice in these traditional Yankee strongholds. A contributing factor in the greater intolerance displayed by the white residents was that the later stream of Cape Verdean settlers were more easily differentiated as nonwhites than the initial group had been. The earlier Cape Verdean arrivals had all come from the island of Brava, where the inhabitants tended to be light-skinned and, therefore, could more readily pass as "white" Portuguese. In the late 1890s the first newcomers from Fogo and São Tiago, who generally have darker complexions, began to arrive.

Nonetheless, for the most part, the Cape Verdean cranberry pickers were depicted by local Cape Cod writers as industrious, law-abiding, honest, and thrifty.[56] Yet they were immigrants with unmistakable African as well as Portuguese roots and, as such, were targets of white racism. A 1906 New Bedford newspaper account of the arrival of the Schooner *Flor de Cabo Verde,* whose passengers were primarily Fogo island immigrants bound for the cranberry bogs, carried this commentary:

> The news has spread in the islands that there is work to be had near this city and everybody in the islands who can get together the price of a passage and enough money to show on arrival at this port is coming this fall.
>
> While the owners of the cranberry bogs and others interested in the property wish to see the immigrants come to pick the cranberries, it is said they do not like to see them remain on the Cape, and the problem is how to make the pickers all go away from the places where they pick berries.[57]

As early as 1905, in the Cape Cod town of Harwich, there was talk of establishing segregated schools. Later that year in Marion, Massachusetts, a town directive was issued against further employment of Cape Verdeans in public works.[58] Also in 1905, the theme of a commencement address by a Wareham high school girl was the problem of the incoming "half-blood" Portuguese to the area. In her speech, entitled *"Drifting Backwards,"* she deplores the influx of "cheap labor," bemoaning the fact that "our poor American girls are obliged to labor side by side with these half-civilized blacks."[59]

Several years later, in 1917, another young woman was to give her valedictory speech at Wareham High School. On this occasion, it was Belmira Nunes Lopes. Her essay, "The Ideal Town," in contrast to the 1905 address, made the point that the perfect community would have no prejudice. In her autobiography, Lopes discusses at length the difficulties and isolation she experienced throughout her years of schooling:

> I suffered many a humiliation. I was the only dark-skinned person in the entire high school. . . . I had friends when it came to doing the work in school, but otherwise, I had no social contacts with the other students. On the contrary, sometimes when we were going home on the trolley, I'd be sitting by myself and there would be a student standing rather than sitting down beside me. Or some girl might say something disparaging, as on one occasion when a girl made a remark about Roy Archibald, the other Cape Verdean pupil. . . . I guess I must have been embarrassed at the remark she made because she turned around then to the other girls, laughed, and said, "Oh! Even Mary's color can blush." They called me Mary although my name is Belmira, but we never knew what the possible translation of Belmira could be, so I answered to Mary all through high school.
>
> I used to eat lunch by myself because the other girls used to have lunch with each other or they used to go off and sit somewhere else. Oftentimes, I preferred to eat by myself because my lunch was not like the lunches the other girls carried. . . . I can ascribe my associations almost wholly to the fact that I was the leading student in the class.

When her high school class was planning a special trip to Washington, D.C., the following racial incident occurred:

> When I was going through high school, they had trips to Washington in the springtime. We used to sell cakes and all kinds of things to try to raise money for the trip to Washington. I remember with what difficulty I was able to bring a cake a week as all the other students did. I am sure that most of the time the cakes I took to school were not so good as some of the other cakes that were brought in by students in the class. Nevertheless, I did my share, but when the time came to go to Washington, the principal called me into the office and said that they wouldn't be able to take me to Washington with them because there was discrimination in Washington that would not permit them to take me all the places where the other students would be able to go. So they gave me my share of the money. They gave me twenty-seven dollars and I stayed home.

Lopes's greatest disappointment occurred later when, after gradua-
tion with honors from Radcliffe College, she learned that Wareham
High School needed a Spanish teacher. She returned to her home town
to apply, armed with a superb recommendation by the head of the
Romance Languages Department at Harvard University. Despite the
excellence of her credentials, she was denied the job. The Superintendent of Schools explained that the parents of the students would
object to having her teach because she was not of Anglo-American
descent. It was only then that Lopes realized the extent of the discrimination against her and her people.[60] In 1919, in Onset, Massachusetts, where the Cape Verdean neighborhood was disparagingly
termed "Jungle Town," racial tension escalated to the point of violence
and a young white man died as a result. An eleven-year-old Brava boy,
Joseph Lomba, was charged with manslaughter after hitting his assailant,
John Cook, in self-defense, causing the older boy to fall and break his
neck. In asking the court for leniency in the matter of bail, Attorney
Lewis said he understood that Lomba had been provoked, that Cook
had called him "nigger," and that when Lomba grabbed him, he said,
"Take your black paws off me."[61]

Despite these examples of racist attitudes toward the Cape Verdeans,
Albertina Fernandes felt that there was less prejudice in the earlier days
of settlement than currently exists in Plymouth County. Following are
her recollections of shared respect among the differing nationalities:

"There were, maybe a few racial remarks or something like that,
but we all got along fine. Here in town were the Yankees, the Finnish
and the Cape Verdeans. Three groups. And the Finnish people and the
Cape Verdeans were immigrants. We had a lot more in common, while
the Yankees had been here longer and most of them were the owners. . . . The town was so small. We were in school together. We so-
cialized. There were so few of us, only 900 altogether. We got along
fine. Everyone knew each other."[62]

Lucillia Lima also looked back favorably on relations with the Finnish
settlers in particular. "The Finnish were always there. They were friends.
Two groups pretty much on the same plane. So many were such good
friends and good neighbors. And we lived like a family, too.[63] However,
this close association between the groups stopped short of complete
integration as endogamy prevailed. According to Albertina Fernandes
"there was no intermarrying. I don't think there is today, not with the
Finnish. There is more with the Yankees than the Finnish people. I
don't think we even thought of intermarrying. No one was supposed
to marry anyone who wasn't Cape Verdean."[64]

And not all of the oldtimers carry such pleasant memories of mutual acceptance. Lawrence Peters, a Cape Verdean immigrant who has built his own construction firm on the Cape, recalled that when he grew up in Falmouth, Massachusetts, his neighbors constructed a gate "to keep out the Jews and blacks and Catholics." As a builder, he found it difficult to buy land, "The money didn't amount to anything. It was a very shocking thing. There were a lot of problems. The prejudice was not like down in the South. Down South, it's more open. Up here, it's not in the open and that's more difficult to deal with." Peters currently resides near the neighborhood that was closed to him in his youth.[65]

In the rural areas, racial divisions were not so pronounced as in the cities. As long as the Cape Cod Cape Verdeans "stayed in their place," associating with their own kind in their own sectors, a semblance of cooperation and tolerance between groups was maintained. But true acceptance and an end to discrimination on the basis of color has been a long, slow, ongoing process.

In addition to the obstacle of bias in the sale of real estate on the Cape, the newcomers did not, for the most part, consider purchasing land for bog development because they did not see themselves as permanently relocating. If there was extra money to be saved, these earnings would go back to the Cape Verde Islands to purchase property there, rather than trying to buy acreage locally. As Albertina Fernandes explained it,

> The best cedar swamp land at that time was only $5 an acre. Then they would build the bog themselves. This was all hand labor. There were no bulldozers or anything else at that time. Yet that same $5 would be sent back to the old country. . . . The Finnish people worked on the cranberry bogs like we did, but eventually they ended up buying and building bogs. And now in Carver they are a large majority of the good cranberry growers. Anybody could have bought bogs at the time. Cape Verdeans would have been the biggest bog owners now, but they didn't have their minds set on living in this country.[66]

The tie to their homeland was so compelling that, although the connection served as a source of strength to the Cape Verdean Americans during the years of immigration, it may have hurt them in the end, interfering with the success of a more permanent settlement here. After working for over sixty years for the Hammond Cranberry Company, both as picker and foreman, Tony Jesus expressed what was his only regret in life: "That's the biggest mistake I made. I had a chance to buy a bog. Wish I had a bog today. I have a friend now in Osterville who has three-quarters of an acre himself. He works it himself. Can't speak English very well. He's got a nice home. . . . So, you see, today the cranberry business is wonderful. Which is a mistake I made. I didn't want to have to worry about anything when I got to be an old man."[67]

Converting the swamp lands to productive bogs is a process that takes from three to five years. Most of the immigrants simply could not afford to invest the time and money into a project with delayed financial return. If they did own property, the larger land holding companies such as Makepeace or Hammond would try to buy them out. Yet, a few individuals were successful in obtaining land suitable to bog conversion. In 1925, Dr. Henry J. Franklin, director of the Cranberry Experiment Station in East Wareham, noted that Cape Verdeans owned no more than a total of one hundred acres but that this was at least a start in the right direction.[68] Lucillia Lima, a descendant of cranberry growers, described how her family went about it:

> You have to give credit to a lot of those old Fogos. My grandfather's brother started out with a section here. And the following year he'd buy another section. Then my grandfather and all the brothers would go out and work on it. . . . Another piece and another piece. They keep adding on. And every year my grandfather and his father and his uncle would work and encourage him to add a piece. . . . And he bought all that land for about $200, in those days. Now it's worth a small fortune.
>
> A lot of the old timers that worked on the bogs invested their money. The people from Fogo are clever people. Very enterprising and great organizers. Very thrifty. They prepared for their children. And gave them a little push ahead. You find quite a few down on the Cape. Like the Pina brothers in Falmouth. They had their own business. They had their own bogs and they did very, very well.[69]

Some immigrants, like the Pina brothers, who owned homes and businesses in the cranberry region, would build a small bog adjacent to the house for their own use and to supplement their income. Antonio Canto Barboza became one of the first Cape Verdeans to own a retail business in the Falmouth area. He came to the Cape in 1906 and set up a store where berry truckers waited for their loads from nearby bogs. At various times, he also ran a gas pump, an ice cream parlor, the Beer Barrel bar, a restaurant, a barber shop, and a pool hall. He was the first Cape Verdean in the area to obtain a liquor license. In addition to these business ventures, the family had a small cranberry bog as well as strawberry fields.[70] In Wareham, Massachusetts, another enterprising Fogo islander set up a store and a dance hall near the bogs, while also keeping a small piece of land to grow his own cranberries.[71]

Those who grew up in the rural areas had particularly fond memories to share in the interviews:

> We had a large hen house a short distance from the house on the other side of two apple trees. We had mostly Rhode Island Reds, Plymouth Rocks, and a few Bantys. Ma fed the chickens in the morning when we kids went to school. There were a lot of fox and weasels—boy, oh, boy! Cy set traps everywhere. It was all woods. Mother loved horses and we had a Clydsdale. He was so gentle. The old man used to talk to that horse to plow and the horse knew just what to do! Smart? You bet. We had pigs, too.

> My favorite cheese was the one made after the first milking of the nanny goat following the birth of her kid. It was a mild, sweet cheese and good served cold, white as snow, with little or no aroma of cheese. . . . Services such as plowing, harvesting and wood chopping were shared with all the neighbors. Each week a group would meet at the home of whomever needed one of these services. All the families would spend the day together with the receiver of the service. They would prepare full meals for everyone for that entire day until the job was done.

> On the cranberry bogs, there was storytelling at night, playing the guitar, music, singing, dancing, parties. We always had a party after picking time. We had a square dance and they would call the dances in crioulo. Contra-dances we call it.[72]

Edward Lopes of Point Road in Marion, Massachusetts, seventy years of age at this writing and still harvesting cranberries, grew up in the same house by the bog that he lives in today. His three adult sons are all college educated and hold professional jobs. His thoughts on cranberry picking: "I liked it. In fact sometime on a rainy day you get ready to go to the bogs and they wouldn't let you pick. We were young and we used to tell stories or raise cane with each other. And it was nice. When cranberry time came we always gathered there. That's what we have now—a memory. I have good memories of the bogs. I couldn't help it. I was born into it. That was family there."[73]

Listening closely to the voices of the cranberry harvesters, even the seasonal laborers, demonstrates that the strong positive recollections are as crucial as the memories of hardship in our understanding of the work culture and family experience of this ethnic group. In the early 1930s, at age thirteen, Manuel E. Costa made the eight-hour trip from New York with his father and two brothers driving in their reconstructed Model A Jalopy to pick cranberries on Makepeace's Frogfoot Bog in Wareham. At one moment he described the abysmal housing conditions where they stayed during the harvest: "Our shanty had 10 men. The one room on the bottom was a kitchen, with no sink, no water, a stove and a table. Upstairs was two long bunk beds where the 10 of us slept. Two windows. Talk about poor air circulation. With the residue heat that stayed there, you'd practically die from it. The windows were nailed shut. You didn't want them open because of the mosquitoes. The kitchen area was so crowded and hot because of the wood stove, especially in mid-August, that you couldn't stay there. When the food was cooked we'd sit outside on the ground on logs." But in the next breath, he declared, "It was a great time. It was a festive time. When cranberry time came, everybody looked forward to it. We knew there was work and money to be made. It was family. You ate well that time of year. There was always food."[74]

Of the many Cape Verdeans that I have spoken to during the course of this research, I have found that those who managed to purchase land in the cranberry district and to turn their property into productive bogs constitute the primary success stories of this immigrant group. Brought up as peasants on the islands, their connection to the land has endured. At the same time, with the cranberry industry still booming today, they have been able to achieve economic security. Their children may not chose to stay in the cranberry business but they typically go on to college and achieve middle-class occupations.

This is no small feat, particularly in a society where people of color who have worked the land have traditionally been able to do so only as slaves, tenants, or sharecroppers, not as proprietors, and have otherwise been ghettoized into the larger cities. They have not had the opportunity, as the Cape Verdean cranberry growers have had, to sink down roots in the vast American soil and to carve a small piece for future generations.

Albertina Fernandes, from the island of Fogo, and her son Domingos are long-standing cranberry bog owners in South Carver, Massachusetts. She described the quality of her life this way:

> We just enjoy it out there. It's beautiful to walk around the bog. You see all kinds of animals—deer, muskrat, rabbits, fox. And it's yours. You go up and walk around and it makes you feel free and airy. It's just a beautiful feeling. . . . All during the time the kids were growing up, we used to go camping out there. Like early in the spring, my husband would come home and say, "Oh, let's take a ride." We'd

go up there and walk around the bogs. It was just nice, relaxed, no stress. No matter what you have to do, you're not under complete stress all the time. The boys are all college graduates and they still love to go out there. They really don't have to do it. They enjoy it like I do."[75]

NOTES

1. Albert Ernest Jenks, "Cranberry Bogs of Cape Cod: Their Workers," *Dearborn Independent,* 3 Jan. 1925, p. 14.

2. Joseph Ramos in Kathleen Megan, "Whaling: Cape Verdean Memories," *Sunday Standard Times,* 18 July 1982, p. 17.

3. Albert Ernest Jenks, "New Englanders Who Came from Afric Isles," *Dearborn Independent,* 27 Dec. 1924, p. 5.

4. *Morning Mercury,* 25 Aug. 1900, p. 12.

5. Interview with Antonio Jesus, 20 Nov. 1983.

6. Interview with Antonio "Tote" Cabral, 16 Oct. 1985.

7. Interview with Flora Monteiro, 30 Nov. 1983.

8. Interview with Cecelia Perry Vieira, 24 Oct. 1985.

9. Interview with Mary Da Rosa Barros, 12 Dec. 1984.

10. Joseph Ramos, quoted in *Spinner* II, p. 108.

11. William P. Dillingham, "Recent Immigrants in Agriculture," in *Immigrants in Industries: Report of the Immigration Commission,* 22 pp. 548–549.

12. Josiah C. Folsom, *Farm Labor in Massachusetts, 1921,* U.S. Department of Agriculture Bulletin no. 1220 (Washington, D.C.: Apr. 1924), pp. 19–20.

13. Ibid., p. 19.

14. Ibid., p. 8.

15. Nunes, *A Portuguese Colonial in America,* pp. 39–40.

16. Interview with Flora Monteiro, 30 Nov. 1983.

17. Interview with Albertina Fernandes, 5 Dec. 1983.

18. Interview with Antonio Jesus, 20 Nov. 1983.

19. Victor Safford, "Cape Cod Africans," *Falmouth Enterprise,* 18 Aug. 1944, p. 5.

20. Nunes, *A Portuguese Colonial in America,* p. 57.

21. Ibid., p. 55.

22. Lewis Hine, Richard K. Conant, and Owen R. Lovejoy, "Child Labor on the Cranberry Bogs of Massachusetts," 19 Aug.–20 Sept. 1911 (Notes), pp. 5–6.

23. Interview with Lucillia Lima, 25 Jan. 1984.

24. Nunes, *A Portuguese Colonial in America,* p. 50.

25. Interview with Albertina Fernandes, 5 Dec. 1983.

26. Interview with Lucillia Lima, 25 Jan. 1984.

27. Interview with Mary Barboza, conducted by Ron Barboza, Jan. 1984.

28. Interview with Mary Da Rosa Barros, 12 Dec. 1984.

29. Jenks, "Cranberry Bogs of Cape Cod," p. 14.

30. Interview with Lucillia Lima, 25 Jan. 1984.

31. Nunes, *A Portuguese Colonial in America*, p. 28.

32. Interview with Anthony Barboza.

33. Interview with Flora Monteiro, 30 Nov. 1983.

34. Interview with Albertina Fernandes, 5 Dec. 1983.

35. Jessamine Whitney, *Infant Mortality, Results of a Field Study in New Bedford, Mass.* (Washington, D.C.: Department of Labor, Children's Bureau, 1920), pp. 18–20.

36. Chas, H. Verrill, "Infant Mortality and Its Relation to the Employment of Mothers in Fall River, Massachusetts," Transactions of the 15th International Congress on Hygiene and Demography (Washington, D.C., 1913), pp. 318–37.

37. New Bedford, Massachusetts Board of Health, *Annual Report*, 1915, p. 23 and 1918, p. 23.

38. New Bedford, Massachusetts Board of Health, *Annual Report*, 1924, p. 43.

39. Interview with Antonio Jesus, 20 Nov. 1983.

40. *Population and Resources of Cape Cod*, Massachusetts Department of Labor and Industries (Boston: Wright and Potter Printing Co. 1922), pp. 33–34; L. B. Boston, "Strawberry Culture on Cape Cod," *Cape Cod Magazine* 1, no. 4 (Aug. 1915): 25–26; "Where Your Strawberries Come From," *Cape Cod and All the Pilgrim Land* 5, no. 2 (June 1921): 34–36.

41. Interview with Lucillia Lima, 25 Jan. 1984.

42. Nunes, *A Portuguese Colonial in America*, pp. 35–38.

43. Interview with Lucillia Lima, 25 Jan. 1984.

44. "Riot Among No. Carver Cranberry Pickers," *Morning Mercury*, 12 Sept. 1900, p. 8.

45. *Wareham Courier*, 8 Sept. 1933, pp. 1, 2.

46. Doug Meyers and Donald Glickstein, "Striking Workers in the Cranberry Bogs: The Depression Years," *Bowsprit, The Sunday Standard Times*, 3 Sept. 1978, p. 4.

47. LeBaron L. Briggs, "The History of the Cranberry Industry in Massachusetts" (Honors thesis, Harvard University, 1941), p. 47; Meyers and Glickstein, "Striking Workers."

48. Interview with Flora Monteiro, 3 Nov. 1983.

49. "Shot in Berry Strike," *New York Times*, 14 Sept. 1933, p. 48.

50. *Wareham Courier,* 22 Sept. 1933, p. 1, 2; 29 Sept. 1933, p. 1.

51. *A Voz Caboverdeana,* 15 Sept. 1933, p. 4.

52. Interview conducted by Joe Thomas with Larry Cole, Nov. 1989.

53. Interview with Flora Monteiro, 30 Nov. 1983.

54. Interview with Antonio Jesus, 20 Nov. 1983.

55. Interview with Lucillia Lima, 25 Jan. 1984.

56. See, for example, Katherine Smith and Edith Shay, *Down Cape Cod* (New York: Robert M. McBride and Co., 1936), pp. 26–27; Millard C. Faugh, *Falmouth, Mass.* (New York: Columbia University Press, 1945), p. 152; Agnes Rothery, *Family Album* (New York: Dodd, Mead and Co., 1942), pp. 43–45; Cooper Gaw, "The Cape Verde Islands and Cape Verde Immigration," *Evening Standard,* 29 July 1905, p. 10; Dillingham, "Recent Immigrants in Agriculture, p. 551; Folsom, *Farm Labor in Massachusetts, 1921,* p. 6. A notable exception to the favorable portrayal appears in E. Garside, *Cranberry Red* (Boston: Little, Brown and Co., 1938).

57. *Morning Mercury,* 19 Sept. 1906, p. 8.

58. Gaw, "Cape Verde Islands," p. 3.

59. Herbert D. Bliss, "Feeling on Cape Is Not Inimical to Cape Verdeans," *New Bedford Sunday Standard,* 28 Aug. 1921, p. 5; Gaw, "The Cape Verde Islands," p. 3.

60. Nunes, *A Portuguese Colonial in America,* pp. 54–60.

61. "Brava Boy Held for Death of White Man, *Evening Standard,* 25 Aug. 1919, p. 1.

62. Interview with Albertina Fernandes, 25 Dec. 1983.

63. Interview with Lucillia Lima, 25 Jan. 1984.

64. Interview with Albertina Fernandes, 5 Dec. 1983.

65. Lawrence Peters quoted in "Cape Verdeans hold fast to roots," *Cape Cod Times,* 13 Aug. 1983.

66. Interview with Albertina Fernandes, 5 Dec. 1983.

67. Interview with Antonio Jesus, 20 Nov. 1983.

68. Jenks, "Cranberry Bogs of Cape Cod," p. 14.

69. Interview with Lucillia Lima, 25 Jan. 1984.

70. Conversation with Ron Barboza.

71. Interview with Mary Da Rosa Barros, 12 Dec. 1984.

72. Interview with Lucillia Lima, 25 Jan. 1984.

73. Interview with Edward Lopes, 17 July 1989.

74. Interview with Manuel E. Costa, conducted by Joseph Thomas, 25 Aug. 1989.

75. Interview with Albertina Alves Fernandes, 5 Dec. 1983.

Living—Just Enough for the City

4

Work on the cranberry bogs drew large numbers of Cape Verde Islanders to Plymouth County, Buzzards Bay, and Cape Cod; most of the newcomers, however, settled in urban areas. Together the cities of New Bedford, Massachusetts, and Providence, Rhode Island, drew just over half the immigrants. From early on, New Bedford encompassed the largest concentration of Cape Verdeans, with a third of the arriving passengers listing the Whaling City as their intended destination. The town became known as the Cape Verdean capital of the New World. Table 7 shows frequency totals of the various destinations recorded from the ship manifest data.

At the turn of the century when the bulk of the Cape Verdean immigrants were beginning to arrive in New Bedford, the city was booming with prosperity. While the whaling industry, which had brought such wealth to New Bedford in the nineteenth century, continued to steadily decline, the growth in production of fine cotton goods was enabling the city to flourish once again. Construction of mills and mill housing, banks and businesses was occurring at a rapid pace, including the appropriation in 1903 of thirty thousand dollars to build an immigration shed at the head of City Wharf.[1] In the first decade of this century alone, seventeen new corporations were founded in New Bedford. The expanding textile industry required a large work force and immigrants were pouring into New Bedford to fill the demand for labor in the cotton mills. In 1901, the city's population of eighty thousand was double what it had been a decade before, and by 1905, less than one-fifth of the people in New Bedford were of Yankee ancestry.[2] The largest of the immigrant groups were the Portuguese, and among them the Cape Verdean settlers began to have an increasingly significant presence in the city (see table 7).

Almost half of all the Cape Verdeans who came to live in New

Bedford were from the island of Brava. So many of the packet ships sailed in and out of her harbors that the term "Brava Packet Trade" was often used to describe the movement. São Nicolau was the next most frequently recorded last residence of the Cape Verdean settlers in New Bedford. Of the total immigration from São Nicolau, almost three-fourths planned to live in New Bedford.[3] Also noteworthy is that almost half (48.5 percent) of all the women who arrived in this country from the archipelago listed New Bedford as their intended destination. Table 8 correlates those who cited New Bedford as their destination with island of last residence.

Once landed in New Bedford, the Cape Verdean immigrants clustered in the city's South End, roughly from South Water Street eastward to the waterfront. Later, the neighborhood expanded west to South Second Street. In the novel *Chiquinho*, the author portrays the immigrant father of the central character as residing on South Second Street. Cape Verdean newcomers gravitated to the streets of the South End not only

Table 7. Cape Verdean Immigrant Destinations

Destination	Immigrants
Martha's Vineyard and Nantucket	173
Other Rhode Island locations	355
Barnstable County	629
Boston	711
Other Bristol County locations	851
Other New England locations	1,008
Providence	3,961
Plymouth County	5,186
New Bedford	7,825

Table 8. Destination New Bedford, by Island of Residence

Island	Immigrants
Boa Vista, Sal, Maio	160
São Vicente	369
Santo Antão	464
São Tiago	542
Fogo	595
São Nicolau	1,298
Brava	3,653

because of ethnic identification, but also because of the proximity of these streets to the waterfront and to the mills, the most likely work-places of the arriving islanders. Carrie Pina noted that "when a boat would arrive, people would come down to the docks and give you directions telling you that all you had to do is walk from the pier to the first street, turn left and you'd be in the Cape Verdean neighbor-hood."[4] "Tote" Cabral, who grew up in the heart of the South End held this memory: "My father was a whaler. I remember the last time he sailed. I was about twelve years old. He sailed out and I could see the ship going by on the river as I walked along the top of the fence in front of my house on Griffin Court."[5]

Though once one of the more desirable sections of the city in which to live, by the time of the Cape Verdean influx, the South End neigh-borhood was run-down and sorely in need of attention. Dwellings were humble tenements or cottages with inadequate lighting and sanitation facilities. In her investigation of the area as part of the citywide study on infant mortality in 1920, Jessamine Whitney reported that two or three Cape Verdean families were living in houses that had once served as single-family dwellings for Anglo-American families.[6]

Often, already settled families would take in boarders to supplement their income, thus providing a familiar environment to the many single men who were steadily arriving to New Bedford from the Cape Verde Islands. Housing and feeding unmarried coethnics was a standard prac-tice among families of the foreign-born in this period; Cape Verdeans were no exception. The married women of the community played an essential role through the provision of household services to bring in extra money, an exchange that became crucial to the maintenance of the family economy. Both Lucillia Lima's grandmother and mother ran boarding houses in the community:

> My grandmother and her cousin had boarding houses. . . . The old Cape Verdeans were very protective of their own. They didn't want ever to have one of their own walking the streets or denied a place to sleep or food. It was a way of life and it was a means of money for a lot of poor people.
>
> The children's godmother and her two cousins helped my mother get a boarding house started right there on Cannon Street. The house is gone now. It's all Bay Village. She ran the house and liked being home with the family again. Money was coming in and Ma saved, bought new furniture, sewed, did a lot for us.[7]

Another recounted growing up in a family of lodgers as well:

When the immigration started mostly men came over, and there were very few families. The men had no place to go, so my mother ran a boarding house. They were mostly relatives. Paying boarders. We had maybe twenty men—sailors, musicians, and even a painter. Not very many of them could speak English. When we were kids we used to imitate them. One man we used to call "Cigarette" because he always had a cigarette hanging out of his mouth, even while he played the violin. My father was very good hearted; my mother was the shrewd one. She took care of money matters.[8]

In some instances the women operating the boarding houses would also be delegated the responsibility of managing the insurance policies and wills of their boarders: "My mother was running a sort of boarding house—paying rent for the building. Three or four whaling men, working at the same time with my father, roomed there. They would leave their policies in my mother's name. Metropolitan used to have collectors come to the door—the only company at the time, I think, that worked here."[9] The other option for the many unattached men, particularly those involved in industries supplied by the wharfs, was to stay at the dockside lodging houses located on the streets leading down to the harbor.

When young unmarried females arrived without close relatives to sponsor them, they would often stay at first with already established Cape Verdean families in the capacity of housekeepers and cooks. Known as *kriadas,* these women were provided the opportunity to have some legitimate connection here until they were married or ready to live on their own. "Tote" Cabral described his household:

> When my mother came from the old country, there were a few women that she knew back there—daughters—and they'd want to come over here. Two or three of them came to stay with her. And when they stayed with her they would take care of the housekeeping. And then when they got on their feet they'd go and some others would come in. We had a big house on Griffin St. where whalers would board. The attic was for them. There was room for about five up there. A lot were part of the family—cousins and nephews. And the *kriadas* would cook for them.[10]

The South End quickly became an ethnically homogeneous and close-knit community, the nucleus of the enclave. In a pattern that stemmed in part from the process of chain migration, relatives tended to live near one another, if not actually residing in the same household. Consanguineal and affinal kin bonded together through domestic and economic exchanges as well as sharing in the socialization of the children. It was common practice for neighbors to informally watch one anothers' youngsters, always making sure they had a hot meal. A kettle of *manchupa, jagacida,* or *canja* would steadily simmer on the stove for whoever came into the house, but the young people were especially encouraged to partake and, if it was mealtime, would not be allowed to leave the house without eating. "Very often a child's eating style will approximate that of a smorgasbord—soup with mom, main course with auntie and dessert with grandma," wrote one commentator.[11] In the case of grandparents, this close relationship was formalized in the ritual of asking for blessings. Grandchildren and grandparents traditionally greeted one another with the child requesting to be blessed and the grandparent responding with a touch to the forehead.

The shared child care arrangement extended to disciplining one another's children as well. As one of those interviewed complained, "We could never get away with *anything*. If your mother didn't see you do it, then you'd get caught by one of the neighbors or your aunt, who would then tell your mother and you'd be in worse trouble!"[12] Cousins, brothers, and sisters formed intimate bonds of friendship and were often the primary peer group as the children matured.

Ritual bonds of kinship, particularly the role of godparent or *cumpad,* served to further the cohesiveness of the neighborhood. While the naming of godparents originated in the religious sphere with participation in the Catholic baptism ceremony, the functions of the *cumpad* spilled over to the social and affective arenas, much like the ties of blood relatives. It was quite common to choose a relative as a godparent, thus bringing even greater integration to the kin system. Relatives and godparents lived in close proximity, but non-kin could also participate in this rhythm of daily life.

The children of the South End attended the neighborhood school, but typically dropped out as soon as they were old enough to work. State guidelines allowing children to quit school at age fourteen facilitated this pattern. In 1910, twelve hundred working papers for minors were issued in New Bedford.[13] For some, like "Tote" Cabral, the sheer embarassment of being poor discouraged them from continuing their education: "When I was high school age, I went to the ninth grade. I didn't graduate because I said, 'jeez, I can't afford to go dressed up every day to school.' I had to go to work. There were quite a few kids like that. Nowadays you put on overalls and go to school, you're all set. Back then you were ashamed to go to school unless you could dress right."[14]

Another of "Tote's" contemporaries, also a former longshoreman, had a similar experience: "My father used to tell us he was embarrassed about going to school. He used to have to wear his step-mother's shoes to school. He only went on to the fourth grade."[15]

Others who emigrated as adults reported having taken advantage of night school classes to assist in learning the English language. In general, however, despite the value placed on literacy among the Cape Verdean immigrants, once settled, the necessity of finding paid work took precedence over the importance of acquiring an education beyond the primary level.

Employment of Cape Verdeans in New Bedford during the years of mass migration was confined to three major areas of unskilled labor. Most men were employed in maritime-related occupations or in the cotton mills. Women also labored in the mills or as domestics in the homes of the wealthier families in the city. In addition, despite permanent residence in an urban center, most of the city dwellers interviewed still relied on seasonal employment in the cranberry industry to supplement their wages and would at various times in their lives temporarily relocate for the duration of the cranberry harvest. Almost all of the workers had sporadic employment histories due both to the nature of the occupations available to them and to the ups and downs of the textile trade.

After whaling ceased to be a lucrative business, it passed into the hands of Cape Verdean seamen. This endeavor plus control of the packet trade eased the Cape Verdean immigrants into work on merchant vessels. The men filled positions on lighthouse tenders, tugs, coastal boats, and tramp merchant ships as stewards, cooks, firemen, and crewmen. By the late 1930s, they were working off-shore for the major oil companies such as Shell and Standard. Cape Verdean deck hands were hired exclusively by the local river and excursion steamboat companies because "they are sober and orderly, and these qualities have been preferred to certain characteristics of white deck hands."[16]

The work at sea naturally led to Cape Verdean domination in the dockside jobs as well. Many retained their seaman's cards so that if activity slowed down on the waterfront they could always ship out again. They worked as longshoremen, coalboat shovelers, riggers, coopers, and in the ropeworks as well as in related jobs requiring heavy manual labor, such as hod carriers and construction workers. Kin networks played an important part in occupational clustering on the docks. Once a man became a stevedore, it was an accepted fact that any of his male offspring would join on when they came of age. One of the longshoremen put it this way, "Well, I went to work on the waterfront. Why? That was the logical thing for Cape Verdean kids, or Cape Verdean–American kids to do. Number one you could walk from your house to the docks, basically. You knew people that worked there. You knew that they would help you out on the docks. And you make good money."[17]

The job of loading and unloading was physically demanding and, especially before unionization, was completely lacking in occupational safety standards. As a result, casualties were frequent. John "Toy" Fernandes described the work:

> My father became a longshoreman and then I became one in 1927. It was hard work. Cape Verdeans were hired. They were people who could be depended on. . . . They knew how to rig the ship. You had to know how to rig the ships—knowing the tonnage of the booms. In those days booms were rigged for five tons, if there was more you took your chances. Because at that time you didn't have safety— there was no safety check during the unloading process. . . . It was the only way we could survive. No one else wanted to do it—there was great discrimination at that time.[18]

By the early 1930s the longshoremen began to agitate for better wages and working conditions. In 1933, the longshoremen of Providence organized the first black labor union in New England, the International Longshoremen's Association, Local 1329. Although this effort coincided with the agricultural workers organizing on the bogs, there is no evidence to suggest that the two movements were related. Three years after the longshoremen organized, the New Bedford dockworkers unionized. They congregated at the city's Liberty Hall one day in 1936 with a delegate from Washington, D.C., to discuss unionization and within weeks had formed their own bargaining unit. Retaining a largely Cape Verdean membership, the longshoremen continue to be a significant voice in the local labor movement to this day. Toy Fernandes continued: "Before we were organized, we worked all kinds of hours, all weather—rain or shine. . . . In 1927 we got paid 50 cents an hour. After 5 o'clock, we got paid 70 cents an hour. Just like slavery they worked you. We had no control. . . . When we started to agitate there were a few of us and there was a one dollar fee to belong. . . . Organizing gave us strength and kept us from being abused. And we were being abused!"[19]

Cape Verdean men and women also constituted the great majority of the labor force in the rope works. The New Bedford Cordage Company employed so many of the newcomers that it was nicknamed "Brava College." In the story of "Antone Fortes, Whaleman," the author writes that after his last whaling stint, "Tony searched for a job and found one in a rope factory where he worked, from seven to five, each day through the winter. When the five o'clock whistle blew, Tony and his fellow workers hurried out of the mill; slipping, jostling, and pushing each other, they plowed through the snow, until they parted to go their several ways."[20]

By the end of the whaling era, profits were so meager and conditions aboard the ships so unbearable that it became difficult to recruit seamen. Even the most desperate were reluctant to sign on, resulting in the unscrupulous practice of having the crew shanghaied. "Tote" Cabral recounted how these captures usually took place: "There was a guy, 'Shanghai Joe.' He shanghaied a lot of the guys here in New Bedford. He'd get them drunk and they would pass out. Then he'd put them over his shoulder and throw them on the boat. When they woke up they were out to sea. He got paid by the company to bring them in. Any drunk he caught—he's going whaling."[21]

Another common approach was for the captain to deceive a green crew from the islands by telling them that they would not be admitted to this country permanently unless they made a repeat voyage. This was how Joseph Ramos was coerced into signing on for a second stint: "When the *Wanderer* returned to New Bedford, the captain pulled a trick on us. He took us to Boston and pretended to be preparing papers for us to be able to stay in the country. Instead, he arranged for us to go on another ship. . . . After the second trip, we said no to what the captain wanted us to say to immigration. He got mad! He didn't pay us when we first came here. When we refused to go back out—then he paid us."[22]

Although many of the Cape Verdean settlers were experienced mariners and logical candidates for the work force of the budding commercial fishing industry in New Bedford, they never were able to make inroads in this area of employment.[23] In the early part of the century, commercial fishing was hampered by the absence of a fish house in the city to handle a large catch, and the small fleet was dominated by immigrants from the Canadian Maritime Provinces and Scandinavia. As the fishing industry began to grow, the Azoreans also became heavily involved.

Fishing for a living during this period was not necessarily more lucrative than the dockside occupations, but it was definitely steadier work and therefore more desirable. Furthermore, unlike the earlier whaling crews, which were larger and had well-defined hierarchical structures with Cape Verdeans holding the lowest positions, the fishing boats were tiny, taking on a maximum of six seamen. Usually the crew consisted of the owner and one or two kinsmen working in very close quarters. Acquiring enough capital to buy a commercial fishing vessel was beyond the means of most of the Cape Verdean immigrants, while at the same time, the owners of the existing fishing fleet had no interest in integrating their crews.

At the same time that commercial fishing was getting off to a slow start, the manufacture of cotton goods in New Bedford reached its pinnacle. During World War I, especially, when a demand for coarse cotton goods such as bandages and uniforms was added to the production of fine cotton fabrics, mill jobs were plentiful. Many of the newly arrived Cape Verdean immigrants took advantage of this need for unskilled labor. Work in the factories, however, was stratified in such a way that each operation became the exclusive turf of a particular ethnic group. For example, the highest paying positions, such as the weavers and mule-spinners, were the domain of the English and French, while the Poles were primarily involved in the dying process. Cape Verdeans were relegated to the least desirable categories—in particular, breaking bales and cleaning the cotton. They also were most likely to work the night shift. Although they were invariably excluded from the better jobs reserved for the white immigrant groups, the Cape Verdeans managed to find a place for themselves. "Tote" Cabral "worked in the Quissett Mill. It wasn't hard getting a job in the mill. You didn't run a machine at first. They put you doing some kind of work carrying cans or something like that and you learn to operate a machine as you go along. A lot of people worked until they died on the job. Tuberculosis was rampant in those days. That mill was a killer."[24] His wife Julia's father was also a mill operative:

> My father worked in the cotton mills. He worked in one mill—the Sharp Mill—until they closed down in 1927.... Then, it must have been in the '30s, he got a job at the Hathaway Mill. And he stayed there until he retired. He worked days. I know a lot of the Cape Verdeans worked nights. He was a comb tender.... I used to take his lunch to him in the afternoons. I would come home from school and have to run down there and it was a little distance. You'd run like a son of a gun when you're small and you'd get there and everything's spilled inside the pail! I brought *jag* and stew. Cape Verdean food.[25]

In some cases, those who had received professional training in the Cape Verde Islands were forced to work in manual jobs in the United States because nonwhites were not hired in the skilled occupations. Fluent in Portuguese as well as *Crioulo* and trained as a secretary, Jose

Santos arrived in this country at the turn of the century and was unable to find work in the secretarial field. He ended up in the cotton mills where even there the better positions were not open to him.[26] Similarly, Jesuino DeBarros had been educated in Cape Verde and was employed in a bank before emigrating, but found no such opportunities when he reached the United States.[27] "Tote" Cabral confirmed the racism that existed toward Cape Verdeans in hiring practices, particularly during the depression years: "I did all kinds of work: stevedore, construction, pick and shovel and cement. It was hard getting a job. The color had a lot to do with it—the color line. The gas company and the telephone company didn't hire any people of color. Even a pick and shovel job for 25 cents an hour was hard to get. I worked in the cotton mill. That's the only place you could get a job."[28]

There were positions for women in the factories as well, albeit under the worst conditions. Antonia Enos "worked at the Wamsutta mill which is all dilapidated now. I had to go early in the morning to clean the cotton. The job is dirty. If the cotton wasn't clean, then they'd send you to the office. Then the higher up would check it. If you didn't pass inspection, you were fired.[29] The female Cape Verdean immigrants faced the doubly oppressive situation of discrimination in employment based on race and sex. In the absence of organized provisions for child care, work in the textile mills for women had to be periodic and consequently, they tended to be the last hired. "Tote's" wife, Julia Cabral, recounted her mother's work history: "My mother worked in the mills. She first started in the Yarn mill up the north end. Then she worked in the Potomska mill. But after she would have a child, she would have to leave and then she'd have to look for a job some place else because somebody would have taken her place."[30]

Other than discrimination based on gender, often difficult working conditions, and overly demanding bosses, women often faced an even more taxing problem within the workplace: sexual harassment. The mother of Lucilla Lima simply refused to continue working in the mills because she would not tolerate the level of such harassment.

Ma got a job in City Mill as a speeder tender. Now the speeders had to run around those machines connecting threads with the machine still running. It was a dirty, lousy job and long hours with low pay. No union in those days compared to today. No benefits, no workman's compensation, nothing. . . . Ma didn't like the idea of the men and women sharing the same toilet, so she complained. The super told her she could take it or quit, so she quit. Leaving her children alone left her uneasy anyway. She told us the women were treated with no dignity and harassed sexually and verbally. Some of the supers liked patting the women on the behind. Most of the women put up with it because it could mean their jobs if they complained. Bad language was used when mistakes were made or orders mixed up. A mistake meant doing the job over, and once she told me one of these men pushed a young girl, and she tripped and fell into one of the carts that carried spools of thread.[31]

A widow, with several children, this enterprising woman subsequently managed to start a boarding house and supplemented that income by operating a small business with her brother, carrying hot lunches she had prepared on a wagon to sell at the Pairpoint mills.

Besides employment in the textile industry, the other choices open to female Cape Verdean immigrants in the city were to work as housekeepers and laundresses. The wealthier sections of New Bedford were in close enough proximity to the South End to enable the domestic workers to maintain their own homes as well as those of the rich, rather than having to live in with their employers. Maria "Baba" Barros, "worked for the same family for fifty years off and on. Even when I worked in the mill, I went to their house after work to cook and clean. I worked like a horse."[32] In addition to laboring in the mills, Antonia Enos also did domestic work: "I came to stay with my sister. At first I worked in the homes of rich people. I worked for a French lady up the north end. That was before I went to work in the mills. After working in the mill for awhile, the boss asked me to come and work for his wife at home. I washed and ironed the clothes for them. I washed and ironed for several families—The Delanos—and others on Hawthorn Street."[33] The Hawthorn Street area is the most elegant section of New Bedford, with mansions built by whaling captains during the height of the industry lining the boulevards.

The mid–1920s marked the beginning of the irreversible fall of the textile industry, due primarily to competition from the South, which by 1925 had surpassed New England in number of active spindles. Widespread layoffs and wage cutbacks were occurring in New Bedford's cotton mills well before the 1929 Depression. At the very same time, the final chapter in the saga of the whaling industry was drawing to a close as the last active whaling vessel, the bark *Wanderer*, set sail from New Bedford in August 1924. She was to head directly for the island of Brava to fill out her crew, as so many ships had done before her, but the trip ended in disaster when the boat was wrecked on the treacherous Sow and Pig reef off the coast of Cuttyhunk, almost within sight of New Bedford's shores. During the days the *Wanderer* had been in port outfitting for this concluding voyage, word came that the Cape Verdean packet, the *Matthew S. Greer,* carrying some of the last of the island immigrants, lay anchored off the coast. Called "The Ship of Blasted Hopes" in the headlines of the local newspaper, its passengers would not be permitted entry because of the new quotas. This remarkable convergence of events, signifying the end of an era, prompted one contemporary observer to set forth this commentary on the Cape Verdean American connection, "Thus the curtain was rung down simultaneously in New Bedford on as thrilling and perilous a romance as ever made a city prosperous and deservedly famous, and on the immigration of one of our unique, though in numbers, lesser immigrant peoples."[34]

And there were more endings. In 1925, in the South Central neighborhood, the last of the gas street lights were extinguished to be replaced by the less costly electrical lamps. The following year marked the closing of the only remaining local whale oil refineries with the Delano Oil Works on South Street and the oil refinery of William A. Robinson and Company, being sold to a New York firm and removed from competition.[35]

By the latter part of the 1920s, as the mill owners struggled to stay in operation, Cape Verdeans were generally the first to be laid off. In 1928, thousands of mill operatives went out on strike in response to the announcement of an overall 10 percent wage cutback in twenty-seven local mills. Yet, despite heroic organizing efforts by the workers, more and more mills continued to shut down. By the time of the Great Depression, almost 50 percent of Cape Verdeans were out of work, with an eighteen-month average duration of unemployment.[36] Many immigrant workers fled the area, with half of the French-Canadian population leaving New Bedford between 1926 and 1928.[37] However, some, including almost all the Cape Verdean settlers, simply could not afford to relocate or had no other place to go and were forced to find alternative ways of surviving. "Tote" Cabral spoke of the Depression years: "The depression was tough. I was stevedoring at the time. If you could catch a boat on a Sunday, you'd make as much as working all week in the mill. And in between working on the docks, I'd pick cranberries. Some days when there wasn't any work, we'd go down and pick."[38]

Harvesting cranberries proved to be the one of the best ways for the Cape Verdean workers in the city to make it through the Depression years. By the late 1930s, the New Bedford pickers could commute to Wareham in automobiles whose owners charged a small fee. Even in the more prosperous times, seasonal bog work often made the difference for the Cape Verdean urban dweller in ensuring that the family stayed afloat financially. "Many city workers would ask for time off from their jobs in order to harvest the crop. A good scooper could earn three times the amount earned in a factory," recalled one seasonal picker.[39] Often, the entire family would pack up and transport themselves down to the bogs to stay for the season as Joaquim Pina's, Lucillia Lima's and Julia Cabral's families did:

> You'd load up a truck with mattresses. You took your food, canned goods, anything that was a staple and wouldn't spoil and head down to pick for the harvest.[40] (Joaquim Pina)

> Every cranberry season, it was like a ritual with Cape Verdeans, even in the cities. They would migrate as a group and go off to these bogs to pick. That was big money for them. It was a lump sum. We survived on credit until we were paid. You had a grocer who knew you very well. We'd go down with all our provisions. I remember with my grandmother, even after we moved to New Bedford and I was in my teens, she would pack all the food and go down there from September until about the last week in November.[41] (Lucillia Lima)

> The mill where my father worked closed down in 1927 or '28. He was off about six months. In the meantime we went down to the Cape, to Wareham, and we picked cranberries. We stayed in somebody's house near Blackmur's Pond. . . .They had an empty tenement downstairs. It was a family from Finland. Then we came back home and my father got a job at the Hathaway mill.[42] (Julia Cabral)

A very few Cape Verdeans were able to secure employment in semi-professional or professional occupational categories while others operated small businesses. An informal survey conducted in 1924 showed three lawyers, two physicians and two dentists.[43] Alfred Gomes was the first Cape Verdean to practice law in the city, while in later years two of the attorneys held judgeships, James Bento in Wareham's Third District Court and George Leighton as a Circuit Court Judge in Illinois. Lawyer Roy Texeira provided legal counsel to a good number of the packet captains and owners concerning the intricacies of immigration law and, in this way, made it possible for many Cape Verdeans to gain entry into this country.[44] A Cape Verdean professional and business-men's association, which sponsored scholarships under the name of "The Seaman's Fund" to assist college-bound Cape Verdeans, was also founded at this time.[45]

During this period, at least one furniture store was Cape Verdean owned, as were two or three variety stores in the South End. There was a Cape Verdean photographer, a trunk maker, several barbers from Brava, and in later years, a funeral home.[46] But severely limited access to the better jobs due to racial bias and, in later years, high unemployment kept the vast majority of Cape Verdeans from occupational advancement.

For the most part, the immigrants, whether rural or urban — working the bogs, the docks, the factories or the households of the wealthy — all occupied the lowest strata of the economy. Hence, stratification within the community was minimal. Issues of hierarchy among Cape Verdean workers do not readily lend themselves to the usual model employed by labor historians of the white working class. Stratification, where it did exist, was much more likely to be based on skin shade or island of origin than on economic or occupational position.

The easy association among compatriots in New Bedford was sometimes tempered by an overruling identification with one's particular island homeland. This loyalty stemmed from the fact that, by and large, before emigration, Cape Verdean Americans rarely had dealings with the inhabitants of islands other than their own. Travel between islands was infrequent and difficult to achieve. Each island became a nation unto itself. Though sharing a similar history and culture, immigrants from different islands were strangers to one another upon arrival in this country. This situation sometimes led to residential grouping by native island as well as to minor intergroup rivalries. When, in 1920, Elsie Clews Parsons was collecting Cape Verdean folktales, she was informed that "inter-island marriage is disapproved. . . . In this country there is a marked tendency for immigrants from the same island to keep together. A group of Fogo men will board in a Fogo family, S. Antao men in a S. Antao family, etc."[47] Because the dialects of *Crioulo* varied from one island to the next, pride in speaking the "better" form of the language would also be expressed as well as arguments over whose background was more superior. Moreover, island identification was also at times associated with color and phenotype. At least one social club formed exclusively for Brava islanders also determined membership on the basis of "whiter" features and lighter shade.

Thus, social status was complicated by issues of color and racial identification. Yet, the evidence indicates that these internal differences were not significant as compared to the level of racial and ethnic segregation and discrimination to which the Cape Verdean population as a whole was subjected. Belmira Nunes Lopes:

When the Cape Verdeans came to this country, we had to find

various ways of earning a living in which we didn't have to depend too much on the help of the Anglo-Americans. We did not know the language, and we had a number of strikes against us. We were dark for the most part in a country where most people were, if not blondes, of light complexion. We were professed Catholics, especially undesirable in a section of the country that had been settled mostly by Protestants who had left England in search of freedom of religion. We had religion against us, we had color against us, and of course, were were poor, and that has never been an asset.[48]

The racist attitudes that restricted employment opportunities for the Cape Verdean settler pervaded other facets of immigrant life as well. Attempts were made to enforce Jim Crow–type regulations on streetcars and trains as well as in the movie houses. The 1911 Dillingham Commission reported, "A few years ago it was easily possible to put a Brava on the back seat in a street car. . . . Now the Brava who knows his importance refuses to move back or forward or anywhere else until he pleases to do so, much to the annoyance of the conductor.[49]

"Tote" Cabral, who was an infant when his family came to New Bedford in 1896 remembered that as a young teenager, "I used to go to the movies. It cost a nickel but the Cape Verdeans weren't allowed to sit downstairs. We had to go up to the balcony seats."[50] "Separate but equal" was also the norm in the haircutting establishments. The most vivid memory of discrimination in this former whaler's life history occurred at the barber shop: "One time my brother-in-law who looks white and has blue eyes walked into a white barber shop. When he finished, he called his father in. Because his father was dark, the barber wouldn't cut his hair. He said to my brother-in-law, 'You're OK, but if I let your father sit in the chair, all my other customers will walk out.' "[51]

Unlike the racism that the Cape Verdeans experienced in the cranberry district, which came directly from the Yankee population, the ethnic and racial divisions in New Bedford were much more complex. In urban areas, Cape Verdeans became the target of prejudice from both Yankee and white immigrant groups, whereas on Buzzards Bay and Cape Cod, "white" and "black" tended to be lumped in the same category of Portuguese "foreigners." Actually, in the popular local history accounts and memoirs of the Cape during this period, it is very difficult to ascertain whether the condescending and sometimes derisive tone that is invariably used to describe the resident Portuguese is aimed toward the Cape Verdean bog workers or the Azorean fishermen of lower Cape Cod.[52]

In the city, there was no such ambiguity. From very early on, in residential, occupational, and social patterning, segregation of the "white" and "black" Portuguese was evident. This distinction, which the Cape Verdean newcomers did not choose for themselves, had a significant effect on their adaptation in the United States. They had immigrated to this country as Portuguese colonials with Portuguese surnames. They came as followers of the Catholic faith, speaking a dialect of the Portuguese language and were often fluent in standard Portuguese as well. If they had any other strong identification, it was to *nha terra* (my land), a reference to their particular island of origin. Certainly they did not see themselves as "black" Portuguese or even necessarily as Cape Verde Islanders. Yet, they were entering a society that had a well-defined bipolar racial structure with no recognized place for those of mixed ethnic or racial background or for those of varying skin color. This was a harsh reality that the Cape Verdean arrivals were quick to perceive, but that nonetheless was a situation for which they were not well prepared.

The system of racial classification in their home islands was much more fluid and varied. In Machado's anthropological research, she found over 250 different phenotypical categories in Cape Verdean society, the result of widespread intermarriage. She further demonstrated that, unlike the United States, membership in the upper social strata of the archipelago depended on a combination of factors including phenotype, but wealth, education, and background were also important.[53] In some cases, those who were darker in complexion but who had attained more prestigious positions in the society were nevertheless referred to as "white." In the Cape Verde Islands, skin color was a social as well as a racial designation.

By contrast, in the United States, no matter what an individual's ethnic background or physical characteristics, any person with known African ancestry at that time was considered to be "Negro" or "black." And "black" in our society meant severely restricted upward mobility. When given the choice, the Cape Verdean immigrants have tried to emphasize their Portuguese or "white" identity, rather than being forced to endure the same type of oppression that African Americans have had to face. As one immigrant expressed it, "the first thing Cape Verdeans learn is that black people sit at the bottom of the American totem pole. We found out quickly that America doesn't believe in shades—only black and white."[54] Another explained: "When my father learned the way that blacks were treated in the United States he didn't want that kind of treatment for him or his family."[55]

Thus, the Cape Verdean arrivals attempted to distinguish themselves from American blacks by stressing their differing language and cultural heritage and by segregating themselves from the local black population, which included those who had come to the city chiefly by way of the West Indies and from the South. A few of the African American residents of the West End were descendants of those who had settled in New Bedford before the American Revolution.

Yet, the so-called white Portuguese immigrants from mainland Portugal, the Azores and Madeira, would not allow their Cape Verdean counterparts to settle in their neighborhoods, join their social clubs, or attend their places of worship. They too were quick to recognize the stigma of being labeled nonwhite in the United States and feared that in a system with such a rigid color line, they would also be classified as black by virtue of association with the Cape Verdean settlers. They were acutely aware that if all of the island immigrants were identifying themselves as Portuguese and some were seen as black, the entire group would then be stereotyped as such. The vulnerability of the Portuguese to this kind of racial prejudice surfaced in an altercation in the early 1920s, following a soccer match between Portuguese-American and Irish teams. The scuffle was precipitated by the hurling of racial slurs, including reference to being "Negro," by a blond woman to an Azorean woman of equally fair coloring, who proceeded to slap the blond in the face for her remarks.[56]

The animosity did not just point in one direction, however. In the Cape Verde Islands, the white Portuguese had often been the object of ridicule, looked down upon by the Cape Verdeans as intellectually inferior. Yet, this was not simply a matter of reverse discrimination, but rather the cultural expression of resistance to Portuguese racial prejudice. At certain points historically, it does appear that the Cape Verdean level of literacy was, in fact, higher than that of Portugal.[57] When they arrived in this country, the Cape Verdeans assigned the pejorative term *nhambobs* to the Azoreans, which translated means "yam growers," a reference to one of the staple foods of the Azores.

The degree to which the other Portuguese immigrants disassociated themselves from the Cape Verdeans was also heightened by competition in the job market. Antonia Enos, a former mill operative, recalled the following incident at her workplace:

> There were only a few Cape Verdeans at the mill. The *nhambobs* thought they were better than we were. I used to inspect the cotton. If the cotton wasn't clean, well then they had to go to the office to have it checked and they could lose their job. They held that against me. . . . One time, I'll never forget this, they said to me, "We saw

some of your people on the stage at the Olympia theatre." Vaudeville days. They were the colored people. I said to them, "You're stupid. Those are not my people. I wish we could be smart like them, but we're not."[58]

The unofficial policy of reserving all newly constructed mill housing, which was readily available to the "white" Portuguese during the prosperous first quarter of the century, further crystallized the pattern of segregation between Cape Verdean and Azorean immigrants.

But nowhere was the tactic of exclusion more evident than in the circumstances that precipitated the founding in 1905 of the first Cape Verdean Catholic parish in the United States, Our Lady of the Assumption. Before that time, most of the South End residents who regularly attended church worshipped at St. John the Baptist, where the congregation was made up primarily of white Portuguese. It soon became clear that the Cape Verdeans were unwelcome participants in the St. John's religious community. They were not allowed to serve on the governing board or in any other administrative capacity.[59] Even those communicants who were not interested in exerting an influence on parish policy received an icy reception. Consequently, many of the Cape Verdean newcomers simply stopped going to church at all.

On 6 April 1905, in part as an attempt to rectify this situation Bishop Stang of Fall River wrote an official letter to Father Stanislau Bernard, member of a Belgian religious order, the Sacred Hearts Fathers, declaring, "You have the spiritual care of all Catholics known as Cape Verdeans living in New Bedford." By 15 August 1905, an old chapel was acquired in the name of the Bishop and the Cape Verdean parish was opened on Water Street near the harbor. The building was purchased on the Feast of Our Lady; hence the name "Our Lady of the Assumption" (OLOA). It began with only a handful of worshippers. Five people were in attendance when the Bishop arrived to dedicate the church, but by the time the service began, the number had increased to about twenty.[60] "Tote" Cabral recalled that "there weren't too many who went to OLOA in the beginning. I was baptised at St. John's. After OLOA was built, if you tried to christen a child there, they'd tell you to go to Our Lady of Assumption. They figured, that's your church, now you go there—don't bother us. They didn't want the Cape Verdeans there. The people were poor. They didn't have too much to donate to the church.[61]

Slowly, more and more of the local lay people became involved in all aspects of the functioning of the parish:

The church on Water Street was heated by an old coal furnace. . . . Mr. Theodore Almeida was in charge of seeing that it kept running and Mr. Antone "Sunshine" Ramos was in charge of ringing the bell to call parishioners to church on Sundays and for other services during the week. Aunt Jenny was in charge of seeing that the church remained clean and also that the altar cloths and priest's garments were ready for the services. . . . Aunt Jenny taught the children of the parish catechism in English in her home, while Mrs. Ana Araujo taught it in Portuguese. Later, as the number of parishioners grew, the classes were held in the church with the assistance of other women in the parish. Classes were taught orally because there were no books and no money to purchase English books.[62]

The same discrimination that the Cape Verdean immigrants initially confronted in finding a place to worship surfaced again in the 1950s when they wanted to secure a larger facility. The owner of the proposed site for the new church would not sell it to a Cape Verdean. It became necessary for a white friend to purchase the property first and to in turn sell it to the church. Recently, the OLOA parish celebrated the eighty-fifth anniversary of its founding at this graceful structure located at the corner of Madison and South Sixth Streets.

The *de facto* segregation within the local Catholic establishment spurred some of the Cape Verdean settlers to turn to Protestant sects for religious enlightenment. Evangelical communities had particular appeal. On Cape Cod, discrimination in other area churches was the catalyst to the establishment of the Harwich Massachusetts Church of the Nazarene founded by Pastor Joseph DeGrace, a Cape Verdean.[63] One group of newly arrived immigrants converted to the Nazarene faith, and brought their beliefs back to the Cape Verde Islands. In collaboration with another sect, the Sabbatarians, they built two Protestant churches on the island of Brava and began to translate the Gospels into *Crioulo*.[64] In his tour of the archipelago in the 1930s, Archibald Lyall had this to say about the transplanted evangelists: "The mere existence of these peculiar American sects in this remote African island of half-caste Portuguese seemed as incongruous as a Shinto cult in some Norfolk village.[65]

Back in southeastern Massachusetts, Protestant revivalism had captured the spirited interest of a young man hailing from Brava, the flamboyant, "Sweet Daddy" Grace, who was to engender more notoriety than any other Cape Verdean American immigrant. Founder of the United House of Prayer for All People, this charismatic evangelical leader established hundreds of congregations in numerous cities throughout the United States, with an estimated following of half a million by the late 1930s.

Records of the parish of Our Lady of Mount Brava show Grace's given name to be Marceline Manoel da Graca, born to Manuel da Graca and Gertrude Lomba, in 1881. He arrived in New Bedford with his family in the year 1900, at first working in the city and on Cape Cod as a cook and then as a peddler of patent medicines on the streets of New Bedford and Wareham, Massachusetts. Later, he also operated a small grocery store. His evangelical career began in the South, where he traveled in his "gospel car" preaching to primarily black followers at rural tent meetings. Grace erected his first church building, however, back in the Wareham area. Finding that the community there did not respond with enthusiasm to his brand of Protestantism, he returned to New Bedford in 1921, having just proclaimed himself a bishop. There, he organized a House of Prayer, bringing his unorthodox style of baptism and faith healing to all who would listen. Before long the neighbors were complaining to the police about the level of noise coming from the church building. "The ecstasies of the worshippers were audible throughout the neighborhood," reported the local newspaper. For the mass baptismal ceremonies, Grace brought his converts to area beaches and to Clark's Cove.

Dressed in suits of bright purple, chartreuse, and yellow with four-inch-long manicured fingernails painted in similar colors, this cult figure rose to prominence almost overnight. Sweet Daddy became more and more extravagant as the numbers in his flock swelled and as he began to amass hundreds of thousands of dollars. On the subject of race, he declared, "I am a colorless man. I am a colorless bishop. Sometimes I am black, sometimes white. I preach to all races." This statement was made in an article from *Ebony* magazine entitled "America's Richest Negro Minister." Shortly after his death in 1960, a writer for the *Boston Globe* proclaimed that he "was easily the most effective evangelist money-maker of all time." Among his many teachings was the singular claim that God first came to America in 1900 when Sweet Daddy immigrated here.[66]

While the House of Prayer drew some Cape Verdean members, most of the immigrants remained faithful to the Catholic religion. Their allegiance was motivated in part by a desire to hold on to a tradition distinct from the largely Protestant African American religious experience. Despite white Portuguese attempts to disclaim them, whenever possible, first-generation Cape Verdeans presented themselves as Portuguese-Americans to the larger society.

This social identity was not only reserved for the public. Most of the immigrants felt much more in common with the other Portuguese groups than they did with the African Americans. Although clearly an Afro-Portuguese people, they had learned, over four hundred years of Portuguese rule, to identify with the colonizer. In addition, they had historically served in the role of colonial agents on the Guinea coast, in some cases as middlemen in the slave trade and then, after slavery was abolished, as administrators, teachers, and missionaries. The positions they held in the service of the Portuguese led the Cape Verdeans to look down on the local African population. European influence pervaded their daily life both on the islands and in the African colonies.

Moreover, in *Crioulo,* the word for "Negro," *blac,* has the same insulting connotation as "nigger." No Cape Verdean, no matter what the color of his skin or status in the society, would choose to be described as such. Thus, they arrived in this country with a complex and unique history as both the victims and perpetrators of Portuguese colonialism, who shared a physical resemblance and ancestral link with the existing black population (although some individuals could easily pass for white Portuguese) but who held a predominantly Portuguese self-concept.

A study done of the black communities in New Haven, Connecticut, before World War II depicted the Cape Verdean residents holding themselves aloof from the African American population: "The Portuguese have an even stronger tendency to live elsewhere than in Negrotown. They scarcely appear at all in Negro society and, despite their pigmentation, often deny that they are Negroes. These foreigners mingle with the other immigrants in industrial wards or are found elsewhere in run-down sections."[67]

Likewise, young Cape Verdeans in New Bedford were strongly discouraged by their parents from socializing with the West End people of color:

> We had rivalries between the Cape Verdeans in the South End and the American colored in the West End. Your mother couldn't see you going around with a girl from the West End. And their people couldn't see their daughter going with a guy from the South End, a Cape Verdean, Portuguese. We had that funny feeling we were better than they were. And they thought they were better than we were. . . . You'd get a beating if they catch you talking to one of them. We were all black but they thought there was a difference back then. We wouldn't go into the West End for nothing. There were fights every Saturday night.[68]

The following recollection further describes the conflict that existed between the two groups: "When I was a boy . . . I can recall that whatever kids' fights we got into—you know, group against group—were with the American Negro kids. I guess we tried hard to distinguish ourselves from them. It wasn't until some of us left this community in war time and really experienced, in the South and elsewhere, what it was like to be a "person of color" in this country that we began to identify at all with American Negroes."[69] West End blacks also participated in maintaining the territorial separation, "County Street was the boundary—we wouldn't go South and they wouldn't come West."[70]

Jenks reported that as early as 1924 the leaders of the Cape Verdean community in New Bedford began to prefer the designation of "Cape Verdean" to describe their ethnicity rather than being classed as Portuguese and certainly as an alternative to being known as black Portuguese.[71] This marked the beginning of the long-standing pursuit by various members of the Cape Verdean American community over the years to be recognized by the wider society as a distinct ethnic group with a specific cultural heritage. Not until many years later, on the 1980 federal census forms, was it even possible for Cape Verdean Americans to officially identify themselves as such.

While the endurance of Cape Verdean customs and rituals among the immigrants to the United States was not an exclusively urban phenomenon, a large enough cluster of Cape Verdean settlers converged in the city of New Bedford to establish a viable *Crioulo* subculture. For certain festivals and holidays, those who resided in outlying areas would congregate in the city to celebrate. As Belmira Nunes Lopes put it, "We who lived on the Cape thought of New Bedford as the capital of Cape Cod. We had gone there in our youth to the theaters because the largest theaters were there. We went there frequently for the Christmas holidays because that's where they sang the best *reis*"[72] (traditional *Crioulo* caroling). The survival of the *Crioulo* language, with its accompanying distinctive art forms from the oral tradition such as the *morna*, has contributed significantly to a definition of Cape Verdean culture, but other *Crioulo* remnants were transplanted to this country as well.

The traditional island cuisine has been mentioned in several different contexts as a mark of Cape Verdean American ethnicity. Whether living in the rural areas or in the city, these recipes were not only part of the daily menu for the immigrant family, but they appeared on the table at any of the social gatherings, whether it be a christening, kitchen dance, *festa*, or wake. And the responsibility for preparation of customary *Crioulo* dishes did not fall solely within the women's domain. Cape Verdean mariners were so often employed as cooks that once on shore they brought these talents back with them. The dedication in the recently published *Cozinha de Cabo Verde. . . . A Cape Verdean-American Cookbook* reads "to all the Cape Verdean merchant marine cooks both living and deceased. It has been through the superb cooking of our merchant seamen that the Cape Verdean cuisine has become well known and enjoyed world-wide."

Similarly, the original sound of *Crioulo* music, its nostalgic melodies as well as the folkloric dance tunes, would most certainly be heard on these festive occasions. Many of the newcomers had transported their musical instruments from the old country, primarily fiddles, violas, guitars, and mandolins forming small three- or four-piece bands when they arrived here, performing the familiar music at social events. In later years, brass instruments and the accordion were also added to the harmony.

Sometimes in the process of relocating, modification of the original cultural forms took place. For example, the ingredients used to prepare the popular *jagacida* changed once the immigrants settled here. In the Cape Verdes, corn and beans were used, while in the United States as part of the trend away from using the *pilon* to grind corn (the *pilon* is more symbolic of Africa) the dish is made with rice and beans and the name has been shortened to simply *jag*. Musical forms with African-based rhythms such as those derived from the ceremonies of the *batuque* and the *tabanca* barely survived with the first generation of immigrants since they were native to the island of São Tiago, from which fewer immigrants originated. Furthermore, the lyrics were an expression of the autonomous ex-slave communities indigenous to the São Tiago mountains and a threat to the Portuguese colonizers who proceeded to outlaw them. Traditionally, in the *batuque*, women used cloth wadded up in a ball as well as the *pilon* as percussion instruments to accompany the dancing and singing. The movements were often quite sensual, resulting in both the church and the government discouraging the dances. Only since Cape Verdean Independence has there been a revival of interest in these art forms. However, the melodies and lyrics with European roots have been enthusiastically passed on to this country, though not without some transformation resulting in Americanized versions of traditional pieces. For example, adaptation of the *mornas* to the sound of swing bands among the second generation was apparently especially startling to the ears of the older members of the community.[73]

One popular *festa* that is still alive today in New Bedford and Providence is the *Canta-Reis,* a celebration to welcome the New Year. A small group of musicians roams through the neighborhood serenading from house to house with traditional *Crioulo* tunes. There is a special song that is first played outside the door and translated as, "Won't you please open the door for *Canta-Reis?*" The carolers are invited inside for more singing and to partake of the customary food, usually *canja* or *gufongo* (cornmeal crullers) and spirits before moving on to the next awaiting household. According to one performer, "I can remember when we used to visit as many as seventy-five houses in one night. Many of the Cape Verdean people had altars inside, with statues of saints and candles and traditional green leaves and grass. Back then we would play the songs in front of the altar."[74]

Another cultural survival that derived from the religious tradition is the ceremonial raising of a *Mastro* (mast) at the feast of a saint. A structure resembling the mast of a sailing ship is built, with fruit, baked goods, and candy attached. Children especially enjoy this ritual, with the daring older ones attempting to climb the *Mastro* in order to pluck off the goodies, while the rest await its being lowered before scrambling to snatch the treats. The custom is typically carried out on the feast days of Saint John and Saint Anthony. As one Cape Verdean American described it, "the *Mastro* is like the mast of a schooner that goes from island to island, bringing food and supplies. It's a joyous event and everyone gets involved."[75]

The rich tradition of Cape Verdean folklore has been preserved in this country through informal gatherings, particularly for the children, in which the tales, especially of *Nho Lobo,* the lazy wolf, were repeated over and over again by a storyteller, much to the delight of the young listeners. A Cape Verdean game known as *ouri,* which fascinated the youngsters as well, was also a familiar activity in the neighborhood. The game, played with beans, seeds, or marbles on a wooden board and akin to checkers or chess, is actually over three thousand years old and originated in Northern Africa: Julia Cabral reminisced: "I used to watch them play when I was a kid. They used seeds. I remember watching this man when I was a little girl. He was from Praia. He must have brought the game with him to the house because everytime he got ready to go home, he'd always put the board under his arm to take home. I used to like to play with the little seeds but I'd get a slap on the hand. I learned to play though, by watching."[76]

Weddings, wakes, and baptismal ceremonies also continued to incorporate rituals derived from the old-country traditions. Just as was the case in the islands, the occasion of a baptism could end up being a two-day event. As was mentioned earlier, fictive kin figured strongly in the Cape Verdean familial structure, and the attention given to this ceremony was symbolic of the continued importance attached to the godparent role. Matrimony was also celebrated in traditional ways and could be quite an extravagant affair:

One of the special times of our lives was the wedding of a relative. My aunt got married just like they do in the old country. A real Cape Verdean wedding is really something. . . . They prepared for weeks ahead for the traditional meal. Another of our relatives who played the violin and had a band provided the music. Traditionally, your baptismal Godmother served as Maid or Matron of Honor and the Godfather as Best Man. . . . After the wedding, they had a custom of walking home or getting out of the car or horse and buggy about half a mile from the house and walking the rest of the way while music was played. They were met at the door by their parents and welcomed as "Mr. and Mrs." It was so nice, the mixed emotions of tears and happiness. . . . My mother and dad, who was a chef, prepared the wedding meal. We had *canja,* a kind of chicken in rice, for everyone, especially for the men who had celebrated a little too much. The bride and groom left for their honeymoon. Two weeks later we returned for another house party, this time for the cutting of the wedding cake and the opening of gifts We sure know how to put on a party![77]

The wakes were equally significant occasions that lasted three days and became large family gatherings. An abundance of food and drink was on hand as some of the mourners would stay up for the duration of the event. A traditional form of wailing for the deceased, known as the *guiza,* was also transmitted to this country. It is a mournful lament usually led by a woman who is closely related to the person who has died. As she chants in tribute to the departed loved one, her emotional expression of grief spills over into uncontrolled weeping and elicits from others around her a refraining chorus of sobs. Belmira Nunes Lopes elaborated on this tradition:

Every wake was also an occasion for the whole community's getting together to mourn the dead for several days in succession. . . . Neighbors would cook *canja* or bake and fry dozens of *bufongos* to have with coffee. Wine was passed around and sometimes stronger drinks for the men. There would be the expected wailing on the part of the women. Some of the wailers sounded as if they were singing a sort of monotonous religious chant. Almost always, there was a leader with a reputation for crying the best *guiza.* She had to have a good, strong voice, carry a tune, and at the same time, improvise, citing the

merits of the deceased as she chanted. The wake was no success
without her. After midnight, the storytelling began.[78]

In addition to the gatherings and festivities that derived from the
traditional cultural and religious forms, Cape Verdean expressions of
ethnicity in New Bedford were realized through casual as well as formal
association in organized clubs, mutual aid societies, athletic events, and
neighborhood get-togethers. Part of the incentive for the formation of
these social clubs, much like the founding of the OLOA, stemmed
from the lack of acceptance in the Portuguese associations.

The oldest Cape Verdean organization in the United States, the Cape
Verdean Beneficent Association, was founded in New Bedford in 1916.
The Beneficent Association was a classic example of immigrant societies
in the period before the passage of Social Security legislation, providing
its membership both companionship and emergency economic benefits,
particularly in cases of sickness and death. In addition to affording
mutual assistance in the form of financial as well as emotional support
in times of need, it had an important social function.

Another established institution in the South End community is the
Cape Verdean Ultramarine Band Club, which began in 1917 and is still
active today. Organized less for mutual aid and more for socializing,
the club would host popular bands, hold weekly dances, sponsor beauty
contests and fashion shows, and serve as a recreational facility and
drinking establishment for its many members. The Ultramarine Band,
for which it was named, was a marching ensemble comprised of some
thirty musicians playing brass and percussion instruments. They were
featured in local parades and at outdoor social events and traveled as
well to other Cape Verdean communities in New England to perform.
As one current officer has remarked: "The club originated out of need
and stays together out of love."[79]

Some of the social organizations were intentionally structured to
bring together immigrants from the same island and would be composed
solely of island natives, such as the Brava club and the São Vicente
Sporting Club. The Ladies Auxillary was made up primarily of women
from São Nicolau.

Another popular social form, which was more informally constituted,
was known as the kitchen dance. Held in people's homes, musicians
playing stringed instruments would entertain as the guests danced to
the *Crioulo* tunes for hours on end. Again, *canja* and other traditional
dishes were served. Not only were the dances a sanctioned setting for
the young people to meet and engage in courtship rituals but they also

functioned, when necessary, as a form of mutual assistance, known as "rent" or "dime parties."

Some of the young men of the South End, however, preferred to congregate on the streets instead. Julia Cabral remembered well the "Walnut Street" gang: "In the '20s, they'd all hang out on Walnut Street. They were the Walnut Street boys. You wouldn't want to walk by them, you'd walk down Purchase Street instead. The police would routinely come and break it up."[80]

An unlikely activity that drew many Cape Verdean participants was the game of cricket. The link here is through those who immigrated from the island of São Vicente, the location for many years of a British coaling station that brought the local population into contact with English workers living there. The Cape Verdean players in New Bedford were repeated winners in this traditionally English sport. Most of the intramural teams were organized on the basis of nationality, and year after year the Cape Verdeans, sponsored by the Beneficent Association, captured the championship. "Tote" Cabral recalled, "The Cape Verdeans had a damn good cricket team with some very good players. They were in a league and they used to win a lot of trophies. Mostly those from São Vicente played it. When they would win, they would have parades throughout the Cape Verdean neighborhood."[81] When ships would come in with foreign sailors, the local Cape Verdean team would also challenge them to cricket matches.

There was a Cape Verdean baseball team as well in New Bedford, which regularly played teams on the Cape and in the Wareham area. One of the city's most outstanding athletes, perhaps the best in New Bedford, was a Cape Verdean man, George Michaels, who played basketball, football, and baseball. He was also one of the first Cape Verdean Americans to graduate from high school in the city, but racism barred Michaels—like many other nonwhite athletes of that time—from joining the ranks of the professional ballplayers. "Those were the days when they didn't take too many colored in the big leagues, so he went into the colored league," explained "Tote" Cabral who had been Michaels' boxing trainer.[82]

Once outside the Cape Verdean enclave in New Bedford, which served as a buffer to the racism of the wider society, the immigrants, as exemplified by the experience of George Michaels, were to face a more stern reality. The immigrant generation had been primarily concerned with physical and economic survival accomplished, in part, through the re-creation of a vibrant *Crioulo* community in southeastern New England. While they may have encountered racial intolerance, they could retreat to the safety of the ethnic neighborhood. For the initial group of settlers, social identity was more clearly constructed in ethnic terms. The principal shift was from an island to a broader Cape Verdean identification. Still, most simply thought of themselves as belonging to a global Portuguese civilization, negating any affiliation with African peoples, and were able, for the most part, to keep that assignation intact.

By the 1930s, a combination of factors including the trade and legal restrictions on immigration as well as the economic effects of the Depression led to the close of the packet trade. Thus the integral links of communication to the islands weakened dramatically. The first generation had been insulated by both the protective boundaries of the New Bedford enclave and the strength of the tie to the archipelago. Typically, for the males the turning point was World War II, when many left the sheltering New England region to train and serve in the military. Whatever the route, the second and third generations have been forced to reshape new identities often through a process that has reflected tremendous personal turmoil. The concluding chapter begins to examine what happened to the Cape Verdeans of southeastern Massachusetts once they ventured beyond the geographic area and the time frame that has been the primary focus of this study.

NOTES

1. Judith A. Boss and Joseph D. Thomas, *New Bedford: A Pictoral History* (Norfolk/Virginia Beach: Denning Company Publishers, 1983), p. 160.

2. Boss and Thomas, *New Bedford*, p. 150; Seymour Louis Wolfbein, *The Decline of a Cotton Textile City: A Study of New Bedford* (1944, rpt. New York: AMS Press, 1968).

3. Lobban's obituary analysis shows a similar spread in differential emigration to New Bedford from the various islands. Richard Lobban, "Patterns of Cape Verdean Migration and Social Association: History through Obituary Analysis," *New England Journal of Black Studies* 5 (5 Nov. 1985): 32. His figures based on 777 cases are as follows: Brava—43.3 percent; São Nicolau 17.1 percent; Fogo 16.5 percent; Other Islands—16 percent.

4. Interview with Carrie Pina by Ron Barboza.

5. Interview with Antonio "Tote" Cabral, Jan. 4, 1985.

6. Whitney, p. 11.

7. Interview with Lucillia Lima, 25 Jan. 1984.

8. Susan Sharf, "The Cape Verdeans of Providence" (Honors thesis, Brown University, 1965), p. 17.

9. John "Toy" Fernandes quoted in Sam Beck, *From Cape Verde to Providence,* p. 23.

10. Interview with Antonio "Tote" Cabral, 4 Jan. 1985.

11. June Dicker, "Kinship and Ritual Kinship among Cape Verdeans in Providence" (Master's thesis, Brown University, 1968), p. 19.

12. Interview with Diana Duarte, 21 Feb. 1985.

13. "Immigrants in New Bedford" (Ms., New Bedford Free Public Library, 1911), p. 14.

14. Interview with Antonio "Tote" Cabral, 4 Jan. 1985.

15. Armentine Jackson quoted in Beck, *From Cape Verde to Providence,* p. 13.

16. *Morning Mercury,* 25 Aug. 1900, p.12.

17. Quoted in Sam Beck, "Manny Almeida's Ringside Lounge: The Cape Verdean Struggle for Their Neighborhood" (Ms., 1981), p. 93.

18. John "Toy" Fernandes quoted in Beck, *From Cape Verde to Providence,* p. 23.

19. Ibid., pp. 26–29.

20. Dorothy C. Poole, "Antone Fortes, Whaleman," *Duke County Intelligencer,* 2 May 1970, p. 133.

21. Interview with Antonio "Tote" Cabral, 4 Jan. 1985.

22. Joseph Ramos quoted in *Spinner* II, pp. 108–109.

23. One exception was Cape Verdean ownership of a fishing boat by the Fortes brothers in the 1940s. Thanks to Ron Barboza for this clarification.

24. Interview with Antonio Tote Cabral, 16 Oct. 1985.

25. Interview with Julia Cabral, 15 Oct. 1985.

26. Interview with Mary Santos Barros, 7 Nov. 1985.

27. Interview with Lucillia Lima, 25 Jan. 1984.

28. Interview with Antonio "Tote" Cabral, 16 Oct. 1985.

29. Interview with Antonia Enos, 3 Jan. 1985.

30. Interview with Julia Cabral, 16 Oct. 1985.

31. Lucillia Lima quoted in *Spinner* I, p. 93.

32. Inteview with Maria Lima Barros, 27 Apr. 1983.

33. Interview with Antonia Enos, 3 Jan. 1985.

34. Albert Ernest Jenks, "New Englanders Who Came from Afric Isles," *Dearborn Independent,* 27 Dec. 1924, p. 5.

35. Joyce Maccarone and John Andrade, "The History of the South Central Historic District" (Ms. for the Office of Historic Preservations, New Bedford, Dec., 1978), p. 54.

36. Wolfbein, *Decline of a Cotton Textile City,* pp. 44–47.

37. Boss and Thomas, *New Bedford,* p. 184.

38. Interview with Antonio "Tote" Cabral, 16 Oct. 1985.

39. Letter to the editor from Jose Duarte Ramos, *CVN,* 16–31 Aug. 1985, p. 2.

40. Interview with Joaquim Pina, 26 Jan. 1984.

41. Interview with Lucillia Lima, 25 Jan. 1984.

42. Interview with Julia Cabral, 16 Oct. 1985.

43. Jenks, "Cranberry Bogs," 3 Jan. 1925, p. 9.

44. Raymond Anthony Almeida, *Cape Verdeans in America: Our Story* (Boston: American Committee for Cape Verde, 1978), p. 35.

45. Nunes, *A Portuguese Colonial in America,* p. 55. She adds, "They named the scholarship 'The Seaman's Fund' because, at that time, one of the ships that carried Cape Verdeans to and from the Cape Verde Islands met with disaster at sea, and all the men were lost."

46. Conversation with Ron Barboza.

47. Elsie Clews Parsons, "Folk-Lore of the Cape Verde Islanders," *Journal of American Folklore* 34, no. 131 (Jan.–Mar. 1921): 94.

48. Nunes, *A Portuguese Colonial in America,* p. 35.

49. William P. Dillingham, "Recent Immigrants in Agriculture," in *Immigrants in Industries: Report of the Immigration Commission,* 22:551.

50. Interview with Antonio "Tote" Cabral, 16 Oct. 1985.

51. Interview with Jose Flore Livramento videotaped by Ron Barboza.

52. See, for example, Theodate Geoffrey Suckanesset, *A History of Falmouth* (Falmouth: Falmouth Publishing Co., 1928), p. 152–53; Agnes Rothery, *Cape Cod: New and Old* (Boston: Houghton Mifflin, 1918), pp. 48–51; Rothery, *Family Album* (Dodd, Mead, 1942), pp. 43–45; Katherine Smith and Edith Shay, *Down Cape Cod* (New York: Robert M. McBride, 1936), pp. 26–27; Millard C. Faugh, *Falmouth, Mass.* (New York: Columbia University Press, 1945), pp. 151–52.

53. Deirdre Meintel Machado, "Cape Verdean–Americans: Their Culture and Historical Background" (Ph.D. diss., Brown University, 1978); Machado, "Cape Verdean Americans," in *Hidden Minorities,* ed. Joan Rollins (Washington D.C.: University Press of America, 1981), pp. 234–36.

54. Eugenia Fortes quoted in Colin Nickerson, "Black, white or Cape Verdean?" *Boston Globe,* 30 Sept. 1983, p. 2.

55. Arnold M. Howitt and Rita Moniz, "Ethnic Identity, Political Organization and Political Structure" (Paper delivered at the 1976 Annual Meeting of the American Political Science Association, Chicago, 1976), p. 8.

56. Leo Pap, *The Portuguese-Americans* (Boston: Twayne, 1981), p. 160.

57. Machado, *Cape Verdean Americans,* p. 237

58. Interview with Antonia Baptiste Enos, 3 Jan. 1985.

59. "Church/A Igreja," *TCHUBA Newsletter,* 3, no. 5, (1978) p. 15.

60. Our Lady of the Assumption 75th Anniversary Yearbook, p. 16.

61. Interview with Antonio "Tote" Cabral, 4 Jan. 1985.

62. OLOA Yearbook, p. 18.

63. *TCHUBA Newsletter,* 3, no. 5, p. 17. DeGrace was the brother of the well-known evangelist, Daddy Grace.

64. David Tyack, "Cape Verdean Immigration to the United States" (Honors thesis, Harvard University, 1952), pp. 50–51.

65. Archibald Lyall, *Black and White Makes Brown: An Account of the Journey to the Cape Verde Islands and Portuguese Guinea* (London: Heineman, 1938), p. 151.

66. Biographical information on Daddy Grace was compiled from the following sources: Robert Lovinger, "I Am the Boyfriend of the World," *Standard Times,* 12 Jan. 1985; *Newsweek,* 15 Feb. 1960, p. 32; *New York Times,* 13 Jan. 1960; *Washington Post,* 13 Jan. 1960; Joseph R. Washington, Jr., *Black Sects and Cults* (New York, 1972), pp. 10–12, 15–16, 77, 127, 149, 158–59. "America's Richest Negro Minister," *Ebony* 7, no. 2 (Jan. 1952), pp. 17–23.

67. Robert Austin Warner, *New Haven Negroes* (New Haven: Yale University Press, 1940), p. 197.

68. Interview with Antonio "Tote" Cabral, 4 Jan. 1985.

69. Richard E. Engler, Jr., *The Challenge of Diversity* (New York : Harper and Row, 1964), p. 34.

70. Howitt and Moniz, "Ethnic Identity," p. 8.

71. Jenks, "New Englanders," p. 5.

72. Nunes, *A Portuguese Colonial in America,* p. 143.

73. Tyack, "Cape Verdean Immigration," p. 42.

74. John Barboza quoted in Rona S. Zable, "Cape Verdean Custom of Canta Rez Passes to New Generations, Places," *Providence Journal,* 31 Dec. 1981.

75. Donald Ramos in Cabral and Beck, *Nha Destino.*

76. Interview with Julia Cabral, 16 Oct. 1985.

77. Interview with Lucillia Lima, 25 Jan. 1984.

78. Nunes, *A Portuguese Colonial in America,* pp. 51–52.

79. Interview with Diana Duarte, 21 Feb. 1984.

80. Interview with Julia Cabral, 16 Oct. 1985.

81. Interview with Antonio, "Tote" Cabral, 16 Oct. 1985.

82. Ibid

Identity Matters:
The Immigrant Children

5

Vivid in the recollections of many of the men interviewed for this study was the jolt to their self-concept that was experienced during military service in World War II. For most Cape Verdean American male immigrants, joining the United States armed forces meant a first step out of the protective shelter of their enclave. This critical juncture in their lives brought them face to face with the existence of segregated troops and a wider society that did not know or care about the ethnic identity of a Cape Verdean. Most were sent to black regiments where they were forced to deal directly with the issue of race, both in terms of the racist treatment they received in the military and in having to confront the question of their own racial identification. As one Cape Verdean veteran said: "I grew up thinking of myself as brown-skinned Portuguese, not black at all. I remember telling this sergeant, a black guy, that I was Cape Verdean. He said, 'You ain't Portuguese nothing. You're a nigger.' It sounds incredibly naive, but I'd never thought of myself as black or white. I was both, and neither. I was Cape Verdean. America wants you to choose sides."[1]

Some were assigned to white units where they were not accepted either. Those Cape Verdean recruits who were sent with white regiments into the southern states found it especially painful to try to come to terms with the ambiguity of their own ethnic and racial background and the rigid racial barriers of their surroundings. The immigrants and their children had largely been raised to think of themselves as Portuguese, thus white, but once outside the ethnic community, they faced an indifferent, often hostile world that labeled them black. Interaction beyond the New England region became more problematic. Belmira Nunes Lopes sometimes handled it in this way:

My trips south have been very interesting, but I must admit that every time I went south I always acted as if I wasn't too well acquainted with the English language because I didn't want to be discriminated against on the buses and the trains. I always put on a fake accent and I always managed to get away with it. I didn't want anybody to think I was an American black because I am darker than most so-called white persons. My mother had never been mistaken for a black woman. She had been taken sometimes for an Indian, but she could never speak English well. I decided that I was going to act as if I couldn't speak English well.[2]

The social and political events of the postwar era also penetrated the cocoon of the Cape Verdean enclave. Beginning with the civil rights movement, the 1960s were watershed years for Cape Verdean Americans as the rise of black nationalism and its attendant emphasis on pride in one's African heritage had a transformative effect on many. The domestic social changes coincided with the struggles for liberation from Portuguese colonialism on the continent of Africa as well. At the time, the Cape Verde Islands in collaboration with Guinea-Bissau were engaged in a protracted armed conflict to procure their independence. They did find some support for their cause among Cape Verdean Americans but there was also much resistance to the idea of Cape Verde breaking its long-standing ties with Portugal and switching to an African-identified political and cultural ideology. The process of rethinking racial identifications touched most Cape Verdean families in this period, often creating intergenerational rifts between the parents and grandparents who were staunchly Portuguese and their children who were beginning to ally themselves with the African American struggle not only in political thought but also in cultural expression. Some, who could, would let their hair grow out into Afros; others may have dressed in colorful dashikis, much to the dismay of their Portuguese-identified parents. Writing about the 1960s, Belmira Lopes Nunes explained:

At that time, our idea of Portuguese culture was Cape Verdean culture, and that was the thing that we really wanted to stress. To us, to be Portuguese was synonymous with being Cape Verdean. . . . The Cape Verdeans have been saying they were Portuguese all along. I was brought up to believe that I was Portuguese. My parents said they were Portuguese. Whenever anybody asked us what we were because we spoke a foreign language or because we looked different from any other group, we always said that we were Portuguese. All of a sudden to be told that you are an African, I think, is a shock to most people, certainly to my generation and to many of those of this generation also, the children of Cape Verdean parents who have made their children feel that they had some reason to be proud of the Cape Verdean heritage.[3]

Perhaps the most graphic example I can give to illustrate Cape Verdean ambivalence concerning African origins is the anecdote reported to me about a woman, now middle-aged, whose Cape Verdean father, from the time she was a baby, would continually stroke her nose from the inner edges outward in a pointing motion in order to try to control its shape and development. The girl's mother was African American, and the father feared his daughter would grow up to have a nose of broad and flat contours.

Following are excerpts from the oral histories of two Cape Verdean Americans that cogently illustrate the multifarious and shifting nature of racial meanings. Both Joaquim A. "Jack" Custodio and Lucille Ramos were born in the United States, children of Cape Verdean immigrants and life-long residents in the New Bedford area. Each has a biography that has been punctuated by issues resulting from the ambiguity inherent in belonging to a nonwhite immigrant group. Both demonstrate how they and their families have been subjected to the arbitrary design of racial classification in the United States. In both accounts, the decade of the 1960s looms large. While each individual has a unique story to tell, I have selected these two life histories particularly for inclusion here because their experiences within the arena of racial-ethnic definitions have a universality among the Cape Verdean American population as I have understood it.

When I asked Jack Custodio in July of 1988, "What would you call yourself today in terms of identity?" he replied with his characteristic mixture of dead seriousness and ironic humor, "I'm black—I'm not beautiful, but I'm black. Positively black." How he arrived at this self-designation follows:

> The salient facts of my life are I was born September 6, 1914, a cold water flat, at home, as usual, all the births were in New Bedford. I was born to a Cape Verdean mother and a Cape Verdean father but it has to be noted that my mother was so fair that she could go any place whereas my father would have to get in the back of the bus. He's what we call in my own lingo, *besh roulade cavasa sec,* which means "thick lips and nappy hair" and that is still used by Cape Verdeans.
>
> The South End was the Cape Verdean ghetto but it has to be noted that in New Bedford you had the West End, which was another ghetto, these were Afro-Americans, for the most part, slaves who had

migrated north from the south, after the Civil War and there was *no* intermingling, there was no mixture, there was nothing. If you were in the West End that was it, if you were in the South End, you were in the South End. I grew up and my mother taught me to say, "Those damn niggers in the West End." I said it like any other little white boy.

This is where my identification dilemma was spawned. Because my mother always told me I was white. I went to a Cape Verdean school at which we were all treated as white officially but unofficially we got the worst teachers in regard to competence. The equipment, the material—all obsolete, the hand-me-downs from the other schools.

Now I can see it so clearly. There is a distinction. I have to bring in the white Portuguese here. The white Portuguese have been labeled *nhambobs* by Cape Verdeans. We never referred to ourselves as Portuguese in the context of the *nhambobs*. They were kept separate, not for definitions of race but that's because they were different, they were *nhambobs*. But it was a concession, I can see that so clearly now, to the fact that we, as Cape Verdeans were not white like the *nhambobs* were. Now that I look back on it, we professed to be white. If you asked me my race, I would tell you white, if you pin me down, I would tell you Cape Verdean or Portuguese. But I wouldn't do that until you pinned me down, and then, of course, I wouldn't be able to do that when I went to New Britain, Connecticut. I couldn't get away with saying Portuguese or Cape Verdean there because they didn't know either one.

But it raises the point now of identification which was, of course, cultivated by my own background and environment—I was not black. And when I went to New Britain, Connecticut, and got into fights with these Polish and Italian kids and whipped every one of them. When I left New Bedford and those kids in New Britain called me "nigger," I was outraged. How dare they call me "nigger." I know where the "niggers" are. The "niggers" are in the West End of New Bedford. And I plopped them one. That was it. And, of course, one of the advantages of growing up in the ghetto, you learned how to use your hands real quick. It's a question of survival more than anything else.

I was in the 8th grade. I must have been around 12 or 13 because I always kept pace with the norms. My mother had married again and my stepfather got a good job in Connecticut and he sent for us. I spent a year or two there and when things opened up here again in this area, we moved back because by that time my white aunt owned a house in Fairhaven [across the river from New Bedford] and she allowed us to move into the top floor of her house. I loved Fairhaven. At that time, Fairhaven was tolerant of particularly Cape Verdeans in the context of Portuguese.

Both my mother and father were born in São Vincent. My stepfather was from São Nicolau. But my stepfather could go anywhere. He and my mother made an ideal combination. They could go anywhere. My stepfather was the leader of the Cape Verdean band and they always thought that it was a *nhambob* leading the Cape Verdean band. He was a white man—every definition of the white race—the texture of his hair, the features, the coloring and he was white. I don't know anything about genetics but visibly there are a lot of Cape Verdeans that have been accepted by society as whites and once that happens then they don't want any black relatives. Both my mother and stepfather were firmly convinced in their own minds that they were white. This was not a question of passing. There was no need for them to masquerade.

There was no problem with the older people. The problem is with us who were born here. The dilemma—especially of looking black and being white. And, of course, if you looked white it was all right, but if you didn't look white, then forget about it.

So I grew up in New Bedford and when I went to New Bedford high school, I immediately found out that the cards were stacked against me. Number one, my ambition was to be an attorney. But I ended up in a commercial course. Now had my mother or my stepfather been aware of all these things, they could have advised me. Guidance counselor? I still don't know what a guidance counselor is—at my age. That was unheard of. So I ended up in a commercial course. I ended up typing, shorthand, bookkeeping, I was very good at it. I even took up French as an elective. And, you know, I did very well in French. I went through four years of high school and I didn't flunk a single subject. And I worked. If I hadn't been able to work at the Boys Club, I would never have been able to stay in high school.

Then I got out of high school—and lo and behold—talk about finding a job. That's when I began to have this dilemma of "What am I?" Because I'd call up and I'd make an appointment. I'd show up but I would never be hired. And inferior people were hired in regards to studies. And, of course, college was out of the question. I applied for a salesmen job. These magazines, you know, and they'd send me back a letter. This oil company wanted a salesman in this area. And I'll never forget the letter they sent me back. "Please send a photograph" and when I'd send a photograph and they'd send back a letter, "at this time we cannot consider hiring. We don't think your qualifications . . ."

I can't believe that. This is in the early 1930s. And it was a little more subtle but you couldn't get a job at the *Standard Times,* [the New Bedford daily newspaper]—all white. The banks—all white. I couldn't even get a job driving a cab. Do you know they didn't hire black cab drivers in those days? I tried to get a taxi driver's job in the fifties. Was already married with children. They wouldn't hire me. Union Street Railway. Safety Cab. Wouldn't hire me. And the theory behind this—white women aren't safe with black taxi drivers. Still prevails.

After I got out of high school, it was the usual series of cranberry picking, strawberries, for minimum, for non-existent wages—and dishwashing. All the chefs in this area were Cape Verdeans. That was a good job for us in that sense. We were allowed those jobs. Mills had gone out. Goodyear. Revere Copper and Brass. Even Chamberlain discriminated very blatantly against Cape Verdeans. After I left high school, I ran into all these problems. And, of course, what am I? The confusion was so disconcerting. Tell everybody I'm Cape Verdean and they'd put me in the back of the bus.

In the merchant marine in the early 30s, I was a mess boy. When I went on a ship, I found out that down south, if I were waiting for a trolley, there are two places. Colored and white. Well, I would speak Spanish, well my Portuguese, pidgeon Portuguese and Spanish, I would be with my *cumpads,* male *cumpads,* the firemen who was white, but the motor man would look at me and allow me to sit in front because I was still a Cape Verdean and I was not going to mix with quote "dem niggers." I wasn't going to do it that's all there was to it. They would view me with a suspicious eye, but they wouldn't throw me off the trolley. Then I'd get off the trolley car and I'd go uptown to a show in Newport News or Baltimore, mind you, this was in the early '30s. And they would not sell me an orchestra seat. You know, that's where I found out that that's where "Nigger Heaven" originated.

I've got to tell you this anecdote. In '38 and '39, I worked on this shrub as a relief fireman. And I had the car. And boy, it was a great thing to own a car in '38. All the other crewmen were dependent upon me for rides. From Bristol, Rhode Island, to New Bedford, we'd come home every other weekend. This was the lighthouse service, before it was taken over by the Coast Guard. Well, this guy, God bless his soul, Mach—Seraphim Olivera, Brava, typical Brava who would not identify. Strictly white. We made an agreement. We went to the show in Providence and the agreement was, use my car, my gas but he'd pay for the ticket. And he always prided himself on the fact that he was white. He used to tell me, "I won't go to the show with you—you're too black." He used to tell me this. Mind you, we were supposed to be friends. Of course, he resented the fact that— we had boxing gloves out there and every time we put on the gloves, I would kick the living daylights out of him. And I would do it deliberately, you see, because of his Brava feeling of being superior. We went to this show in Providence. Providence longshoremen told me this afterwards, but this show was notorious for not admitting blacks or Cape Verdeans downstairs. They still had the "nigger heaven" bit. So Mach went up—Mach was his nickname. *Mach* means male. Mach went up to the box and the woman didn't see me. And he asked for two orchestras. "Oh, no, no, no, there was vaudeville on. They're all sold out." So we went upstairs. Unknowing and innocent of the custom of the theater management. We get upstairs and lo and behold, downstairs is vacant. I told Mach, they won't let colored people sit downstairs. He says (all of this in *Crioulo*), "You are colored; I'm not colored." I says, "Well, you bought the tickets." He says, "Animal, the lady must have seen you. And refused to sell me the tickets." Now, I was out of the vision of the lady. I got hysterical. And all this was in his dialect. There he is, he bought the tickets but he's blaming me. He was so embarrassed and humiliated because they refused to accept him as white, which he was. That is a typical Cape Verdean story.

The feeling of animosity between the West End and the South End led to fights. The white Portuguese never, never accepted us in any way, shape or form except they'd do it on superficial basis. We had our own separate little areas. Cape Verdean Band Club, St. Vincent's Sporting Club. And if you weren't Cape Verdean. God forbid, if you married *American d'cor* [pejorative term for African American]. If my mother were alive right now knowing that both of my surviving daughters have married Afro-Americans, my mother would turn over in her grave.

You know, I had an inferiority complex when I was a kid. Of the three sisters' children, me and George were the ugly ones. It had nothing to do with shade. In fact some of my cousins were darker than me. We were nappy headed. It had nothing to do with color. My hair was considered *pret corvasa sec*. They had good hair and even though they may have been darker, their features were better. I was considered ugly and so was George—based on appearance and the texture of the hair.

So eventually, I lived in New Bedford. Public housing came into

existence and I applied for it and was accepted. And Bay Village from
Walnut Street right down to Canon Street was all Cape Verdean except
for two Afro-American families. From Canon Street all the way down
to Grinnell Street was all white. So then I found out, among other
things that they violated the pact, which meant this was Cape Verdean,
why did they have those two Afro-American families in there. Now,
this was in the forties. Which goes to show you the feeling I still
retained — this Cape Verdeanism — even then. In the 1940s, I had to
be in my thirties. I still resented Afro-Americans being brought into
my neighborhood. I still had that in-bred inferiority.

By the time of the "searing" sixties, I had started to change. By
that time I had bumped into Duncan Dottin, a sociologist from
Cambridge, an Afro-American who lived in the West End. He was
fascinated. Here he is talking to me and I'm calling him a "nigger"
and here I am telling him I'm white. One thing I've got to give Duncan
credit for, Duncan has never, never held this against me. He knew
my background. But God bless the man. He knew my potential. He
was able to develop it. If I've got to the stage now where I'm fairly
articulate and fairly knowledgeable, its due to the fact that Duncan
was the springboard.

I'll never forget the time when he said something about Langston
Hughes and I said to him, "Who's Langston Hughes?" He wanted
to hit me. I began to recognize one thing, while I was not a "nigger"
and I was Cape Verdean, they didn't accept Cape Verdeans and the
more and more I looked around — you know the minute you hit
School Street [the Cape Verdean neighborhood in New Bedford] you
know where you are. I don't give a damn what they say, I don't give
a damn if they speak a foreign tongue. You know they're not white.
And if you're not white, man, in this country you've got to be black
and when I say black — it is in the context of the oppression, the
subjugation. So, who am I kidding?[4]

Lucille Ramos, mother of four and foster-mother of twenty-five
children, has an intergenerational outlook on the Cape Verdean dilemma of social identity:

Being a Cape Verdean is special to me and to my children even
more so — because we're a potpourri really, we're a mixture of people.
I think we have both European and African influence. When I was
younger our country was still ruled by the Portuguese government,
we, we've gone through changes, you know. When we were young
we were Portuguese because that was our mother country, and then
we went through the Black part of our lives in the sixties. And now

I think we finally know who and what we are, which is Cape Verdean, and it is something special. And we are different, we're different from the American Blacks and we're different from the Whites. We've taken from both cultures, and that makes us unique.

With the kids, I remember the first time I knew they were proud of being Cape Verdean was when they had clubs, in high school, like International Food and they would ask everyone for ethnic foods, and right away the kids wanted to bring in Cape Verdean dishes. When they were young it wasn't so important, but they began to have more pride as they grew older. When we were young we didn't really know that much about Cape Verdeanism. People just classified us as Portuguese because we were a Portuguese colony. Now since 1975 when Cape Verde gained its independence, I think it's become much more important to us, and in particular to our children.

Here in New Bedford, you know, we just kind of accepted the fact that we were Cape Verdean and that everybody knew what that meant. But when Cape Verdeans began to go away from the community, they began to have problems.

For instance, one of my sons was in the R.O.T.C. and they travel a lot. Everywhere he went he would say, "My name is Ramos," and everybody thought he was Spanish. And he would say, "No, I'm Cape Verdean." "What's a Cape Verdean?" they would all ask, so it became a thing to be able to tell them where the islands were, that we had our own language and dialect, had our own foods, music and culture.

The older people may still say "We're Portuguese." That is how they were raised. But I think the New Bedford Portuguese always objected to us saying we were Portuguese, because they felt we really weren't. . . .

In the sixties we had lots of problems here locally with the labels "Black" and "White." You see, up till then the kids identified themselves as Cape Verdean. But at that point they had to take a stand, especially in high school. You were either Black or you were White, there was no in-between. So you had to decide then, "Am I a Black or am I a White?" And nobody wanted to hear whether you were a Cape Verdean or not. It was just Black or White. The kids had a difficult time then because they had to make that decision.

People may not understand this, but it was very difficult because Cape Verdeans come in shades from pure white to ebony black. For instance when my kids were going to the Greene school [a New Bedford public school in the South End], the teacher would identify the child's race by looking at him. I had three sons all in the school at the same time. I was a carpet joke because I have three sons three shades; and one teacher identified one boy as Black, one teacher identified one as White, and one was identified as Mulatto. So I have three children identified as three different races.

But this kind of confusion was not unusual for me. I'm the fourth child in my family. I have three brothers older, and four of us were delivered by one doctor, and four of us delivered by another. In those days it was not the parent who determined the race — and you know how race goes on your birth certificate? Well, when my brothers went into the service their race was listed as Caucasian. So when I went for my marriage license, I remember the woman there said, "What is your race?" and I said "Caucasian," because I had just assumed I was listed Caucasian too. I remember this very distinctly because the place was crowded at the time, and she went and took out my birth certificate and said, in a very haughty voice "You're not Caucasian, you're colored!" and I said, "Whatever, my brothers were Caucasian." She said, "They must have had different fathers." I said, "No, we all have the same mother and father." She said, "That's impossible." But it was very true, and as far as I know, it is still true that the doctor who delivers the child names the child's race. And the amazing thing was the white doctor listed the children as Caucasian and the Cape Verdean doctor listed the children as Colored.

But my mother and father had no idea what we were listed as until we had to go and get our papers. My husband, who's half and half, was listed as Caucasian in the service. We married when he got out of the service. We went to Dartmouth for his papers, and they said, "What is your race?" and he said, "Caucasian," and they went and said, "You're a Mulatto, you're a mixed breed, your father is a Cape Verdean and your mother is White." So you know you run into these kinds of things.

I remember when my children were born that was a big thing for me. I told the doctor right at the beginning. "I will identify their race, not you." He said, "Fine, you do the whole thing," and it was funny because, with all the trouble my husband and I went through, we could now choose — and these were the choices — it was either Black, White, or Mulatto. We chose Mulatto. It became a crisis for them in the sixties, though, when they had to make a choice. Especially so when you had several kids in the family and one was light and one was dark, because — to us it meant nothing, but to the White person it meant something, or to the person who identified as Black it meant something.

I think the majority of the kids now are coming around to saying they are Cape Verdean. But if it is a choice of identifying White or

Black, I think they would choose Black. I think it was more difficult for the older ones, the parents and the grandparents, to accept that their children identified as Black. Some of the kids were even dropping the Cape Verdean altogether and it was just Black. There was lots of peer pressure and they felt you couldn't be in-between, you had to be one or the other, and if the color of your skin wasn't pure white, that didn't give you much choice to begin with anyway.

But it was very difficult for the parents and grandparents to accept this. Take my father-in-law for instance. He is an extremely dark man, and looking at him there would be no doubt in your mind that this is a Black man. But he does not consider himself a Black man. He was born on the Cape Verdean islands. He is now in his eighties, and he considers himself Portuguese—he does not identify as Cape Verdean. He is Portuguese and Portuguese is White. Do you know the ridicule that a Black man faces when he says, "I'm White, I'm Portuguese."

But you see the kids were not going to be ridiculed that way. They knew what they were, and the thing is, they have been able to accept the pride in it, which is the important thing. Whereas for the older people being White meant being—special. They didn't want to be in the minority. But our kids don't feel that way, they're Black and they're proud. That came about in the sixties. And I think they realize that "Well, I may be Black but I am Cape Verdean and I have my own culture within the Black, and I can be as proud of that as being Black."

So they've gone through a lot of changes, which we have as well, as parents. So racially I think we've had our difficulties, and I think our children still have difficulties, although not so many now.[5]

Over the years, whenever I made a public address on the topic of Cape Verdean immigration, or when my work was covered in the media, invariably I received telephone calls in response from interested Cape Verdeans. While the callers represented divergent backgrounds, their reasons for getting in touch with me were generally of two kinds. Most commonly, the individual wanted to make sure that I, the non–Cape Verdean, *really* did understand what a Cape Verdean is. For example, one woman was particularly adamant about my recognizing that there are white Cape Verdeans too. The rest of the callers were themselves typically in the process of trying to figure out who they *really* are and were looking for a sympathetic outsider's ear. This was the case for a young Cape Verdean woman from California who was frustrated in her attempts to try to educate her classmates about who she was and

was not getting much help from home because she was African-identified and her mother would not accept this position. Matters of identity
are especially troubling in the adolescent years.

I have always welcomed these generous attempts to communicate
with me and I have tried my best here to present the complex construction of Cape Verdean identity with as much accuracy as possible.
Whether or not I have succeeded, I can say with utmost certainty that
what has been consistent in the voices of the Cape Verdeans that I
have heard is a common need to address, to discuss, to figure out these
questions of identity. For the Cape Verdean American, social identity
can never be assumed and is never a given. Rather, the issue is continually being reformulated, sometimes at critical personal cost. Most
often, the individuals see their struggles in personal terms, blaming
themselves or other Cape Verdeans for the psychological strain that
results from feeling invisible or not belonging. However, the phenomenon is so intrinsic to the Cape Verdean experience in America that
it is best to speak of the quest within a sociological framework. The
crisis in racial-ethnic meanings, the clash and confusion, result from
having to juxtapose one's adaptation to new cultural norms within the
suffocating strictures of racial categorization in American society. Perhaps Belmira Nunes Lopes, in her autobiography's closing chapter titled,
"Looking Back: Reflections on Life, Race, Ethnicity and Womanhood,"
elucidated these dynamics most clearly when she pronounced:

> I believe in struggling with other minority groups to get justice for
> all of us, but nevertheless, within this struggle with other minority
> groups, I want to be recognized as my group struggling with other
> groups for the rights of all minorities of my color.
>
> It is more a question of having my culture recognized as opposed
> to the whole blanket viewing of all non-white people as black. I
> belong to a black sorority, and I like the Afro-Americans immensely,
> but I just don't happen to be an Afro-American, and I want people
> to recognize me for what I am. I guess I am just proud of what I
> am, and I do not want to have people think that I am anything else.
> If when people ask me if I am black, the answer is yes, I'm black. If
> anybody who has African blood is black, I am black because there
> is no question about the fact that I have African blood in me. The
> very fact that my ancestors come from islands so close to the African
> continent, the fact that so very many of the people who were brought
> there were from the continent of Africa, the fact that I am the color
> I am, how can I deny that I have African blood in me? It is evident.
> It is something that you can see, and you cannot deny it. Nevertheless,

I want to be recognized as a person with a distinct culture. It is a blend of many races and many cultures dominated by the culture of Portugal. In keeping with the tendency in American society nowadays for ethnic groups to reclaim their roots, this is precisely what I feel Cape Verdeans are doing. It is the basis from which Cape Verdeans are going forward and asking to be recognized as a minority group.[6]

Despite movement outside of their insular neighborhoods, traditional Cape Verdean culture has persisted among the settlers in the United States. One reason for the level of cultural retention has been the failure of the host society to adequately define and assimilate the Cape Verdean immigrant group. Another is the extent of reciprocal communication between Cape Verdean Americans and those remaining on the Islands, such as travel back and forth, the *mantenhas,* and material exchanges. Finally, the long span of migration, which continues to the present, has sustained and replenished the cultural legacy despite decades of curtailment due to restrictive immigration laws.

Yet, it is an oversimplification to conceive of the Cape Verde Islands as an eternal spring that is an ever flowing source of cultural influences. Of course, the culture and society of the Cape Verde islands are not static either. Indeed, Cape Verdean Americans are active participants in the evolution of Cape Verdean island culture—the result of complex interrelationships between the Cape Verdes and emigrant communities around the world. For example, remittances from Cape Verdeans living and working in the United States are such an important source of income for many households in the Islands that they can even be said to make possible, to a significant extent, the very preservation of Cape Verdean society and culture.

As Cape Verdean Americans have moved to other areas of the country, southeastern New England has continued to play a central role in the endurance of *Crioulo* culture on this side of the Atlantic. For all its obscurity, the Republic of Cape Verde has closer ties, particularly of kinship, with the United States in general, and New England in particular, than any nation of black Africa. Nearly as many Cape Verdeans live in Massachusetts, Rhode Island, and Connecticut as on the islands themselves.

To signify the special quality of this bond, the Cape Verdean government, shortly after gaining its independence, presented to the United States the gift of the historic schooner *Ernestina,* the last Cape Verdean packet in existence. It arrived ceremoniously in 1982 at its home in the port of New Bedford with these words from the Ambassador to the United States:

For Cape Verdeans forced by centuries of drought and the politics of colonialism to leave our Islands and make new lives in distant lands, the Schooner ERNESTINA is a symbol of the interdependence which binds us together as one people, united in our relationship to our common reference point, the Cape Verde Islands.

For over a century, the people of Cape Verde have looked to the people of America as a reliable partner whenever we found ourselves caught in the death grip of drought. Our hope is that the ERNESTINA will serve as a tangible symbol of these historic ties and our continuing people-to-people partnership.[7]

The vessel, built in 1894 and named the *Effie M. Morrissey*, had been a fishing schooner and an Arctic exploration ship before it was purchased in 1948 by Henrique Mendes, a native of Fogo. In 1898 at the age 18, Mendes emigrated to the United States by jumping aboard a schooner bound for New Bedford. Once arrived, his occupational history of shoveling coal, shipping out on a whaler, picking cranberries, and working as a deckhand on coastal vessels was classical for a young Cape Verdean man at that time. But Mendes was also an entrepreneur. He managed to save money from his various jobs and to get others to advance him the funds necessary to buy his own boat and enter the packet trade after only a few years in this country. His last venture turned out to be the purchase of the *Morrissey*, which he was able to sail under American registry through the help of his sister, already an American citizen. Mendes brought the vessel from New York to New Bedford and rechristened it *Ernestina* after his daughter. After twenty-eight years of transatlantic trade between the United States and the Cape Verde islands, the schooner was docked at the archipelago. At the age of eighty, Mendes himself returned to Fogo to live out his remaining years.[8]

The newly independent Republic then gave the ship a major overhaul and a crew of Cape Verdeans and Americans sailed it back to the United States as a token of friendship between the two nations. In 1986, the *Ernestina* participated in the Statue of Liberty Centennial worldwide Tall Ships celebration, sailing in the front of the flotilla in recognition of its unique history as the only vessel in the parade that had actually carried immigrants to this country's shores.

The most recent Cape Verdean immigrants now arrive with the intention of staying and increasing numbers are moving out of menial occupations and into white collar jobs. Yet, for so many who have relocated, even those who are prospering in this country, the spiritual and cultural links to Cape Verde remain strong. In the words of one long-standing resident of the New Bedford Cape Verdean American community: "The United States is my country of choice, but Cape Verde is the country of my heart. Her melodies still move within me."[9]

Cape Verdean Americans were one of the earliest populations to be caught between the cracks of race and ethnicity in the now shattered melting pot. Particularly as we examine recent immigration to the United States, the dimensions of race and gender become crucial to the analysis. No longer are the classic works on immigrant adaptation that utilize ethnicity alone sufficient to understanding this process. Since 1930, women have annually outnumbered men in legal migration to the United States, a shift that is largely ignored in immigration scholarship, particularly historical research. Second, the majority of the latest wave of immigrants are arrivals from Central and South America (34 percent) or Asia (34 percent). Differing sharply from the primarily Anglo-European roots of immigrants in the past, these newcomers have mixed racial-ethnic backgrounds—their impact a phenomenon that has been coined "the browning of America."[10] Like the Cape Verdean immigrants before them, recent populations defy binary racial classification and represent widely varied ethnic, racial, and social backgrounds. Neither black nor white, these new arrivals are reshaping the contemporary American social landscape, requiring that their incorporation into the dominant culture be conceptualized in terms of a complex of racial, ethnic, social class, and gender variables. Their odyssey has taken them outside and beyond the rigid boundaries of cultural definition.

NOTES

1. Charles Andrade, Jr., quoted in Colin Nickerson, "Black, White or Cape Verdean?" *Boston Globe*, 29 Sept. 1983, p. 16.

2. Maria Luisa Nunes, *A Portuguese Colonial in America: Belmira Nunes Lopes, the Autobiography of A Cape Verdean-American* (Pittsburgh: Latin American Literary Review Press, 1982), p. 193.

3. Nunes, *A Portuguese Colonial in America*, pp. 144, 201.

4. Interview with Joaquim A. Custodio, 28 July 1988.

5. Lucille Ramos in *Spinner*, I, pp. 34–37.

6. Nunes, *A Portuguese Colonial in America*, p. 202–3.

7. Jose Luis Fernandes Lopes, Ambassador to the United States, July, 1982.

8. Michael Platzer and Michael Cohn, *Black Men of the Sea* (New York: Doad Mead, 1978), pp. 101–2.

9. Jeronimo Barros quoted in Nickerson, "Cape Verde: Country of Their Hearts," *Boston Globe,* 30 Sept. 1983, p. 2.

10. William A. Henry, III, "America's Changing Colors," *Time* 135, no. 15 (9 Apr. 1990), p. 28.

Appendix

Arriving Vessels from the Cape Verde Islands to New Bedford, Mass. 1860–99

Rig	Vessel	Captain	Where From	Arrival Date	Pass.
Bark	Susan Jane	John D. Childs	São Vicente	12 Apr. 1860	2
Bark	Susan Jane	J. W. Nickerson	Brava	23 May 1861	1
Bark	Susan Jane	J. H. Phinney	Brava	6 Oct. 1864	113
Brig	M. Shepherd	John W. Nickerson	Brava	22 Apr. 1867	20
Sch.	Blue Bell	S. D. Pierce	Brava	12 Sept. 1868	8
Bark	Osprey	M. V. B. Millard	Brava	24 July 1871	1
Bark	Islander	J. C. Hamblin	CVI	25 July 1871	8
Sch.	Galena	Joseph Silva	Azores & CVI	9 Sept. 1873	30
Sch.	Irving	Narcisco d'Azevedo	Brava	6 June 1874	4
Bark	Gomez II	J. C. Texeira	Brava	17 Aug. 1874	4
Sch.	Irving	Narcisco d'Azevedo	Brava	24 Sept. 1874	12
Bark	Janet	John Bernard	Brava	28 Nov. 1874	7
Brig	Rescue	Joseph Butler	Azores & CVI	12 Oct. 1875	11
Sch.	Fleetwing	J. J. Godinho	Brava	15 May 1876	21
Brig	Rescue	Joseph Butler	Barbadoes & Brava	6 June 1876	29
Sch.	Fleetwing	J. J. Godinho	CVI	21 Aug. 1876	29
Sch.	Julia & Victoria	Julio Texeira	CVI	2 May 1877	8
Brig	Rescue	Antonio C. Sylvia	CVI	21 Sept. 1877	9
Sch.	Julia & Victoria	? Castro	CVI	4 June 1878	7
Brig	Rescue	Narcisco d'Azevedo	São Tiago	1 Mar. 1880	26
Brig	Bogota	Narcisco d'Azevedo	São Vicente	3 Jan. 1881	8
Brig	Bogota	Narcisco d'Azevedo	Brava	1 Nov. 1881	11
Brig	Bogota	J. C. Texeira	São Tiago	17 June 1882	32
Sch.	Little Lizzie	John Gonsalves	São Vicente	1 May 1883	1
Sch.	Adelaide	Antonio Joaquim Lopes	São Vicente	18 Aug. 1883	16
Sch.	Kate Florence	A. R. Woodhouse	Brava	24 Mar. 1884	30
Bark	Veronica	J. C. Texeira	CVI	24 May 1884	17
Sch.	Adelaide	Antonia Joaquim Lopes	Brava	19 Sept. 1884	4
Sch.	Onward	John Gonsalves	Brava	20 May 1885	—
Sch.	Spring Bird	John Gomes	Brava	1 May 1886	41
Brig	Bogota	J. C. Texeira	São Tiago	20 May 1886	24
Sch.	W. E. Terry	John A. Silva	Brava	31 May 1887	13
Sch.	Carolina	Ayres Jose de Senna	Brava	13 June 1888	28
Sch.	Carolina	Hendrick Oliveira	Brava	17 Apr. 1889	28
Sch.	Emma O. Curtis	George S. Johnson	Brava	20 Apr. 1889	34
Sch.	Rebecca J. Evans	Joaquim O. Perete	Brava	22 Apr. 1889	43

Rig	Vessel	Captain	Where From	Arrival Date	Pass.
Sch.	*Carolina*	Henrique Oliveira	Brava	24 July 1889	27
Sch.	*Vale A. Pina*	Joao A. Silva	Brava	27 July 1889	25
Sch.	*Forest Fairy*	Bras Thomas Pina	Brava	29 Apr. 1890	49
Bark	*Raposa Do Mar*	Henrique S. Oliveira	Brava	30 Apr. 1890	51
Sch.	*Rebecca J. Evans*	Joaquim D. Perete	Brava	5 May 1890	45
Sch.	*Rebecca J. Evans*	Julio M. Fernandes	Brava	5 Aug. 1890	3
Bark	*Raposa Do Mar*	Henrique d'Oliveira	Brava	1 Oct. 1890	10
Bark	*Raposa Do Mar*	Henrique d'Oliveira	Brava	20 Apr. 1891	105
Sch.	*Rebecca J. Evans*	Julio M. Fernandes	Brava	18 May 1891	35
Sch.	*Forest Fairy*	Joao Jose d'Oliveira	Brava	10 June 1891	71
Bark	*Raposa Do Mar*	Henrique d'Oliveira	Brava	17 Oct. 1891	18
Bark	*Raposa Do Mar*	Henruque d'Oliveira	Brava	25 Apr. 1892	80
Sch.	*Forest Fairy*	Joao Jose d'Oliveira	Brava	25 Apr. 1892	76
Sch.	*Rebecca J. Evans*	Julio M. Fernandes	Brava	5 May 1892	23
Sch.	*Vale A. Pina*	J. A. Silva	Brava	6 May 1892	12
Sch.	*Carolina*	Gaudencio Joaquim d'Oliveira	Brava	17 May 1892	22
Bark	*Maria Lila*	Henrique Morse	Brava	11 July 1892	16
Sch.	*Forest Fairy*	Joao Jose d'Oliveira	Brava	13 Aug. 1892	3
Bark	*Raposa Do Mar*	Henrique S. d'Oliveira	Brava	25 Aug. 1892	6
Sch.	*Wellena D.*	J. C. Texeira	São Tiago	11 May 1893	23
Bark	*Raposa Do Mar*	H. S. d'Oliveira	Brava	18 May 1893	80
Sch.	*Forest Fairy*	J. J. Oliveira	CVI	20 May 1893	71
Sch.	*Rebecca J. Evans*	Julio Fernandes	CVI	8 Aug. 1893	26
Bark	*Raposa Do Mar*	Henrique S. d'Oliveira	CVI	11 Sept. 1893	35
Sch.	*Forest Fairy*	J. J. Oliveira	CVI	11 May 1894	60
Bark	*Raposa Do Mar*	A. J. Lopes	CVI	19 May 1894	30
Sch.	*Rebecca J. Evans*	A. H. Brito	CVI	26 July 1894	15
Sch.	*John E. Shatford*	J. M. Fernandes	CVI	15 Aug. 1894	2
Sch.	*Zulmira*	J. J. Oliveira	CVI	3 Oct. 1894	14
Sch.	*Joseph P. Johnson*			29 Apr. 1895	—
Sch.	*Zulmira*	J. J. Oliveira	CVI	14 May 1895	30
Sch.	*Augustine Kobbe*	Henrique S. d'Oliveira	CVI	15 May 1895	46
Sch.	*Julia II*	J. C. Ferreira		20 May 1895	—
Sch.	*J. E. Shatford*	Julio M. Fernandes	CVI	27 May 1895	22
Sch.	*Fannie Spurling*	John A. Silva	CVI	18 Sept. 1895	6
Sch.	*Zulmira*	Joao Jose d'Oliveira	CVI	14 Oct. 1895	30
Sch.	*John C. Shatford*	J. M. Fernandes	CVI	2 May 1896	50
Sch.	*Zulmira*	J. J. d'Oliveira	CVI	2 May 1896	19
Sch.	*General Scott*	J. D. Leighton	CVI	2 May 1896	40
Sch.	*Carolina*	Luiz Antonio Mercis	CVI	16 June 1896	30
Sch.	*Longwood*	Isaac Asulay	CVI	17 June 1896	30
Sch.	*Zulmira*	J. J. d'Oliveira	CVI	31 Aug. 1896	34
Sch.	*Ethel & Addie*	Antonio J. Lopes	CVI	14 Sept. 1896	4
Sch.	*John A. Shatford*	J. M. Fernandes	CVI	12 Apr. 1897	56
Sch.	*Zulmira*	A. F. Camacho	CVI	1 May 1897	75
Sch.	*John E. Nickerson*	Abraham Azulay	CVI	18 May 1897	44
Sch.	*Cabo Verde*	J. L. Sylvia	CVI	19 May 1897	24
Bark	*Augustine Kobbe*	H. S. Oliveira	CVI	24 May 1897	118

Rig	Vessel	Captain	Where From	Arrival Date	Pass.
Sch.	*Carlota*	A. J. Lopes	CVI	31 July 1897	9
Sch.	*Zulmira*	A. F. Camacho	CVI	9 Oct. 1897	20
Sch.	*Serpa Pinto*	A. da Roza	CVI	2 May 1898	30
Sch.	*Ziulmira*	A. F. Camacho	CVI	2 May 1898	24
Sch.	*Olive H. Robinson*	L. Dos Santos	CVI	22 Apr. 1898	37
Sch.	*Cabo Verde*	J. L. Sylvia	CVI	20 May 1898	29
Sch.	*Dois Irmos*	J. J. Oliveira	CVI	7 June 1898	30
Sch.	*Olivia*	Luiz dos Santos	CVI	1 Aug. 1898	27
Sch.	*Zulmira* .	H. S. Oliveira	CVI	24 Aug. 1898	24
Sch.	*Cabo Verde*	J. L. Sylvia	CVI	27 Sept. 1898	5
Sch.	*Zulmira*	H. S. Oliveira	CVI	13 May 1899	59
Sch.	*Olivia*	Isaac Azulay	CVI	31 May 1899	43
Sch.	*Vera Cruz II*	J. Fernandes	CVI	1 June 1899	50
Sch.	*Dois Irmos*	J. J. Oliveira	CVI	16 June 1899	30
Sch.	*Serpa Pinto*	Antonio da Rocha	CVI	7 June 1899	20
Sch.	*Carlota*	A. J. Lopes	CVI	7 Aug. 1899	2
Sch.	*Zulmira*	H. S. Oliveira	CVI	20 Sept. 1899	26
Sch.	*Serpa Pinto*	A. da Roza	CVI	14 Oct. 1899	4
Sch.	*Vera Cruz II*	J. Whamon	CVI	16 Oct 1899	1

Arriving Vessels from the Cape Verde Islands to New Bedford, Mass. 1901–20

Rig	Vessel	Captain	Where From	Arrival Date	Pass.
	Bryton		Brava	13 May 1901	100
Sch.	*David A. Story*	Luiz d'Oliveira	Brava	3 May 1902	53
Sch.	*America*	Joao Pereira	Brava	3 May 1902	48
Sch.	*Zulmira*	Joao Jose Galvao	Brava	5 May 1902	30
Sch.	*Freeman*	Joao Jose d'Oliveira	Brava	16 May 1902	76
	Hattie & Lottie	John L. Silva	Brava	1 July 1902	22
Bark	*Vera Cruz*	Julo Manoel Fernandes	Brava	4 Aug. 1902	52
Sch.	*David A. Story*	Luiz d'Oliveira	Brava	7 Sept. 1902	58
Sch.	*America*	Joao Pereira	Brava	13 Sept. 1902	9
Sch.	*Zulmira*	Francisco Silva	Brava	24 Sept. 1902	23
Sch.	*Freeman*		Brava	28 Oct. 1902	2
Sch.	*David A. Story*	Luiz d'Oliveira	Brava	11 May 1903	54
Sch.	*Esperanca*	Gaudencio J. Oliveira	Brava	11 May 1903	44
Bark	*Vera Cruz*	Julio M. Fernandes	Brava (to N.C.)	12 May 1903	435
Sch.	*Luiza*	Joao Fonseca	Brava	14 May 1903	60
Sch.	*America*	Joao Pereira	Brava	14 May 1903	60

Rig	Vessel	Captain	Where From	Arrival Date	Pass.
Sch.	Flor de Cabo Verde	Luis Santos	Brava	15 May 1903	87
Sch.	Freeman	Joao Oliveira	Brava	15 May 1903	60
Sch.	Unique	Joseph J. Oliveira	Brava	15 May 1903	56
Sch.	Belle Bartlett	Antonio Gamboa	Brava	15 May 1903	60
Sch.	Zulmira	Joao Galvao	Brava	17 May 1903	77
	D. A. Small	Manoel Rosa	Brava	18 May 1903	75
Sch.	Pilgrim	Joseph Gaspar Conceicao	São Vicente	8 July 1903	34
Sch.	Luiza	Joao Fonseca	Brava	14 Sept. 1903	45
Sch.	Flor de Cabo Verde	Joao Gamboa	Brava	14 Sept. 1903	23
Sch.	Zulmira	Joao Jose Galvao	Brava	15 Sept. 1903	3
Sch.	Esperanca	Sebastiao Mascarenhas	CVI	15 Sept. 1903	29
Sch.	David A. Story	Luiz d'Oliveira	Brava	16 Sept. 1903	45
Sch.	Freeman	Joao d'Oliveira	Brava	1 Oct. 1903	7
Sch.	Flor de Cabo Verde	Francisco da Silva	Fogo	26 Apr. 1904	49
Sch.	Esperanca	Sabastiao Mascarenhas	Brava	30 Apr. 1904	52
Sch.	Zulmira	Joao Jose Galvao	Brava	2 May 1904	66
	Luiza	Joao Baptiste de Fonseca	Brava	3 May 1904	101
Sch.	Freeman	John Joseph Oliveira	Brava	3 May 1904	49
Sch.	David A. Story	Luiz Oliveira	Brava	3 May 1904	52
Sch.	David A. Story	Alfredo Neves	Brava	22 Aug. 1904	48
	Belle Bartlett	Antonio Gamboa	Brava	22 Aug. 1904	48
Sch.	Esperanca	Sebastiao Mascarenhas	Brava	22 Aug. 1904	28
Sch.	Flor de Cabo Verde	Jorge Wahnon	CVI	9 Sept. 1904	26
Sch.	Freeman	Manuel Roza	Brava	21 Sept. 1904	8
Sch.	Luiza	Francisco da Silva	Brava	4 May 1905	54
Sch.	Cameo	Jose P. da Costa	Brava	8 May 1905	48
Sch.	Flor de Cabo Verde	Jorge Wahnon	CVI	11 May 1905	54
Sch.	David A. Story	Alfredo Neves	Brava	18 May 1905	51
Sch.	Sarah E. Lee	Theophilo F. Gonsalves	CVI	14 June 1905	54
Brig	Vera Cruz III	Antonio Santos Redondo	Brava	4 Aug. 1905	52
Brig	Vera Cruz III	Antonio Santos Redondo	Brava	6 Sept. 1905	25
Sch.	Flor de Cabo Verde	Jorge Wahnon	Brava	6 Sept. 1905	19
Sch.	Cameo		Brava	11 Oct. 1905	1
Sch.	David A. Story	Manuel Jose Andrade	Brava	2 May 1906	50
Sch.	Flor de Cabo Verde	Jorge Wahnon	CVI	3 May 1906	54
Sch.	I. J. Marrett, jr.	John A. Oliver	Brava	9 May 1906	62
Sch.	Esperanca	Francisco da Silva	Brava	9 May 1906	68
Sch.	Nannie C. Bohlen	Manuel F. Gonsalves	Brava	19 May 1906	68
Sch.	Inaos Amigos	S. F. Mascarenhas	CVI	21 May 1906	56
Sch.	Vera Cruz VI	Vincente Luiz d'Aguiar Silva	Brava	25 May 1906	47
Sch.	Zulmira	Vincente Constantine Soares	Brava	27 May 1906	44
Sch.	Sarah E. Lee	Theophilo Gonsalves	CVI	30 May 1906	32
Sch.	Cameo	Manuel Roza	Brava	13 July 1906	53
Sch.	Sunbeam		CVI	24 July 1906	2
Sch.	Esperanca	Francisco da Silva	Brava	1 Sept. 1906	49
Sch.	Flor de Cabo Verde	Manuel Cyrillo dos Reis	CVI	18 Sept. 1906	47
Sch.	I. J. Merritt	John A. Oliveira	Brava	19 Sept. 1906	43
Sch.	David A. Story		Brava	20 Sept. 1906	25

Rig	Vessel	Captain	Where From	Arrival Date	Pass.
Sch.	*Sarah E. Lee*	Theophilo Gonsalves	CVI	11 Oct. 1906	39
Sch.	*Meteor*	Alex ?	Brava	3 May 1907	39
Sch.	*David A. Story*	Jose Manuel Domingos	Brava	9 May 1907	48
Sch.	*Cameo*	Manuel Roza	Brava	14 May 1907	50
Sch.	*I. J. Merritt, jr.*	John A. Oliveira	Brava	19 May 1907	50
Sch.	*Sarah E. Lee*	Antonio Oliveira Rodrigues	CVI	21 June 1907	56
Brig	*Luzo*	Manuel Cyrillo dos Reis	CVI	26 June 1907	109
Sch.	*David A. Story*	Jose M. Domingos	Brava	19 Aug. 1907	55
Sch.	*I. J. Merritt, jr.*	John A. Oliveira	Brava	9 Sept. 1907	65
Sch.	*Inaos Amigos*		CVI	13 Sept. 1907	1
Sch.	*Meteor*	Alex ?	Brava	13 Sept. 1907	59
Sch.	*Cameo*	Manuel Roza	Brava	22 Oct. 1907	47
Sch.	*Inaos Amigos*	Jorge Wahnon	Fogo	20 Apr. 1908	54
Sch.	*Meteor*	Joao J. Roza	Brava	24 Apr. 1908	53
Sch.	*David A. Story*	Jose Manoel Domingos		27 Apr. 1908	65
Sch.	*Ramona*	Luiz d'Oliveira	Brava	30 Apr. 1908	54
Sch.	*Talisman*	Fernando Neves	Brava	30 Apr. 1908	50
Sch.	*I. J. Merritt, jr.*	John A. Oliveira	Brava	1 May 1908	52
Sch.	*Mary E. Simmons*	Joseph J. Oliveira	Brava	1 May 1908	55
Sch.	*Sarah E. Lee*	Benjamin Costa	Fogo	3 May 1908	57
Sch.	*Adelia Chase*	Alfred Neves	Brava	10 May 1908	60
Sch.	*A. E. Whyland*	Antonio J. Perry	Fogo	13 May 1908	64
Sch.	*Belle Bartlett*	Joao Baptiste Fernandes	Fogo	24 May 1908	37
Brig	*Luzo*	Manuel Cyrillo Dos Reis	Fogo	1 June 1908	56
Sch.	*Eleanor B. Conwell*	Manuel Roza	Brava	1 June 1908	50
S.S.	*Maria Luiza*	Alvaro F. Camacho	Brava	8 June 1908	212
Bark	*Charles We. Morgan*		Fogo	5 July 1908	3
Sch.	*Irmaos Amigos*	Jorge Wahnon	Fogo	6 Aug. 1908	51
Sch.	*Talisman*	Alfred Neves	Brava	3 Sept. 1908	57
Sch.	*Mary E. Siommons*	Pedro Jose Pinheiro	Brava	9 Sept. 1908	31
Sch.	*A. E. Whyland*	Silveiro Mascarenhas	Fogo	18 Sept. 1908	52
Sch.	*Belle Bartlett*	Joao B. Fernandes	Brava	19 Sept. 1908	6
Sch.	*I. J. Merritt, jr.*	John A. Oliveira	Brava	20 Sept. 1908	47
Sch.	*Sarah E. Lee*	Benjamin Costa	Brava & Fogo	2 Oct. 1908	37
S.S.	*Maria Luiza*	Alvaro F. Camacho	Brava	16 Apr. 1909	210
Sch.	*Foster Rice*	E. H. Pitman	Brava	20 Apr. 1909	54
Sch.	Sarah E. Lee	Benjamin Costa	Fogo	21 Apr. 1909	34
Sch.	Manoclinho	Joao B. Fernandes	Brava	3 May 1909	53
Sch.	Puritan	Jose Manuel Domingos	Brava	12 May 1909	28
S.S.	Maria Luiza		Brava	11 June 1909	167
Sch.	*A. H. Whyland*	Benjamin J. Oliveira	Fogo	29 June 1909	53
Brig	*Luzo*	Luiz Mercis	Fogo	6 July 1909	57
Sch.	*Sarah E. Lee*	John F. Pina	Fogo	3 Nov. 1909	38
S.S.	*Maria Luiza*		Fogo	17 Apr. 1910	192
S.S.	*Pescador*	Luiz Antonio Mercis	Fogo	24 Apr. 1910	122
Brig	*Luzo*	Joao da Silva Gamboa	Fogo	6 May 1910	58
Bark	*Charles G. Rice*	Luiz d'Oliveira	Brava	24 May 1910	318
S.S.	*Maria Luiza*	A. F. Camacho	Fogo	28 June 1910	186

Rig	Vessel	Captain	Where From	Arrival Date	Pass.
S.S.	*Maria Luiza*	A. F. Camacho	Fogo	15 Apr. 1911	189
Bark	*Sunbeam*	J. L. Silva	Fogo	18 Apr. 1911	68
Brig	*Luzo*	Joao Gamboa	Fogo	11 May 1911	59
Sch.	*Diana*	Joao Jose Galvao	Brava	23 May 1911	53
Sch.	*Elizabeth T. Doyle*	Lewis Greene	Brava	23 May 1911	214
Sch.	*Frederick Schepp*	Benjamin Costa	Brava	27 May 1911	76
Bark	*Charles G. Rice*	Luiz d'Oliveira	Brava	28 May 1911	291
Sch.	*Irmaos Amigos*	Jorge Wahnon	Fogo	31 May 1911	59
S.S.	*Maria Luiza*	A. F. Camacho	Fogo	18 June 1911	186
Bark	*Sunbeam*	J. L. Silva	Fogo	19 Aug. 1911	68
Sch.	*Elizabeth T. Doyle*	Manuel F. Caneca	Fogo	19 Sept. 1911	174
Brig	*Luzo*	Joao Bamboa	Fogo	29 Sept. 1911	54
Sch.	*Elizabeth T. Doyle*	Manuel F. Caneca		5 May 1912	318
Sch.	*William A. Grozier*	J. L. Silva	Fogo	5 May 1912	60
Bark	*Plantina*	Benjamin Costa	Brava	13 May 1912	79
S.S.	*Fortuna*	Joao Sacramento Monteiro	São Vicente	23 May 1912	311
Bark	*Charles G. Rice*	Luiz d'Oliveira	Brava	27 May 1912	327
	Ellen A. Swift		São Vicente	7 Aug. 1912	11
Bark	*Plantina*	Benjamin Costa	Brava	9 Oct. 1912	68
Sch.	*William A. Graber*	J. L. Silva	Fogo	28 Oct. 1912	60
Sch.	*William A. Graber*	J. L. Silva	Brava	22 Apr. 1913	58
S.S.	*Evelyn*	Jorge Wahnon	São Tiago	28 Apr. 1913	333
Bark	*Platina*	Benjamin Costa	Brava	12 May 1913	63
Sch.	*William A. Graber*	Joao Lucio Souza	Fogo	13 May 1913	58
Sch.	*Diana*	Joao da Silva Gamboa	Brava	14 May 1913	58
Bark	*Luzo*	Pedro Mariano Azevedo	Brava	6 June 1913	145
Bark	*Charles G. Rice*	Luiz d'Oliveira	Brava	8 June 1913	305
Sch.	*Irmaos Amigos*	Manuel Cyrillo dos Reis	Fogo	14 July 1913	88
Sch.	*William A. Graber*	Arthur Souza Silva	São Nicolau	9 Aug. 1913	62
Sch.	*America*	Alfredo Piedade	São Vicente	13 Aug. 1913	34
Sch.	*Diana*	Joao Gamboa	Brava	25 Aug. 1913	59
Bark	*Platina*	Benjamin Costa	Brava	11 Oct. 1913	96
Bark	*Platina*	Benjamin Costa	Brava	14 Oct. 1913	96
Sch.	*Ideal*	Sebastiao Mascarenhas	São Vicente	12 Apr. 1914	83
Sch.	*Elector*	John A. Oliveira	Brava	13 Apr. 1914	63
S.S.	*Insulano*	A. F. Camacho	Fogo	14 Apr. 1914	544
Bark	*Savoia*	Arthur Silva	Fogo	18 Apr. 1914	264
Sch.	*Indiana*	Manuel Roza	Brava	23 Apr. 1914	59
Brig	*Daisy*	John J. Roza	São Nicolau	1 May 1914	142
Sch.	*Diana*	Joao da Silva Gamboa	Fogo	23 May 1914	58
Sch.	*Lizzie Lee*		Brava	24 May 1914	61
Bark	*Charles G. Rice*	Alfred Neves	Brava	24 May 1914	322
S.S.	*Insulano*	A. F. Camacho	Fogo	14 June 1914	266
S.S.	*Cecil H. Low*	Julio Gonsalves	Brava	5 July 1914	48
Sch.	*Elector*	John A. Oliveira	Brava	8 July 1914	60
S.S.	*Indiana*	Manuel Roza	Brava	3 Aug. 1914	61
Bark	*Savoia*	Joao da Silva Gamboa	Fogo	4 Oct. 1914	161
Sch.	*Mystic*	Benjamin Costa	Brava	16 May 1915	167

Rig	Vessel	Captain	Where From	Arrival Date	Pass.
Bark	Savoia	Joao Gamboa	Fogo	25 May 1915	272
Sch.	Mary Curtis	Valentine Roza	São Nicolau	26 May 1915	71
Sch.	Mary Curtis		CVI	26 May 1915	—
Brig	Daisy	Joao de Freitas	Brava	30 May 1915	227
	Margaret		Brava	8 Aug. 1915	1
S.S.	Indiana	Manuel Roza	Brava	14 Aug. 1915	57
	A. M. Nicholson	Charles Church	São Nicolau	12 Sept. 1915	6
Brig	Viola		São Nicolau	30 Sept. 1915	1
Bark	Savoia	John Freitas	São Vicente	15 Oct. 1915	35
Sch.	Mystic	Benjamin Costa	Brava	17 Oct. 1915	68
Bark	Savoia		São Vicente	15 Apr. 1916	1
Sch.	A. E. Whyland	Joaquim Rene	Brava	5 May 1916	72
Sch.	Cameo	Jose Domingos	Brava	10 May 1916	15
Sch.	Mystic	Benjamin Costa	Brava	15 May 1916	150
Sch.	Bertha D. Nickerson	John A. Oliveira	Brava	20 May 1916	106
	Adelia T. Carleton	? Soares	São Vicente	25 May 1916	136
Sch.	Emma & Helen	James Silva	Brava	15 June 1916	62
Sch.	Diana		Brava	18 June 1916	3
Sch.	Diana	Joao Gamboa	Brava	19 June 1916	59
Sch.	Indiana	Sebastiao Mascarenha	Brava	30 June 1916	63
Sch.	Bertha D. Nickerson	John A. Oliveira	Brava	16 Sept. 1916	103
Sch.	Cameo	Jose Domingos	Brava	7 Oct. 1916	141
Sch.	Bertha D. Nickerson		CVI	10 Oct. 1916	1
Sch.	Emma & Helen		CVI	17 Oct. 1916	2
Sch.	Emma & Helen	James Silva	Brava	17 Oct. 1916	53
Sch.	Diana	Joao Gamboa	São Vicente	3 Nov. 1916	36
Sch.	Ambrose Snow	Arthur Silva	São Nicolau	10 Nov. 1916	59
Sch.	Adelia Carleton	Henrique Scccorro	São Vicente	17 Nov. 1916	82
Sch.	Cameo	Jose M. Domingos	Brava	24 May 1917	111
Sch.	A. E. Whyland	Isaac Azulay	Brava	25 May 1917	79
	Bertha D. Nickerson	Joaquim J. Senna	Brava	27 May 1917	85
Sch.	Ambrose Snow	Arthur Silva	São Vicente	30 May 1917	60
Sch.	Emma & Helen	Manuel Rosa	Brava	31 May 1917	65
Sch.	Normanhal	Alfred Neves	Brava	4 June 1917	74
Sch.	Santiago	Joao Fonseca	CVI	9 June 1917	70
Sch.	Adelia T. Carleton	Henrique	São Vicente	16 June 1917	149
Sch.	Carleton Bell	Albertino J. Senna	Brava	28 June 1917	73
Sch.	Elector	Antonio Francisco d'Oliveira	Fogo	9 July 1917	56
Sch.	Diana	Legismos Ferr. Santos	Fogo	15 July 1917	75
Bark	Bertha	Luiz d'Oliveira	Brava	16 July 1917	50
Sch.	Edith M. Prior	Francisco Pinheiro	Brava	22 Sept. 1917	11
	Bertha D. Nickerson	Manuel Faria	São Vicente	19 Oct. 1917	53
Sch.	Cameo		Brava	20 Oct. 1917	1
Sch.	Ambrose Snow	Arthur Silva	São Vicente	20 Oct. 1917	54
Sch.	Cameo	Jose M. Domingos	São Vicente	20 Oct. 1917	70
	Charles W. Morgan		Brava	22 Oct. 1917	9
Sch.	Carleton Bell		São Vicente	24 Dec. 1917	8
Sch.	Cameo		Brava	11 Feb. 1918	—

Rig	Vessel	Captain	Where From	Arrival Date	Pass.
	A. M. Nicolson		São Vicente	10 June 1918	14
Bark	*Wanderer*		São Nicolau	10 June 1918	18
Bark	*Greyhound*		Sõa Nicolau	23 June 1918	15
Sch.	*Ambrose Snow*		Sõa Vicente	29 July 1918	54
Sch.	*Cameo*	Jose M. Domingos	São Vicente	14 Sept. 1918	99
	A. V. S. Woodruff		São Vicente	21 Sept. 1918	18
Sch.	*Atalanta*	Manuel Rosa	São Vicente	26 Sept. 1918	48
Sch.	*Diana*		Brava	29 Nov. 1918	—
Sch.	*Nourmahal*	John A. Oliveira	São Vicente	3 May 1919	52
Sch.	*Emma & Helen*		São Tiago	31 May 1919	1
Sch.	*Ralph L. Hall*	Fernando Neves	Brava	24 July 1919	31
Sch.	*Ambrose Snow*	Arthur Silva	São Vicente	31 July 1919	33
Sch.	*Volant*	Julius Gonsalves	São Vicente	18 Aug. 1919	33
	A. M. Nicolson		São Vicente	22 Aug. 1919	
	Evolution	Manuel Araujo	São Vicente	18 Oct. 1919	41
Sch.	*Marguerite Haskins*	Hipolito Lemos	Brava	22 May 1920	24
Sch.	*Volant*	Julius Gonsalves	Brava	28 May 1920	38
Sch.	*Venus*	Joao ?	Brava	2 June 1920	45
Sch.	*Melissa Trask*	John A. Oliveira	Brava	2 June 1920	110
Sch.	*Edith M. Prior*	Joao D'Senna Oliveira	Brava	8 June 1920	77
Sch.	*William H. Draper*	Joseph J. Mont	CVI	9 June 1920	139
Sch.	*Lottie S. Morton*	John L. Souza	Fogo	29 June 1920	39
Sch.	*Emma & Helen*	Francisco Pinheiro	Fogo	12 July 1920	48
Bark	*Charles W. Morgan*		São Nicolau	15 July 1920	30

Bibliography

Documents

Atlas of the City of New Bedford, Massachusetts. Boston: Walker Lithograph & Publishing Co., 1911.

New Bedford and Fairhaven Directories, 1836–1971. Various Publishers.

U.S. Customs Service. Record Group 36. Records of the New Bedford Collector of Customs. *Inward Passenger lists, 1823–99.* National Archives Microfilm (3 rolls) in New Bedford Free Public Library, New Bedford, Massachusetts.

U.S. Department of Justice, Immigration and Naturalization Service. *Crew Lists of Vessels Arriving at New Bedford, Mass., 1917–1943.* Microcopy No. T–942. 2 rolls.

————. *Index to Passengers Arriving at New Bedford, Mass., July 1, 1902–November 18, 1954.* Microcopy No. T–522. 2 rolls.

————. *Passenger Lists of Vessels Arriving at New Bedford, Mass. 1902–1942.* Microcopy No. T–944. 8 rolls.

————. *Passenger Lists of Vessels Arriving At Providence, R. I., 1911–1943.* Microcopy No. T–1188. 49 rolls.

U.S. Department of State. *Despatches from United States Consuls in Santiago, Cape Verde, 1818–1898.* Microcopy No. T–434. 7 rolls. Washington: The National Archives and Records Service, 1960.

Oral Histories and Interviews

Joseph R. Andrade, 10 Oct. 1983
Elizabeth Araujo, 23 Oct. 1985
Joanie Andrews, 26 Feb. 1984
Mary Santos Barboza, videotaped by Ron Barboza, Jan. 1984
Mary Da Rosa Barros, 12 Dec. 1984
Mary Santos Barros, 7 Nov. 1985
Maria "Baba" Lima Barros, 27 Apr. 1983
Lena Britto, 27 Mar. 1984

Antonio "Tote" Cabral, 4 Jan. 1985, and 16 Oct. 1985
Julia Cabral, 16 Oct. 1985
Joaquim A. Custodio, 28 July 1988, and 2 July 1990
Manuel E. Costa, interviewed by Joe Thomas, 25 Aug. 1989
Mike DaCosta, 9 Mar. 1984
Kenneth N. DeSilva, 27 Feb. 1984
Diana Duarte, 21 Feb. 1985
Antonia Baptiste Enos, 3 Jan. 1985
Albertina Alves Fernandes, 5 Dec. 1983
Archangel Mary "Canja" Fortes, 7 Aug. 1990
Caesar Galvin, videotaped by Ron Barboza
Antonio "Geech" Gomes and Lydia (Freitas) Gomes, 30 May 1986
Joli Gonsalves, 21 Aug. 1989
Richard A. Gonsalves, 1, 10 Mar. 1984
Antonio Jesus, 20 Nov. 1983
Lucillia Lima, 25 Jan. 1984
Jose Flore Livramento, videotaped by Ron Barboza, June 1984
Edward Lopes, 17 July 1989
Flora Monteiro, 30 Nov. 1983
Jose Mello, 9 Apr. 1985
Zira Perry, 4 Oct. 1986
Carol Jean Pimentel, 5 July 1990
Carrie Pina, 21 June 1985
Joaquim Pina, 26 Jan. 1984
Tony Pinto, 3 Mar. 1984
Joel Pires, 27 Feb. 1984
Lucille Ramos, 19 Jan. 1984
Arthur Santos, 7 Nov. 1983
Mary Shaw, 26 Apr. 1987
Francisco Benholiel Silva, videotaped by Ron Barboza, 1983
Florence "Angie" Souza, 22 Apr. 1986
Antonia Silva Teque, 4 May 1983
Cecelia Perry Vieira, 24 Oct. 1985

Newspapers

Cape Verdean, 1969–present
The CVN, 1979–present
New Bedford Evening Standard, 1850–1932
New Bedford Morning Mercury, 1807–1942
New Bedford The Standard-Times, 1932–present
Tchuba Newsletter, 1975–78

Books, Articles, Theses, and Typescripts

Abshire, David, and Michael Samuels, eds. *Portuguese Africa: A Handbook.* New York: Praeger, 1969.

Almeida, Carlos. *Portuguese Immigrants: The Centennial Story of the Portuguese Union of the State of California.* San Leandro, Calif.: Supreme Council of U.P.E.C., 1978.

Almeida, Raymond Anthony. *Cape Verdeans in America: Our Story.* Boston: TCHUBA — American Committee for Cape Verde, 1978.

————, and Patricia Nyhan. *Cape Verde and Its People: A Short History.* Boston: TCHUBA — American Committee for Cape Verde, 1976.

"America's Richest Negro Minister." *Ebony* 7, no. 2 (Jan. 1952): 17–23.

Anderson, Grace, and David Higgs. *A Future to Inherit: Portuguese Communities in Canada.* Toronto: McClelland & Stuart, 1976.

Anderson, Margo J. *The American Census: A Social History.* New Haven: Yale University Press, 1988.

Andrade, Elisa. *The Cape Verde Islands: From Slavery to Modern Times.* Eugene, Oreg.: Coalition Press, 1974.

Appel, John, Jr. "American Negro and Immigrant Experience: Similarities and Differences." *American Quarterly* 18 (Spring 1966): 95–103.

Araujo, Norman. *A Study of Cape Verdean Literature.* Chestnut Hill: Boston College, 1966.

Archdeacon, Thomas. *Becoming American: An Ethnic History.* New York: Free Press, 1983.

Arnesen, Eric. "Learning the Lessons of Solidarity: Work Rules and Race Relations on the New Orleans Waterfront, 1880–1901." *Labor's Heritage* 1, no. 1 (Jan. 1989): 26–45.

Bailey, W. B. "The Bird of Passage." *American Journal of Sociology* 18 (Nov. 1912): 391–97.

Bailyn, Bernard. *The New England Merchants in the 17th Century.* Cambridge: Harvard University Press, 1955.

Banfield, Edward. *The Unheavenly City Revisited.* Boston: Little Brown, 1974.

Bannick, Christian John. *Portuguese Immigration to the United States: Its Distribution and Status.* Berkeley: University of California Press, 1971.

Barboza, Ron. "Cape Verde Primed for Friday's Celebration." *Standard-Times* (New Bedford, Mass.), 4 July 1985, pp. 1, 7.

————, and Karen Lee Ziner. "Cape Verde." *Sunday Journal Magazine* (Providence, R.I.), 3 Feb. 1986, pp. 6–11.

————, and Cindy Nickerson. "The Face of Cape Verde." *Sunday Cape Cod Times,* 13 Oct. 1985, pp. E-65, E-67.

Barboza, Stephen. "Cape Verde: Islands in Limbo." *Islands* 3, no. 1 (Mar.–Apr. 1983): 66–75.

Barrera, Mario. *Race and Class in the Southwest: A Theory of Racial Inequality.* Notre Dame: University of Notre Dame Press, 1979.

Barrows, Paul W. "The Historical Roots of Cape Verdean Dependency, 1460–1990." Ph.D. diss., University of Minnesota, 1990.

Barton, Josef J. *Peasants and Strangers: Italians, Rumanians and Slovaks in an American City, 1890–1950.* Cambridge: Harvard University Press, 1975.

Baxter, David. "Approaches to Studying Ethnicity among Cape Verdeans in New Bedford, Massachusetts." Paper presented at the Northeastern Anthropological Association Annual Meetings, Worcester, Mass., 1974.

Beck, Sam. "Manny Almeida's Ringside Lounge: The Cape Verdean Struggle for Their Neighborhood." Ms., 1981.

_____, and the members of Local 1329. *From Cape Verde to Providence.* Providence: International Longshoremen's Association, Local 1329, 1983.

Bell, Robert R. "The Lower-Class Negro Family in the United States and Great Britain: Some Comparisons." *Race* 2 (Oct. 1969): 173–81.

Bennett, Norman R., and George E. Brooks. *New England Merchants in Africa: A History through Documents, 1802 to 1865.* Boston: Boston University Press, 1965.

Berger, Josef (pseud. Jeremiah Digges). *Cape Cod Pilot.* 1937. Cambridge: M.I.T. Press, 1969.

_____. *In Great Waters.* New York: Macmillan Co., 1941.

Bliss, Herbert D., "Feeling on Cape Is Not Inimical to Cape Verdeans." *New Bedford Sunday Standard,* 28 Aug. 1921, pp. 1, 3, 5.

Blu, Karen I. *The Lumbee Problem: The Making of an American People.* Cambridge: Cambridge University Press, 1980.

Bodnar, John. *The Transplanted.* Bloomington: Indiana University Press, 1985.

_____. *Workers' World: Kinship, Community and Protest in an Industrial Society, 1900–1940.* Baltimore: Johns Hopkins University Press, 1982.

_____, Roger Simon, and Michael P. Weber. *Lives of Their Own: Blacks, Italians, and Poles in Pittsburgh, 1900–1960.* Urbana: University of Illinois Press, 1982.

_____, Michael Weber, and Roger Simon. "Migration, Kinship and Urban Adjustment: Blacks and Poles in Pittsburgh, 1900–1930." *Journal of American History* 66 (1979): 548–65.

Boss, Judith A., and Joseph D. Thomas. *New Bedford: A Pictorial History.* Norfolk/Virginia Beach: Denning Co., 1983.

Boston, L. B. "Strawberry Culture on Cape Cod." *Cape Cod Magazine* 1, no. 4 (Aug. 1915): 25–26.

Boxer, C. R. *Race Relations in the Portuguese Colonial Empire, 1415–1825.* London: Oxford University Press, 1963.

Briggs, John W. *An Italian Passage: Immigrants to Three American Cities, 1890–1930.* New Haven: Yale University Press, 1978.

Briggs, Le Baron R. "The History of the Cranberry Industry in Massachusetts." Honors thesis, Harvard University, 1941.

Brooke, James. "As Whalers They Left; as Yankees They're Back." *New York Times,* 16 Feb. 1989, p. A4.

Brooks, George R. *Yankee Traders, Old Coasters and African Middlemen.* New York: Homes and Meier, 1970.

Brown, Aycock. "The Mystery of the Vera Cruz." *News and Observer* (Raleigh, N.C.), 9 Dec. 1934.

———. "The Vera Cruz: Her Death at Ocracoke Inlet." *Durham Morning Herald,* 11 Mar. 1951.

———. "50th Anniversary of Coastal Shipwreck Passes Unnoticed." *Citizen* (Ashville, N.C.), 15 May 1953.

Bruskin, Gene. "Hospitals Laundry Workers Organize." *Forward Motion* 7, no. 3 (May–June 1988): 19–25.

Bryce-LaPorte, Roy Simon. "Black Immigrants: The Experience of Invisibility and Inequality." *Journal of Black Studies* (Sept. 1972): 29–56.

———, and Dolores Mortimer, eds. *Caribbean Immigration to the United States.* Research Institute on Immigration and Ethnic Studies, Occasional Papers No. 1. Washington, D.C.: Smithsonian Institution, 1976.

Burness, Donald, ed. *Critical Perspectives on Lusophone Literature from Africa.* Washington, D.C.: Three Continents Press, 1981.

———. *FIRE: Six Writers from Angola, Mozambique and Cape Verde.* Washington D.C.: Three Continents Press, 1977.

Burrows, Fredriks A. *Cannonballs and Cranberries.* Taunton, Mass.: William S. Sulkwood, 1976.

Busch, Briton Cooper. "Cape Verdeans in the American Whaling and Sealing Industry, 1850–1900." *American Neptune* 45, no. 2 (Spring 1985): 104–16.

Cabral, Amilcar. *Unity and Struggle.* New York: Monthly Review Press, 1979.

Cabral, Stephen, and Sam Beck. *Nha Distino.* Providence, R.I.: Roger Williams Park Museum Publications, No. 5, 1982.

Cahan, Abraham. *The Rise of David Levinsky.* 1917. New York: Harper and Row, 1960.

Cahoon, R. H. "Agricultural Possibilities on Cape Cod." *Cape Cod Magazine* 1, no. 9 (Jan. 1916), p. 5.

Camarillo, Albert. "Comparative Perspective on Race and Ethnicity: Mexicans, Blacks, and Europeans, 1900–1940." Paper presented at the Organization of American Historians, Washington, D.C., 23–25 Mar. 1990.

Cape Verde Islands. Boulogne, France: Delroisse. *Dix Ans Édition.* 1985.

"Cape Verdians: *Our World* Visits New Bedford." *Our World* 1, no. 5 (Sept. 1946).

Carmel, Jeffrey. "Cape Verdeans Build a New Life on New England's Shore." *Christian Science Monitor,* 14 Feb. 1983.

Carreira, António. *Cabo Verde: formação e extinção de uma sociedade escravocrata* (1460–1878). Porto: Imprensa Portuguesa, 1972.

————. *Migraçoes Nas Ilhas De Cabo Verde.* 2d ed. Instituto Cabo-Verdeano do Livro, 1983.

————. *The People of the Cape Verde Islands: Exploitation and Emigration.* Trans. and Ed. Christopher Fyfe. Hamden, Conn.: Archon Books, 1982.

Carreras, Luís. "A Cape Verdean Kinship Analysis." Paper presented at the Southern Anthropological Society's Annual Meeting, Blacksburg, Va., Apr. 1974.

Charig, Margaret A., and Ron Barboza. "Glimpses of Cape Verde." *The Standard Times* (New Bedford, Mass.) 20 Oct. 1985, pp. 47–48.

Chippendale, Captain Harry Allen. *Sails and Whales.* Cambridge, Mass.: The Riverside Press, 1951.

Chudacoff, Howard P. "The New Immigration History." *Reviews in American History* 4, no. 1 (Mar. 1976): 99–104.

Clarence-Smith, Gervase. *The Third Portuguese Empire, 1825–1975: A Study in Economic Imperialism.* Dover, N.H.: Manchester University Press, 1985.

Clifford, James, and George E. Marcus, eds. *Writing Culture: The Poetics and Politics of Ethnography.* Berkeley: University of California Press, 1986.

Coli, Waltraud Berger, and Richard A. Lobban. *Cape Verdeans in Rhode Island.* Providence: The Rhode Island Heritage Commission and the Rhode Island Publication Society, 1990.

Cordasco, Francesco. *The Immigrant Woman in North America: An Annotated Bibliography of Selected References.* Metuchen, N.J.: Scarecrow Press, 1985.

Crain, Robert L., and Carol Sachs Weisman. *Discrimination, Personality and Achievement: A Survey of Northern Blacks.* New York: Seminar Press, 1972.

"Cranberries." *Ebony* 4, no. 1 (Nov. 1948): 31–33.

Cressey, Paul Frederick. "Population Succession in Chicago, 1898–1930." *American Journal Of Sociology* 64 (July 1938).

Cumbler, John T. *Working-Class Community in Industrial America: Work, Leisure and Struggle in Two Industrial Cities, 1880–1930.* Westport, Conn.: Greenwood Press, 1979.

Curtain, Philip D. *The Atlantic Slave Trade: A Census.* Madison: The University of Wisconsin Press, 1969.

Da Cruz, Eutrópio Lima. "Cape Verde and Its Music." *The Courier* no. 68, Sept.–Oct. 1981, pp. 77–80.

Dash, Leon. "Cape Verde Confronts Racial Colonial Legacy." *The Washington Post,* 24 June 1981, p. A13.

———. "The Women's Movement Comes to Cape Verde." *The Washington Post,* 26 June 1981, p. D4.

Davidson, Basil. *The Fortunate Isles: A Study in African Transformation.* Trenton, N.J.: Africa World Press, 1989.

Davie, Maurice R. *A Constructive Immigration Policy.* New Haven: Yale University Press, 1923.

DeCicco, Michael, interviewer. "Joseph Ramos." In "Twentieth-Century Whaling Tales." *Spinner: People and Culture in Southeastern Massachusetts.* Vol. 2. Ed. Donna Huse. New Bedford: Spinner Publications, 1982, pp. 107–10.

Daniels Roger. *Coming to America: A History of Immigration and Ethnicity in American Life.* Princeton, N.J.: HarperCollins, 1990.

DePorte, J. V. "Inter-Racial Variation in Infant Mortality." *American Journal of Hygiene* 5 (1925), pp. 479–80.

De Sousa, Jose Maria, trans. and ed. *Hora Di Bai: Morna e Coladeira de Cabo Verde,* 2 vols. Providence, Rhode Island: Capeverdean-American Federation, 1973.

Deutsch, Sarah. *No Separate Refuge: Culture, Class, and Gender on an Anglo-Hispanic Frontier in the American Southwest, 1880–1940.* New York: Oxford University Press, 1987.

Dicker, June. "Kinship and Ritual Kinship among Cape Verdeans in Providence." Master's thesis, Brown University, 1968.

Di Leonardo, Micaela. *The Varieties of Ethnic Experience: Kinship, Class, and Gender among California Italian-Americans.* Ithaca, N.Y.: Cornell University Press, 1984.

Dillingham, William P. "Cape Cod, Massachusetts: Bravas, or Black Portuguese, Cranberry Pickers," chapter 7 in *Immigrants in Industries, Report of the Immigration Commission, Recent Immigrants in Agriculture,* vol. 22 (1911), p. 540.

———. "Recent Immigrants in Agriculture." *Immigrants in Industries:*

Report of the Immigration Commission, 22:539–54, 9, *Dictionary of Races or Peoples*, 1911.

Dinnerstein, Leonard, Roger Nichols, and David M. Reimers. *Natives and Strangers: Ethnic Groups and the Building of America*. New York: Oxford University Press, 1979.

Dixon, Heriberto. "Black Cubans in the United States: A Case of Conflicts between Race and Ethnicity." Paper presented at the annual meeting of the American Studies Association, Miami, Fla., 27–30 Oct. 1988.

———. "Who Ever Heard of a Black Cuban?" *Afro-Hispanic Review* 1, no. 3 (Sept. 1982): 10.

Dominguez, Virginia R. *White by Definition: Social Classification in Creole Louisiana*. New Brunswick, N.J.: Rutgers University Press, 1986.

DuBois, W. E. Burghardt. *The Souls of Black Folk*. 1903. New York: Vintage Books, 1990.

———. *The Philadelphia Negro: A Social Study*. 1899. New York: Benjamin Blum, 1967.

Duffy, James. *Portugal in Africa*. Cambridge: Harvard University Press, 1962.

Duncan, T. Bentley. *The Atlantic Islands: Madeira, the Azores and the Cape Verdes in Seventeenth-Century Commerce and Navigation*. Chicago: University of Chicago Press, 1971.

Ellen, Maria M. *Across the Atlantic: An Anthology of Cape Verdean Literature*. Center for the Portuguese Speaking World. Southeastern Massachusetts University, 1988.

Ellison, Ralph. *Invisible Man*. 1952. New York: Vintage Books, 1989.

Engler, Richard E., Jr. *The Challenge of Diversity*. New York: Harper and Row, 1964.

Ewen, Elizabeth. *Immigrant Women in the Land of Dollars: Life and Culture on the Lower East Side, 1890–1925*. New York: Monthly Review Press, 1985.

Faugh, Millard C. *Falmouth, Mass*. New York: Columbia University Press, 1945.

Ferst, Susan Terry (Shapiro). "The Immigrant and the Settlement of the Portuguese in Providence: 1890–1924." Master's thesis, Brown University, 1972.

Fields, Barbara J., "Ideology and Race in American History." In *Region, Race, and Reconstruction: Essays in Honor of C. Vann Woodward*. Ed. J. Morgan Kousser and James M. McPherson. New York: Oxford University Press, 1982, pp. 143–78.

———. "Slavery. Race and Ideology in the United States of America," *New Left Review* 181 (May/June 1990): 95–118.

Fogg, Ann. "Cape Verdean Connection." *New Bedford Magazine* 1, no. 1 (Spring 1981): 12–15.

Folsom, Josiah C. "Farm Labor in Massachusetts, 1921." United States Department of Agriculture. Department Bulletin No. 1220. Washington D.C., Apr. 1924.

Foner, Nancy, ed. *Jamaica Farewell: Jamaican Migrants in London.* Berkeley: University of California Press, 1978.

———. *New Immigrants in New York.* New York: Columbia University Press, 1987.

Fraser, Don. "Advance Census Ignores Three Items." *The New Bedford Standard Times.* 6 Mar. 1971, p. 3.

Freilich, Morris, ed. *Marginal Natives: Anthropologists at Work.* New York: Harper and Row, 1970.

Fuchs, Lawrence H. *The American Kaleidoscope: Race, Ethnicity, and the Civic Culture.* Hanover, N.H.: University Press of New England, 1990.

Furstenberg, Frank Jr., Theodore Hershberg, and John Modell. "The Origins of the Female-Headed Black Family: The Impact of the Urban Experience." *Journal of Interdisciplinary History* (Autumn 1975): 211–33.

Fyfe, Christopher. "The Cape Verde Islands." *History Today* 31 (1981): 5–9.

Gabaccia, Donna. *Immigrant Women in the United States: A Multi-Disciplinary Bibliography.* Westport, Conn.: Greenwood Press, 1989.

———. "Immigrant Women: Nowhere at Home?" *Journal of American Ethnic History* 10, no. 4 (Summer 1991), pp. 61–87.

Gabe, Catherine. "Cape Verde Pilgrimage Opened a Dozen Souls to Their Rich Heritage." *The Standard-Times.* (New Bedford, Mass.), 4 Apr. 1984, pp. 1, 7.

Garcia, Maria-Cristina. "Creating Little Havana: Cuban American Women and the Making of an Ethnic Community." Paper presented at the American Studies Association Annual Meeting, Miami, Fla., 27–30 Oct. 1988.

Garside, E. *Cranberry Red.* Boston: Little Brown, 1938.

Gaw, Cooper. "The Cape Verde Islands and Cape Verdean Immigrants." *New Bedford Evening Standard,* 29 July 1905, pp. 3, 10, 12.

"The Gees." *Harper's New Monthly Magazine* 12, no. 70 (Mar. 1856): 507–9.

Geertz, Clifford. *The Interpretation of Cultures.* New York: Basic Books, 1973.

Geller, L. D., ed. *They Knew They Were Pilgrims: Essays in Plymouth History.* New York: Poseidon Books, 1971.

Glassner, Barry. "Cape Verdeans: A People Without a Race." *Sepia* (Nov. 1975): 65–71.

Glazer, Nathan. "Blacks and Ethnic Groups: The Difference and the Political Difference It Makes." *Social Problems* 8, no. 4 (Spring 1971): 441–61.

———, and Daniel Moynihan. *Beyond the Melting Pot: The Negroes, Puerto Ricans, Jews, Italians and Irish of New York City.* Cambridge: M.I.T. Press, 1963.

Glenn, Evelyn Nakano. *Issei, Nisei, War Bride: Three Generations of Japanese American Women in Domestic Service.* Philadelphia: Temple University Press, 1986.

Glenn, Susan A. *Daughters of the Shtetl: Life and labor in the Immigrant Generation.* Ithaca, N.Y.: Cornell University Press, 1990.

Golab, Caroline. *Immigrant Destinations.* Philadelphia: Temple University Press, 1977.

Gordon, Milton. *Assimilation in American Life; The Role of Race, Religion and National Origins.* New York: Oxford University Press, 1964.

Gould, Stephen. *The Mismeasure of Man.* New York: W. W. Norton, 1981.

Greenbaum, Susan. *Afro-Cubans in Ybor City: A Centennial History.* Tampa: University of South Florida Press, 1986.

Greenfield, Sidney M. "In Search of Social Identity: Strategies of Ethnic Identity Management Amongst Capeverdeans in Southeastern Massachusetts." *Luso-Brazilian Review* 13, no. 1 (Summer 1976): 3–17.

Gutman, Herbert. *The Black Family in Slavery and Freedom.* New York: Pantheon Books, 1976.

———. *Work, Culture and Society in Industrializing America.* New York: Random House, 1976.

Hall, Elton. *Sperm Whaling from New Bedford.* New Bedford: Old Dartmouth Historical Society, 1982.

Halter, Marilyn. "Working the Cranberry Bogs: Cape Verdean in Southeastern Massachusetts." In *Spinner: People and Culture in Southeastern Massachusetts,* Vol. 3. Ed. Donna Huse. New Bedford, Mass.: Spinner Publications, 1984, pp. 70–83.

———. "The Cape Verdean–American Left." In *The Encyclopedia of the American Left.* Ed. Mari Jo Buhle, Paul Buhle, and Dan Georgakas. New York: Garland, 1989.

———. "The Cape Verdeans" and "The Labor Strike of 1933." In *Cranberry Harvest: A History of Cranberry Growing in Massachusetts.* Ed. Joseph Thomas. New Beford, Mass.: Spinner Publications, 1990, pp. 98–105, 106–7.

Hamilton, Russell G. *Voices from an Empire: A History of Afro-Portuguese Literature.* Minneapolis: University of Minnesota Press, 1975.

Handler, Mark. "Azoreans in America: Migration and Change Reconsidered." In *Hidden Minorities: The Persistence of Ethnicity in American Life*. Ed. Joan Rollins. Washington, D.C.: University Press of America, 1981.

Handlin, Oscar. *Boston's Immigrants, 1790–1880: A Study in Acculturation*. Cambridge: Harvard University Press, 1959.

———. *The Newcomers: Negroes and Puerto Ricans in a Changing Metropolis* (Garden City, N.Y.: Doubleday, 1962).

———. *The Uprooted: The Epic Story of the Great Migrations that Made the American People*. 2d ed. Boston: Little Brown, 1973.

Haraven, Tamara, and Randolph Langenbach. *Amoskeag: Life and Work in an American Factory City*. New York: Pantheon Books, 1978.

Haraven, Tamara. "The Dynamics of Kin in An Industrial Community." In *Turning Points: Historical and Sociological Essays on the Family*. Ed. John Demos and Sarah Spence Boocock. Chicago: University of Chicago Press, 1978.

Haywood, Carl Norman. "American Whalers and Africa." Ph.D. diss., Boston University, 1967.

Heath, Dwight B., and Richard N. Adams, eds. *Contemporary Cultures and Societies of Latin America: A Reader in the Social Anthropology of Middle and South America and the Caribbean*. New York, Random House, 1959.

Hegarty, Reginald B., comp. *Returns of Whaling Vessels Sailing From American Ports: A Continuation of Alexander Starbuck's "History of the American Whale Fishery," 1876–1928*. New Bedford, Mass.: The Old Dartmouth Historical Society and Whaling Museum, 1959.

Henri, Florette. *Black Migration: Movement North, 1900–1920*. Garden City, N.Y.: Doubleday, 1975.

Henry, William A. III. "America's Changing Colors," *Time* 135, no. 15 (9 Apr. 1990): 28.

Hershberg, Theodore. "Free Blacks in Antebellum Philadelphia: A Study of the Ex-Slaves, Freeborn, and Socioeconomic Decline." *Journal of Social History* 5, (Winter 1971–72): 192–204.

———, et al. *Philadelphia: Work, Space, Family, and Group Experience in the 19th Century*. New York: Oxford University Press, 1981.

Hewitt, Nancy A. "Building a 'Virile' Union: Latin Workers, Politics and the Community of Labor." Paper presented at the Annual Meeting of the Organization of American Historians, St. Louis, Mo., Apr. 1989.

Higham, John, ed. *Ethnic Leadership in America*. Baltimore: John Hopkins University Press, 1978.

_____. *Send These to Me: Jews and Other Immigrants in Urban America.* New York: Atheneum, 1975.

Hine, Lewis, Richard Conant, and Owen Lovejoy. "Child Labor on the Cranberry Bogs of Massachusetts: Aug. 10–Sept. 20, 1911." Field notes.

Holmes, Urban Tigner, Jr. "Portuguese Americans." In *Racial and National Minorities.* Ed. Francis J. Brown and Joseph Roucek. New York: Prentice-Hall, 1937.

Houston, Laura Pires. *Cape Verdeans in the United States: Continuing a Story of Struggle, Creativity, and Persistence.* Cape Verdean–American Scholarship Committee, Sept., 1978.

_____, and Michael K. H. Platzer. *Ernestina/Effie M. Morrissey.* New York: Friends of the Ernestina/Morrissey Committee, 1982.

Howitt, Arnold M., and Rita Moniz. "Ethnic Identity, Political Organization and Political Structure." Paper presented at the Annual Meeting of the American Political Science Association. Chicago, 1976.

Ihlder, John. *The Houses of Providence.* Providence: Snow and Farnham, 1916.

"Immigrants in New Bedford." Ms., New Bedford Free Public Library, 1911.

Jackson, Kennell A. "The Old Minorities and the New Immigrants: Understanding A New Cultural Idiom in U.S. History." In *U.S. Immigration and Refugee Policy.* Ed. Mary M. Kritz, Lexington, Mass.: D. C. Heath, 1983. pp. 317–35.

Jenks, Albert Ernest. "New Englanders Who Came from Afric Isles." *The Dearborn Independent,* 27 Dec. 1924, pp. 5, 15.

_____. "Cranberry Bogs of Cape Cod: Their Workers." *The Dearborn Independent,* 3 Jan. 1925, pp. 9, 14.

Jordan, Winthrop D. *White over Black : American Attitudes toward the Negro, 1550–1812.* New York: W. W. Norton, 1977.

Kallen, Horace M. *Culture and Democracy in the United States.* New York: Boni and Liveright, 1924.

Karni, Michael, ed. *Finnish Diaspora II: United States.* Toronto: Multicultural History Society of Ontario, 1981.

Kelley, Robin D. G. *Hammer and Hoe: Alabama Communist During the Great Depression.* Chapel Hill: University of North Carolina Press, 1990.

Kessner, Thomas. *The Golden Door: Italian and Jewish Immigrant Mobility in New York City, 1880–1915.* New York: Oxford University Press, 1977.

Kirk, William. *A Modern City: Providence, Rhode Island and Its Activities.* Chicago: University of Chicago Press, 1909.

Kiser, Clyde Vernon. *Sea Island to City: A Study of St. Helena Islanders in Harlem and Other Urban Centers.* New York: AMS Press, 1967.

Kittredge, C. H. *Cape Cod: Its People and Their History.* Boston: Houghton Mifflin, 1930.

Kohn, Hans. American Nationalism: An Interpretative Essay. 1954. New York: 1961.

Kristol, Irving. "The Negro Today Is Like the Immigrant of Yesterday." *New York Times Sunday Magazine,* 11 Sept. 1966, pp. 50–124.

Kritz, Mary M., ed. *U.S. Immigration and Refugee Policy.* Lexington, Mass.: D. C. Heath, 1983.

Lamphere, Louise. *From Working Daughters to Working Mothers: Immigrant Women in a New England Industrial Community.* Ithaca, N.Y.: Cornell University Press, 1987.

Lawless, Robert "Haitian Migrants and Haitian-Americans: From Invisibility into the Spotlight," *The Journal of Ethnic Studies,* 14, no. 2 (1986): 29–70.

Levine, Lawrence W. *Black Culture and Black Consciousness: Afro-American Thought from Slavery to Freedom.* New York: Oxford University Press, 1977.

Lewis, Earl. *In Their Own Interests: Race, Class, and Power in Twentieth-Century Norfolk, Virginia.* Berkeley: University of California Press, 1991.

Lieberson, Stanley. *A Piece of the Pie: Blacks and White Immigrants since 1880.* Berkeley: University of California Press, 1980.

Lima, Lucillia. *"Lembrança: Crioulo Memories."* In *Spinner: People and Culture in Southeastern Massachusetts.* Vol. 1. Ed. Donna Huse. New Bedford, Mass.: Spinner Publications, 1981.

Littman, Minna. "Only Appeal from Kind Hearts Can Save Father His Daughter." *New Bedford Sunday Standard,* 23 Oct. 1921, p. 1.

Lobban, Richard. *Historical Dictionary of the Republics of Guinea-Bissau and Cape Verde.* Metuchen, N.J.: The Scarecrow Press, 1979.

Lobban, Richard, and Marilyn Halter. *Historical Dictionary of the Republic of Cape Verde.* Metuchen, N.J.: Scarecrow Press, 1988.

———. "Patterns of Cape Verdean Migration and Social Association: History through Obituary Analysis." *New England Journal of Black Studies* 5 (Nov. 1985): 31–45.

———, Waltraud Coli, and Robert J. Tidwell. "Cape Verdean Life Expectancy." Ms., 1985.

Loewen, James W. *The Mississippi Chinese: Between Black and White.* Cambridge: Harvard University Press, 1971

Lopes, Baltasar. *Chiquinho.* S. Vicente, Cabo Verde: "Claridade," 1947.

Lovinger, Robert. "I Am the Boyfriend of the World." *New Bedford Standard Times,* 12 Jan. 1960.

Lyall, Archibald. *Black and White Makes Brown: An Account of the Journey to the Cape Verde Islands and Portuguese Guinea.* London: W. Heineman, 1938.

Maccarone, Joyce, and John Andrade. "The History of the South Central Historic District." Manuscript for the New Bedford Office of Historic Preservation, 1978.

MacDonald, John S., and Leatrice MacDonald. "Urbanization, Ethnic Groups and Social Segmentation." *Social Research* 29 (1962): 433–48.

Machado, Deirdre Meintel. "Cape Verdean–Americans: Their Culture and Historical Background." Ph.D. diss., Brown University, 1978.

―――. "Cape Verdean Americans." In *Hidden Minorities: The Persistence of Ethnicity in American Life.* Ed. Joan Rollins. Washington D.C.: University Press of America, 1981.

Macris, Gina, and Michael J. B. Kelly. "From the Islands and the Mainland, a Proud, Loyal People Live among Us." *Sunday Journal.* (Providence, R.I.) 18 May 1980, pp. A–1, A–22.

―――. "Portugal/Cape Verde." *Sunday Journal.* (Providence, R.I.) Special Issue. 18 May 1980, pp. 2–68.

Marshall, Paule. *Brownstone, Brown Girl.* 1959. New York: Feminist Press, 1981.

Martin, Jane, contributing ed. *Global Studies: Africa.* Guilford, Conn.: Dushkin Publishing Group, 1985, pp. 34–35.

Marques, A. H. de Oliveira. *The History of Portugal from Lusitania to Empire.* 2 vols. New York: Columbia University Press, 1972.

Massachusetts Department of Labor and Industries. *Population and Resources of Cape Cod.* Boston: Wright and Potter, 1922

Mass. House Document #2300. Commission on Immigration. Mar., 1914, pp. 32–33.

McCabe, Marsha. "Julio J. Alves, Sr., July 2, 1917–Oct. 18, 1980." In *Julio J. Alves, Sr. Scholarship Souvenir Booklet.* New Bedford, Mass.: Spinner Publications, 1984.

McCarthy, Joseph M. *Guinea-Bissau and Cape Verde Islands: A Comprehensive Bibliography.* New York: Garland, 1977.

Margaret Mead et al., *Science and the Concept of Race.* New York: Columbia University Press, 1968.

Megan, Kathleen. "Whaling: Cape Verdean Memories." *New Bedford Sunday Standard Times,* 18 July 1982, p. 17.

Meintel, Deirdre. *Race, Culture and Portuguese Colonialism in Cabo Verde.* Syracuse: Syracuse University Press, 1984.

Meyers Doug, and Donald Glickstein. "Striking Workers in the Cranberry Bogs—the Depression Years." *New Bedford Sunday Standard Times*, 3 Sept. 1978, p. 4.

Mintz, Sidney. "Groups, Group Boundaries and the Perception of Race." *Comparative Studies in Society and History* 13, (1971): 437–50.

Modell, John. *The Economics and Politics of Racial Accommodation.* Urbana: University of Illinois Press, 1977.

Mohl, Raymond, "An Ethnic "Boiling Pot": Cubans and Haitians in Miami," *The Journal of Ethnic Studies* 13, no. 2, (1985): 51–74.

Moran, Emilio. "The Evolution of Cape Verde's Agriculture." *African Economic History* 2 (1982): 63–86.

Mormino, Gary, and George E. Pozzetta. *The Immigrant World of Ybor City: Italians and Their Latin Neighbors in Tampa, 1885–1985.* Urbana: University of Illinois Press, 1987.

Mortimer, Delores M., and Roy S. Bryce-Laporte, eds. *Female Immigrants to the United States: Caribbean, Latin American, and African Experiences.* RIIES Occasional Papers No. 2. Research Institute on Immigration and Ethnic Studies. Washington, D.C.: Smithsonian Institution, 1981.

Moser, Gerald M. *Essays in Portuguese-African Literature.* University Park, Pa.: The Pennsylvania State University, 1969.

New Bedford, Mass. Board of Health. *Annual Reports.* 1915, p. 23; 1918, p. 23; 1924, p. 43.

Neyland, Harry. "Harry Neyland's Log of His Cape Verde Voyage." *New Bedford Sunday Standard*, 26 Feb. and 4, 11 Mar. 1928.

———. "The Isles of Volcan." *The New Bedford Times.* 16, 17, 19, 20, 23, 24, 25, 26, 28, 30 Sept. and 1–5, 7, 8, Oct. 1929.

Nickerson, Colin. "Cape Verde: A Struggle for survival." *Boston Globe,* 28 Sept. 1983, p. 2.

———. "Cape Verde: Country of Their Hearts." *Boston Globe,* 29 Sept. 1983, p 16.

———. "Black, White or Cape Verdean?" *Boston Globe,* 30 Sept. 1983, p. 2.

Novak, Michael. *The Rise of the Unmeltable Ethnics: Politics and Culture in the Seventies.* New York: Macmillan, 1972.

Nunes, Maria Luisa. "A Different Vision of a New England Childhood: The Cape Verdean Experience on Cape Cod." In *Women in Portuguese Society: Proceedings of the Second Annual Symposium on the Portuguese Experience in the United States.* Fall River, Mass.: National Assessment and Dissemination Center, 1976.

———. *A Portuguese Colonial in America: Belmira Nunes Lopes, the*

Autobiography of a Cape Verdean-American. Pittsburgh: Latin American Literary Review Press, 1982.

————. "Portuguese and Cape Verdean Women in Fiction and Family History." In *Culture, Education and Community: Proceedings of the Second National Portuguese Conference.* Fall River, Mass.: National Assessment and Dissemination Center, 1977.

Nyhan, Patricia, and Raymond Anthony Almeida. *Nho Lobo: Folk Tales of the Cape Verdean People.* Trans. The Cape Verdean Educators Collaborative. Boston: TCHUBA—American Committee for Cape Verde.

Omi, Michael, and Howard Winant. *Racial Formation in the United States from the 1960s to the 1980s.* New York: Routledge & Kegan Paul, 1986.

O. L. O. A. Seventy-Five Years, 1905-1980. Yearbook. Our Lady of the Assumption Church, New Bedford, Mass.

Osofsky, Gilbert. *Harlem: The Making of a Ghetto, Negro New York, 1890-1930.* New York: Harper & Row, 1963.

Palmi, Stephan. "Spics or Spades? Racial Classification and Ethnic Conflict in Miami." *Amerikastudien,* 1989.

Pap, Leo. *The Portuguese-Americans.* Boston: Twayne, 1981.

Parsons, Elsie Clews. *Folk-Lore from the Cape Verde Islands.* 2 vols. Cambridge, Mass.: The American Folk-Lore Society, 1923.

Patterson, K. David. "Epidemics, Famines and Population in the Cape Verde Islands, 1580-1900." *International Journal of African Historical Studies* 21, no. 2 (1988): 291-313.

————. "Folk-Lore of the Cape Verde Islanders." *Journal of American Folklore* 34, no. 131 (Jan.-Mar. 1921): 89-110.

Peace Handbooks. Vol. 19. *Portuguese Possessions,* No. 117, Cape Verde Islands. London: H.M. Stationery Office, 1920; rpt. Wilmington, Del.: Scholarly Resources, 1973.

Peace, Zephaniah W., and George A. Hough. *New Bedford, Massachusetts. Its History, Industries, Institutions and Attractions.* New Bedford: Mercury Publishing, 1889.

Pedraza, Silvia. "Women and Migration: The Social Consequences of Gender." *Annual Review of Sociology* 17 (1991): 303-25.

Pedraza-Bailey, Silvia. *Political and Economic Immigrants in America: Cubans and Mexicans.* Austin: University of Texas Press, 1985.

Pires, Joao, and John Hutchinson. *Disionariu Preliminariu Kriolu (Preliminary Creole Dictionary) Cape Verdean/English.* 1st ed. Boston, 1983.

Platzer, Michael, and Michael Cohn. *Black Men of the Sea.* New York: Dodd Mead, 1978.

Pleck, Elizabeth H. *Black Migration and Poverty: Boston, 1865–1900*. New York: Academic Press, 1979.

————. "The Two-Parent Household: Black Family Structure in Late Nineteenth Century Boston." *Journal of Social History* 6, no. 2 (Fall 1972): 1–31.

Polacheck, Hilda Satt. *I Came a Stranger: The Story of a Hull-House Girl*. Urbana: University of Illinois Press, 1989.

Poole, Dorothy C. "Antone Fortes, Whaleman." *Duke County Intelligencer* 2 (May 1970): 129–52.

Preto-Rodas, Richard A. "Cape Verde and São Tomé Príncipe: A Search for Ethnic Identity." In *Critical Perspectives on Lusophone Literature from Africa*. Ed. Donald Burness. Washington, D.C.: Three Continents Press, 1981.

Radford, John P. "Blacks in Boston." *Journal of Interdisciplinary History* 12, no. 4 (Spring 1982): 677–84.

Ramos, Lucille. "Black, White or Portuguese? A Cape Verdean Dilemma." In *Spinner: People and Culture in Southeastern Massachusetts*. Vol. I. New Bedford: Spinner Publications, 1981, pp. 34–37.

Reid, Ira A. *The Negro Immigrant: His Background, Characteristics and Social Adjustment, 1899–1937*. 1939. New York: AMS Press, 1970.

Reimers, D. M. *Still the Golden Door: The Third World Come to America*. New York: Columbia University Press, 1985.

Rodrigues-Taylor, Kathy. "Cabo Verde: A Personal Travel Memoir." *Black Elegance* 2, no. 4 (Sept. 1987): 16–20.

Rodriguez, Clara E. *Puerto Ricans: Born in the U.S.A.* Boston: Unwin Hyman, 1989.

Rogers, Francis M. *Americans of Portuguese Descent: A Lesson in Differentiation*. Beverly Hills: Sage Publications, 1974.

Rolle, Andre. *The Italian Americans: Troubled Roots*. New York: Free Press-Macmillan, 1980.

Roseberry, William. "Balinese Cockfights and the Seduction of Anthropology." *Social Research* 49, no. 4 (Winter 1982): 1013–28.

Rosenzweig, Roy. *Eight Hours for What We Will: Workers and Leisure in an Industrial City, 1870–1920*. Cambridge: Cambridge University Press, 1983.

Rothery Agnes (Edwards). *Cape Cod: New & Old*. Boston: Houghton Mifflin, 1918.

————. *Family Album*. New York: Dodd Mead, 1942.

Safa, Helen I., and Brian M. Du Toit. *Migration and Development: Implications for Ethnic Identity and Political Conflict*. The Hague: Mouton Publishers, 1975.

Safford, Dr. Victor. "Cape Cod Africans." *Falmouth Enterprise,* 18 Aug. 1944, p. 9, 25 Aug. 1944, pp. 5, 11.

Saloutos, Theodore. "Causes and Patterns of Greek Emigration to the United States." In *Perspectives in American History: Dislocation and Migration—The Social Background of American Immigration.* Vol. 3. Ed. Donald Fleming and Bernard Bailyn. Cambridge, Mass.: Charles Warren Center for Studies in American History, Harvard University, 1973.

Sanchez-Korrol, Virginia E. *From Colonia to Community: The History of Puerto Ricans in New York City, 1917-1948.* Westport, Conn.: Greenwood Press, 1983.

Sanjek, Roger. *Fieldnotes: The Makings of Anthropology.* Cornell University Press, 1990.

Scheiner, Seth. *Negro Mecca: A History of the Negro in New York City, 1865-1920.* New York: New York University Press, 1965.

Scott, Joan Wallach. *Gender and the Politics of History.* New York, Columbia University Press, 1988.

Sharf, Susan. "The Cape Verdeans of Providence." Honors thesis, Brown University, 1965.

Shippee, Lester B. *Some Aspects of the Population of Providence.* Providence: E. L. Freeman Co., 1921.

Simone, Timothy Maliqalim, *About Face: Race in Postmodern America.* New York: Autonomedia, 1989.

Smith, Judith Ellen. *Family Connections: A History of Italian & Jewish Immigrant Lives in Providence, Rhode Island, 1900-1940.* Albany, N.Y.: SUNY Press, 1985.

Smith, Katherine, and Edith Shay. *Down Cape Cod.* New York: Robert M. McBride, 1936.

Smith, M. Estellie. "A Tale of Two Cities: The Reality of Historical Differences." *Urban Anthropology* 4, no. 1 (1075): 61-72.

Smith, Timothy L. "Immigration in Twentieth-Century America." *American Historical Review* 71 (July 1966): 1265-79.

————. "Native Blacks and Foreign Whites: Varying Responses to Educational Opportunity in America, 1880-1950." *Perspectives in American History* 6 (1972): 309-35.

Spickard, Paul R. *Mixed Blood: Intermarriage and Ethnic Identity in Twentieth-Century America.* Madison: University of Wisconsin Press, 1989.

Starbuck, Alexander. *History of the American Whale Fishery from Its Earliest Inception to the Year 1878.* 1898. New York: Argosy-Antiquarian, Ltd., 1964.

Steinberg, Stephen. *The Ethnic Myth: Race, Ethnicity and Class in America.* New York: Atheneum, 1981.

Suckanesset, Theodate Geoffrey. *A History of Falmouth*. Falmouth Publishing Co, 1928.

"A Survey of the Foreign Communities in Providence." Report. Providence, International Institute, July 1935.

Swiegenga, Robert P. "List Upon List: The Ship Passenger Records and Immigration Research." *Journal of American Ethnic History* 10, no. 3 (Spring 1991): 42–53.

Taft, Donald R. *Two Portuguese Communities in New England*. 1923. New York: Arno-New York Times, 1969.

Takaki, Ronald. *Iron Cages: Race and Culture in Nineteenth Century America*. New York: Alfred A. Knopf, 1979.

————, ed. *From Different Shores: Perspectives on Race and Ethnicity in America*. New York: Oxford University Press, 1987.

————. *Americans*. Boston: Little, Brown, 1989.

Taylor, Robert. *Colonial Connecticut*. Millwood, N.Y.: KTO Press, 1979.

Thernstrom, Stephen, ed. *Harvard Encyclopedia of American Ethnic Groups*. Cambridge, Mass.: Belknap Press, 1980.

————. *The Other Bostonians: Poverty and Progress in the American Metropolis, 1880–1970*. Cambridge: Harvard University Press, 1973.

Turner, Victor W. *Dramas, Fields, and Metaphors: Symbolic Action in Human Society*. Ithaca, N.Y.: Cornell University Press, 1974.

————. *From Ritual to Theatre: The Human Seriousness of Play*. New York: Performing Arts Journal Publications, 1982.

————. *The Ritual Process: Structure and Antistructure*. New York: Aldine de Gruyter, 1969.

Topouzis, Daphne, "Determined to Develop." *Africa Report*, Sept./Oct. 1989, pp. 52–54.

Trench, Barney. "Cape Verde: The Sahel in the Sea." *Courier* no. 65, Jan.–Feb., 1981, pp. 17–22.

Tyack, David. "Cape Verdean Immigration to the United States." Honors thesis, Harvard University, 1952.

U.S. Dept. of State. Bureau of Public Affairs. *Background Notes: Cape Verde*. June 1984.

Urdang, Stephanie. *Fights Two Colonialisms: Women of Guinea-Bissau*. New York: Monthly Review Press, 1979.

Van der Merwe, Chris. "Places in the sun." *Flying Springbok*. (Aug. 1984): 21–41.

Verrill, Chas. H. "Infant Mortality and Its Relation to the Employment of Mothers in Fall River, Mass." Transactions of the 15th International Congress on Hygiene and Demography. Washington D.C., 1913, pp. 318–37.

Vosburgh, Mark. "Old Whaler's Stories Are Harpoons That Pin Down Time." *New Bedford Standard Times,* 3 Mar. 1983, p. 5.

Wagley, Charles. "On the Concept of Social Race in the Americas." In *Contemporary Cultures and Societies of Latin America: A Reader in the Social Anthropology of Middle and South America and the Caribbean. New York.* 1959. Ed. Dwight B. Heath and Richard N. Adams. New York: Random House, 1959.

Walters, Ronald G. "Signs of the Times: Clifford Geertz and Historians." *Social Research* 47, no. 3. (Autumn 1980): 537–56.

Warner, Robert Austin. *New Haven Negroes.* New Haven: Yale University Press, 1940.

Washington, Joseph R. *Black Sects and Cults.* Garden City, N.Y.: Doubleday, 1972.

Weiss, Feri Felix. *The Sieve* or *Revelations of the Man Mill.* Boston: Page, 1921.

Whitney, Jessamine. *Infant Mortality: Results of a Field Study in New Bedford, Mass.* Washington D.C., Dept. of Labor, Children's Bureau, 1920.

Wilkes, Charles. *Narrative of the United States Exploring Expedition during the Years 1838–1842.* Vol. 1. Philadelphia, 1850.

Willcox, Walter F. *International Migrations: Statistics.* Vol. 1. New York: National Bureau of Economic Research, 1929.

Wilson, Carlos Guillermo. "The Chombo Odyssey." Paper presented at the Annual Meeting of the American Studies Association, Miami, Fla. 27–30 Oct. 1988.

Wilson, William J. *The Declining Significance of Race: Blacks and Changing American Institutions.* 2d ed. Chicago: University of Chicago, 1980.

Wirth, Louis. *The Ghetto.* Chicago: University of Chicago Press, 1928.

Wolfbein, Seymour Louis. *The Decline of a Cotton Textile City: A Study of New Bedford.* 1944. New York: AMS Press, 1968.

Wolforth, Sandra. *The Portuguese in America.* San Francisco: R. & E. Research Associates, 1978.

Woodson, Carter G. *A Century of Negro Migration.* New York: Russell & Russell, 1918.

X, Malcolm. *The Autobiography of Malcolm X.* 1964. New York: Ballantine Books, 1990.

Yans-McLaughlin, Virginia. *Family and Community: Italian Immigrants in Buffalo, 1880–1930.* Ithaca, N.Y.: Cornell University Press, 1977.

———, ed. *Immigration Reconsidered: History, Sociology and Politics.* New York: Oxford University Press, 1990.

Zable, Rona S. "Cape Verdean Custom of Canta Rez Passes to New Generations, Places." *Providence Journal,* 31 Dec. 1981.

Zarafonitis, Bess. "Cape Verdeans Urged to Leave Their Mark." *Standard-Times* (New Bedford, Mass.) 25 Jan. 1986, pp. 1, 12.

Zunz, Olivier. *The Changing Face of Inequality: Urbanization, Industrial Development and Immigrants in Detroit, 1880–1920.* Chicago: University of Chicago Press, 1982.

Index

MARILYN HALTER is a research associate at the Institute for the Study of Economic Culture, Boston University, where she is also a member of the history department and on the faculty of the American and New England Studies Program. She is the author (with Richard Lobban) of *The Historical Dictionary of the Republic of Cape Verde*.

Books in the Statue of Liberty-Ellis Island Centennial Series